FEB 9 '71

P9-CKX-611

shake
it for the world,
smartass

Books by Seymour Krim

MANHATTAN: STORIES OF A GREAT CITY, Editor, Bantam
Books, 1954

THE BEATS, Editor, Gold Medal Books, 1960

VIEWS OF A NEARSIGHTED CANNONEER, Excelsior Press,
1961; E. P. Dutton, 1968

shake it for the world, smartass

by seymour krim

The Dial Press, Inc.
New York 1970

To three West Village artist-shakers who executed themselves but left their swift as a permanent possession to all who felt the humbling whir of their passage through: William Poster, poet-visionary (1916-1960); Beverly Kenny, jazzsinger (1934-1960); Peter LaFarge, actor-writer-lyricist-folksinger (1932-1965).

Grateful acknowledgment is made to the following, in whose pages some of these essays first appeared.

Playboy: for "The American Novel Made Me," June 1969 (published as "The American Novel Made Us").

The Washington Post Company: for "Frank Harris: The First Hipster," copyright 1964 by The Washington Post Company; "Waiting for the End: Leslie Fiedler's Bronco Ride from Pocahontas to Marjorie Morningstar," copyright 1964 by The Washington Post Company; "Nelson A. and His Monsters," copyright 1965 by The Washington Post Company; "Calling In A Deficiency Expert," copyright 1965 by The Washington Post Company; and "The Troubles I've Seen," copyright 1965 by The Washington Post Company. All first published in *Book Week.* Used by permission of The Washington Post Company.

The Village Voice: for "A Comment on Our Lunacy in America," January 15, 1968; "Who's Afraid of *The New Yorker* Now?" November 8, 1962; Letters to the Editor, February 8, 1968 and September 19, 1968; and "Lindsay's Debut: The Mayor and the Gentle Practitioners," January 6, 1966.

Evergreen Review: for "Hungry Mental Lion," February 8, 1960; "An Open Letter to Norman Mailer," February 1, 1967; "Maverick Head Kick," August 1, 1967; "Should I Assume America Is Already Dead?" June 15, 1969; "The Newspaper as Literature," August 1, 1967.

New York Magazine: for "Ubiquitous Mailer vs. Monolithic Me," April 21, 1969 (published as "Norman Mailer, Get Out of My Head!"); and Letter to the Editor, February 10, 1969.

Coward-McCann, Inc.: for the Introduction to *Desolation Angels* by Jack Kerouac. Copyright © 1960, 1963, 1965 by Jack Kerouac. Reprinted by permission of Coward-McCann, Inc.

Shorecrest, Inc.: for Introduction to *I, Jan Cremer*. Used by permission.

New Politics: for "Black Panther Meets Lox and Bagel Man," Vol. VII, No. 2.

Flying Eagle Publications, Inc.: for "The Unimportant Writer," December 1962; "Lenny," June 1963; "Faggotry Is Super-In," February 1965. All first published in *Nugget*. Used by permission.

The New York Times: for "Literature Makes Plenty Happen," April 14, 1968.

W. C. C. Publishing Company, Inc.: for "St. John's School-in-Exile Opens," January 20, 1966; "They Sang His Praises and His Songs," February 21, 1966 (published as "Mike Quill"); and "Men In Bondage on an Easter Sunday," April 11, 1966. First published in *The New York Herald Tribune*. Used by permission.

New York Element: for "Brother Dave at 38," 1968.

The Smith: for "When We Went to John Steinbeck's Funeral Service, This Is What Happened," May 15, 1969.

contents

to the reader

In 1961 I published my comparatively naked thoughts in
Views of a Nearsighted Cannoneer and then, recoiling
from my own act, dove into the Manhattan magazine-
communications world in the hope that the most exposed
part of my "I" would be buried in the anonymity of work
and then transformed in action.

Eight years later I am as "I" as ever, unfortunately or
even fortunately; but while the self I sought to remake
sticks like my skin, I am not altogether the same being
because of a professional involvement with daily events
that pounded over and through me in their importance
to others. It was because of this involvement—which for
me must always continue as psychological socialism,
therapy, engagement, a place to go, a wage to earn, the
soul's need to touch and be touched—that my private
ambition as a writer got joined to the more crucial issues
of political, moral and imaginative power in society itself.
Since I have always thought of myself as an artist the
eight years of jobs, business action, a cruel walloping every
now and then, turned my thoughts constantly into com-
paring art with reality and I came out believing that the

1

mission of art for this both cracking-up and newborn transitional period should be to impose its values on society and recreate reality itself in the light of literature or truth.

I believe in other words that artists, especially literary artists, now have an unprecedented historical chance to extend their envisioning power into the politics of daily living and set the tempo for the world to come because they are being forced to confront public life in terms of direct action more than ever before in their solitary history; the toll will probably be severe, but those artists or whatever you want to call these leaders of the imagination who can stand up to their original vision in the center of contemporary U.S. chaos will enter this society in a much more central way than has ever been seen before.

This view first expresses itself in my writing in 1964 in the articles on Fiedler, Algren and Paul Goodman and reaches a tentative climax in two sizable pieces completed in 1967 and 68 respectively, "The Newspaper as Literature/Literature as Leadership" and "The American Novel Made Me."

Here then are my hardwritten efforts and a point of view hammered together (maybe too evangelically, but it came out of need not restricted to myself alone) since 1961 with the exception of two pieces written before then which form part of the present pattern. It is the only point of view that I can articulate so far which will force the potency of literature on the decisions of the day and make "the novel" real and novelists themselves the architects of the future; it comes out of the literary impulse joined to the new lifescene around us that calls out for great acts right now more than books. Or at least books that are in themselves acts, which this one wants above all to be and fails the demand of this hour where it is not.

SK
Oct. 26, 1969

the american novel made me

1

I was literally made, shaped, whetted and given a world with a purpose by the American realistic novel of the mid to late 1930s. From the age of 14 to 17 I gorged myself on the works of Thomas Wolfe (beginning with *Of Time and the River*, catching up with *Angel* and then keeping pace till Big Tom's stunning end), Hemingway, Faulkner, James T. Farrell, Steinbeck, John O'Hara, James Cain, Richard Wright, Dos Passos, Erskine Caldwell, Jerome Weidman, William Saroyan, and knew in my pumping heart that I wanted to be such a novelist. To me, an isolated, supersensitive N.Y. Jewish boy given the privacy to dream in the locked bathroom of middleclass life these novels taught me about the America OUT THERE and more than anything I wanted to identify with that big gaudy continent and its variety of human beings who came to me so clearly through the pages of these so-called fictions. I dreamed southern accents, Okies, bourbon-and-branchwater, Gloria Wandrous, jukejoints, Studs Lonigan, big trucks and speeding highways, Bigger Thomas,

3

U.S.A., U.S.A.! Nothing to me in those crucial-irredeemable years was as glamorous as the unofficial seamy side of American life, the smack, brutality and cynical truth of it, all of which I learned from the dynamic novels that appeared in Manhattan between 1936 and 1939.

They were my highschool, my religion, my major fantasy life; instead of escaping into adventure or detective fiction— there were no groovy comic books then, such as Pete Hamill writes about 10 years later when Batman flew into his head over in Brooklyn, or if there were I was already a kid snob tucked into my literary American dreamscene—I escaped into the vision of reality that these fresh and tough pioneering writers were bringing to print from all corners of the country. In an odd way, even though most of these books ended bitterly or without faith, they were patriotic in a style that deeply impressed my being without my being able to break down why: they had integrity to the actual things that people did or said, to the very accents of frustration or despair voiced by their characters, they were all "truthful" in recreating American life. This was a naked freeshow about my real national environment that I damn well did not receive at home—a home full of euphemisms and concealments, typical, with the death of one parent and the breakdown-suicide of the other hanging over the charade of good manners—or in the newspapers, radio or at the movies. Except for the fairytales read to me as a bigeyed child and an occasional boy's classic like *Robinson Crusoe* or *Treasure Island* or the Tom Swift books this was the first body of writing that had ever really possessed me and apparently I was never (and will never) to get over it.

How can I communicate the savage greenness of the American novel of 30 years ago as it was felt by a keenly emotional teenage boy?—or girl, I guess, although it was primarily a man's novel but certainly not totally. I and the other members of my generation who were given eyes and ears and genuine U.S. lifestyle by it knew nothing about its father, Theodore Dreiser, and his beautifully pensive younger brother, Sherwood Anderson, until we became intellectually smart-assed and history-minded 10 and 15 years later. We lived in the perpetual present created by those men named in the first paragraph and were inspired to become prosewriters because of them. It wasn't really a question of "talent"; if you responded to the leaping portrait of American life that these craft-loving realists (superrealists in actuality) were showing with professionally curved words you created the talent out of yourself; at first in imitation of what you creamed over in their style, point of view and impact, then later in painful effort to do equal justice to your own personal testube of experience.

The deservedly legendary American novelists of this raw-knuckled period before the war (they were OUR celebrities, on high!) encouraged an untested, unformed young guy to dig into his own worst personal experience and make something exciting out of it in the form of a story. The whole movement was in the finest and least selfconscious sense the story of myriad personal lives in this country, it encouraged everyone caught in its momentum to look hard at the unique grain of his or her life and its interweave with other lives. None of us who in the late 30s were swept up into the romantic-heroic fantasied career of novelists were in any sense fated for this role, in my opinion; we were baited beautifully by the gusher of skilled novels—Maritta Wolff, John Fante, Dorothy Baker, Bessie Breuer, Daniel Fuchs, Pietro di Donato, Josephine Herbst, (the early) Robert Paul Smith, Tess Schlesinger, Frederic Prokosch, Gladys Schmidt, Irving Fineman, Gale Wilhelm, Albert Halper, Nathanael West, Oakely Hall—that seemed to be goosing each other to shine more truly than the next. To a young, hungering mind once hooked by the constantly fresh stream of national lives that made their debut in these novels—characters from all parts of the country, waitresses, fishermen, intellectuals, lesbians, truck-drivers, salesmen, alcoholics, nymphomaniacs, jazzmen, gener-

als, athletes, everything—it was impossible to call it quits;
once the "real" American scene entered your imagination
through the eyes of these standup individual recorders and
native consciences who seemed to loom up, suddenly, hotly,
with a rush before the 30s decade ended in World War II,
there was nowhere else for the youthful truth-maniac to go
but to the new novels hurrying each other out of the New
York publishing womb. New fiction was the hot form, contested, argued, encouraged from *Story* to the *New Masses* to
Esquire to the (then) *Saturday Review of Literature* to the
New Yorker; the city buzzed with the magazine-unveiling of
any new talent, it was news that traveled with enthusiasm
(Irwin Shaw in the *New Yorker,* Di Donato in *Esquire,* James
Laughlin telling it like it was down at his family's Pittsburgh
steel works in *Story* before he became publisher of New
Directions).

It is very true that as the 30s drew to a vicious close with
the Spanish Civil War and Hitler's preparations for the new
blood-and-iron stomping of Europe, the politicalization of the
U.S. novel became more acute and the bleak international
scene seemed to throw its heavy shadow over our comparatively virginal literary pinethrust. But all of this is seen from
the cool view of later years whereas if you were just coming
alive as a human being in the late 30s it all seemed like one
nonstop fictional ball. As a highschool boy, although I bought
my *New Masses* every week because the Communists were
truly involved with fresh fiction (O Meridel LeSeur, where
are you now?) no matter how slanted their typewriters, I
found the political-propagandistic implications of the new
novels much less important than the powerful concrete punch
they delivered. Each of the exciting 30s novelists, it seemed to
me inside my comet-shooting young head, were pioneers; they
were tackling unrecorded experience in each hidden alley and
cove of the country that I wanted to be a part of, bringing it
to ground for the first time, binding it up and sending it East
for exhibition before the rest of the citizenry. Certainly their

moral flame was ignited and burning steadily or they would not have gone to the huge labor of making almost the entire country and its people accessible to fiction; but apart from the explicitly political base of men like Farrell and Wright (and the poignant Odets in drama, although his politics was a left cartoonstrip compared to the flashing originality of his voice) this flame was used to warm their faith in the value of writing truly rather than held aloft as a defiant gesture.

Their moral integrity—Weidman to his New York garment center, Saroyan to a Fresno poolhall, Faulkner to his luxuriant decaying cottonwood swamps (of the soul)—was concerned with how to verbally break the back of unarticulated and unacknowledged truth, that which has been seen, smelled and suffered but never before written. They were to my imagination outriders, advance scouts, and what they brought back from the contemporary American frontier was as rare and precious to all of us who were waiting as the information now hugged to earth by an astronaut.

I saw it in even more private terms; as a boy of 10 or 11 I had wanted to be an explorer, my fantasy-life taking off in the magic snowtracks made by Robert Peary and F. A. Cook who fought over discovering the North Pole and Admiral Byrd and Roald Amundsen who independently reached the southern one. It was no accident, I believe, that the American novelists of the 30s took over the explorer's role in my mind after the merely geographical aspects of exploration had faded into the bottom drawer of childhood. Who else but these selfelected—selftaught—selfstarting—gutty men and women with the sniff of glory in their proud nostrils were the real explorers of this country's unadvertised life? The novelists who electrified me and hundreds, perhaps thousands, of young kids like myself between 1936 and the outbreak of the war were idealists in the most adventurous sense no matter how stained their material seemed to be on the surface. If you said to somebody, as I soon began to after breaking into print in the DeWitt Clinton highschool lit. magazine, that as an

adult "I wanted to write" it could only mean one thing: the
novel. A bigness impossible to recapture in 1968 attached to
those three power-words, "wanting to write." One had the
image of climbing the jaggedest of the Rockies alone, flying
solo like Lindbergh, pitting one's ultimate stuff against all the
odds of middleclass life and coming out of the toughest kind
of spiritual ordeal with that book-that-was-more-than-a-book,
that was the payoff on just about everything, held in your
hand. It was heavenly combat the way I pictured it, selfcon-
frontation of the most hallowed kind, and if my vision of it
was ultra-ultra then the legendary American Novel itself at
this time was the most romantic achievement in U.S. life for
the dreamer who lived inside everybody with a taste for language, style and—justice!

To have wanted to be a writer in this country in the late
30s had about it a gorgeous mystique that was inseparable
from the so-called American Dream on which every last one
of our good writers was first suckled before being kicked out
in the cold to make it come true. If that phrase, A.D., American Dream, meant going all the way, that the individual in
this myth-hungry society had the option to try and fly above
the skyscrapers, then writing toward "the great American
novel" was not only an act of literature but a positive affirmation of the dreamdust that coated all of us born under the
flag. All the driving personal ambition, energy, initiative, the
prizing of individual conscience and courage, that operated or
was supposed to operate in every other branch of national life
entered strongly into wanting to be a novelist—but with a
twist. The act of writing a novel made use of all these widely
broadcast qualities, yes, but the reward one sought in it was
not palpable gold; bestsellers as such were sneered at unless
they occurred by accident; the goal was one of absolute truth
to the material, to make a landmark on the unmapped moral
and esthetic landscape of America that would somehow
redeem the original intentions of the country and the selves
made by it and represent the purest kind of success-story for
the person who brought it off.

This meant that being a typical good American novelist in the 30s, even wanting to be one, was *not* finally dependent on having an extraordinary gift for telling a story in print. Certainly there were narrative and stylistic "geniuses" like Faulkner, Hemingway, perhaps even the early O'Hara, James Cain, Djuna Barnes, each buff and lover of the period will name his or her own, and their overpowering skill with the craft produced virtuoso performances that set standards and became models to aim at. But the American novel only became a great art in its outward finish and skill, in the 30s, because of the internal spiritual motivation that made wanting to write it perhaps the sweetest gamble in national life. You might almost say that the romantic promise of the country as a unique society of total justice for all, pegged on the limitless possibilities of each individual—all the raging hope that the American Dream meant to the imagination of its most ardent dreamers—was all part of the religion of wanting to be a novelist when I got the call while in highschool. If the idea of the mystical American novel had not been bound up with all of these big national feelings and aspirations that writhed around in the direct center of one's being, if that novel had not been more than "literature," I doubt if I and so many prosewriters my age would have chosen the written word as our badge.

It was the ambition (when the time came at 15 or 16 to tell yourself what you "wanted to be") chosen in the pride of the secret imagination by rebel fantasists, now in their 40s, who believed they could rebuild reality closer to the American soul's desire by writing in the light of a final faith that would transform their portraits of frustration or injustice into the opposite. By this I mean that because they wanted to believe in the promise of the country, were inseparable from its myth, were tied up emotionally and psychologically and every other way with "America" almost as if it were a person—with their own fulfillment as human beings actually dependent upon the fulfillment of the nation at the poetic height at which they conceived it—they felt they could let go in the novel to the full extent of their negative imagination. Everything bad, awful, unjust, painful, stupid, outrageous in their own lives or theirs in relation to the lives around them could be discharged at full intensity in fictional form with the underlying implication that it was just and right to give such ferocious bite to negative expression because it was all an attempt to redeem an invisible, psychic Bill of Rights. Towering idealism, paradoxically shown by the extent of the dark "realism" in the characteristic novel of the time, was the climate in which the fictional life of the 30s grew to bursting; the more the novelist envisioned The Way Things Should Be the more he and his readers felt he had the duty to show the ugly side of the land, the failure of the ideal, the color of the pus, the company goons beating down the strikers.

We kids who wanted to write the American novel knew without analysis, responded totally with our sharpened feelers, to the unspoken values that lay behind any particular book in question; if Weidman's *What's in It for Me?* or O'Hara's *Hope of Heaven* showed heels and weaklings with special corrosiveness of scene, dialogue, action, nailing them to the wall with the brilliance that comes from a mixture of contempt and pity, we shared enthusiastically in the experience because we knew that in writers of O'Hara's and Weidman's stripe the moral judgment was implicit rather than explicit as in a Steinbeck or Wolfe or Wright. It didn't matter to us, implicit or explicit, because we were instinctively clued in to the intention of all the late 30s novelists just by wanting to make the same nittygritty comment on our own experience; we knew by feel that even if a specific book baffled our haughty teenage heads it thrust at us a segment of the country's experience, it was criticizing America under the table in order to purge and lift it, it was forever encroaching on the most taboo, subtle and previously undefined aspects of our mutual life to show a truer picture of the way we lived.

Those of us, then, who couldn't forget what we had already been through—who remembered each hurt, black skin, Yiddish nose, Irish drunk, wop ignorance, too short, too tall, too poor, afraid of girls, afraid of boys, queer, crippled, sissies, young-bud neurotics/psychotics, the most vulnerable and stung of the new generation who could fight back with words—it was we who thought that being novelists would heroically reclaim us by recreating the bitter truth about our personal lives and our environment. Obviously it took sensitivity of the most piercing kind to provide the openings in the personality where painful experience could lodge and stick, so that one day it would all be poured forth in answer against frustration (personal and social both); you must never forget that we who wanted to be novelists not only thought it was the most free and ultimately ethical means of American expression, we were also squeezed by the very existential nuts into NEEDING fiction in order to confess, absolve and justify our own experience. The majority of us who "wanted to write" were already middleclass losers who couldn't make it inside the accepted framework, the thinskinned minority who were set apart in our own psyches to observing when we wanted to act and to thinking when we wanted to participate—the kids who were constitutionally unable to do the saddle-shoed American Thing during the smoking acid-bath of adolescence.

Do I therefore mean, to hit it squarely, that writing fiction for me and my breed was a pimply kind of revenge on life, an outcast tribe of young non-Wheaties failures getting their own back, all the shrimpy, titless, thicklensed, crazyheaded dropouts and sore losers of American youth resolving in the utter misery of the dateless Saturday nights to shoot down their better-favored peers in the pages of a novel? Yes, I flatly mean that in part; the mimetic ability, the gift to recreate lifelike scenes and dialogue, to be good at acute description, even to have one's moral perceptions heightened, is spiced and rehearsed by unhappiness. Wasn't the novel to those of us caught in the emotional hell of American teendom a wish-fulfillment device for would-be lovers banished from the sen-

sual playland that taunted us via radio, billboard, movie marquee and our own famished unconscious? From (in my case)
the big, smooth, "in" gentile world of blue eyes and blond
hair and supple tennis-racket bodies that I felt I could never
be part of and that then seemed like the top of the heap?

Yes, the American novel for those of us who were precocious outsiders—and there were a thousand reasons why each
one of us failed to measure up to the gleaming Robert Taylors
and Ginger Rogerses who star-touched our Loew's Saturday af-
ternoons and made us silently weep into the bathroom mirror
on Sunday—was a magic, lifelike double in which we thought
we could work off our private griefs, transform them into messages of hope and light, and remake our lives themselves by
the very act of writing. This artform, then, for us, was MANY
THINGS: the freest and most total kind of expression for
reality-loving idealists; the place where "truth" could be told
as it could not in real life or in any place but one's mind (psychoanalysis was still a decade off for most of us); and a form
so close to living matter itself that the illusion of personally
controlling experience instead of being its fallguy or victim
could not have been stronger. Sure, the novel was a legitimate
"artform" even for those of us who wanted to use it for the
redemption or glorification of self; but it was a yielding
female art that was responsive to the most private subjective
needs and it provided the only complete outlet for the being
that was choked and distorted in our waking relationship to
society. To us it was the golden cup of a modern fable—one
which we could fill to overflowing with all the repressed
hunger in ourselves and also one which could announce our
fame, toast us to the sky because of our verbal triumph over
the weights that near crushed us, make come true in imagination what could not be realized in the bruising action of daily
life.

Of course it WAS action on a literary level, action with
words, but in the final sense it was substitute or dream-action
carefully clothed with the wrinkles of a photographic realism.

The façade of the great realistic style of the 30s was documentary, bang-bang-bang, everything as hard and metallic as the shiny unyielding materials turned out in our most modern factories; swift as a biplane, lit up like a radio tube, driving as a racing car on the Salt Lake Flats ("James Cain's style is like the metal of an automatic. You can't lay his story down."—*Saturday Review of Literature*). But this was only the outward enameling that we swung with and mentally caressed because it was all so new, fresh, a prose like the artifacts of the country itself—streamlined. Our stripped-down, whipped-down appreciation of power loved that clean line bulleting across the page. Yet behind the lean, aware, dirty knowingness we were stylistically tuned in to was that assumption, as if by divine right, of impossible freedom—the novelist working out his total hidden life before our eyes— which made novel-writing in America such a tremendous adventure no matter how pinchingly personal the original motives might be that drove you to your desk.

I am certain that those of you reading this who came of age in the same late 30s period recognize the excitement about the novel that I am trying to recapture because it made me what I am essentially. Can you imagine a human being actually molded by something as abstract as a literary form? Yet it was quite real, not only in my case but in that of the vulnerable cream of an entire generation who graduated from highschool when the U.S. novel had grown so big that it literally stretched us with its broadshouldered possibilities. Our values, coloring and slant as people were dominated by the overwhelming idea of being novelists, the beautiful obsession that kept us secretly, spiritually high like early Christians. It puffed us up with humility, humbled us with pride, made us into every character we imagined and put us in every story we could cook up; but within, not outwardly as an actor might express it (and there were strong correspondences although we novelists-in-embryo toughly put down actors as childish narcissists) and we coolly loved ourselves for the infinite range

of life that easily gave itself to us and you could be goddamned sure to no one else. When I flunked out of college in
1940 a year after finishing highschool, for example, this was
not even remotely seen as a failure by me and mine but rather
as a new and soon-to-be-significant phenomenon which I
would be able to write about from firsthand experience. The
first time I got laid, drunk, smoked "tea," shipped out (and
jumped ship before we left Sandy Hook), saw death, spent
the night in a hospital-clean Pittsburgh jail, masturbated over
the fantasy of going to bed with my sister, put on women's
panties and silkstockings for kicks, got into my first adult
streetfight and almost had the mortal shit kicked out of
me—all of these "firsts" and a hundred others were special,
fated, grand experiences for me and those like me because I
was a novelist-to-be and I was on a special trip!

What a dream it was, what a marvelous hurtproof vest we
all wove in the name of the novel (which was another name
for religion or faith in the nonchurchly modern sense).

2

I did not, finally, write novels as anyone familiar with my
output knows; but I was made as person and mind and writer
in their image, just as a newer generation (and even my own
exact contemporary, Tony Curtis, né Bernard Schwartz) has
been created by the movies. The reasons why I never added
my own byline to that passionate list are many, some personal
as well as cultural; I may not have had the "talent"—
although I published my small share of vivid short stories—or
what is more likely the needs of the post-World War II
period SHIFTED in my eyes and those of my friends and we
put much more importance on trying to understand the new
world zooming up around us than expressing what we already
knew. We became, in manner, crisply intellectual instead of
openly lyrical but much of that same apocalyptic sense of possibility that we once felt in the U.S. novel now went into its

examination (the name of the game was literary criticism)
until the work of fiction became for us a means to examine
life itself. Wasn't that what it was all about anyway?—at least
so ran our sincere and often troubled rationalization at the
time. But even though the form began to slowly change in the
late 40s and the early 50s for a radar-sensitive minority of us,
nonfiction instead of fiction, the goal remained essentially the
same: the articulation of American reality by individuals who
really, personally cared because their own beings were so helplessly involved in this newly-shifting, remarkably unstable,
constantly selfanalyzing and selfdoubting society that had
shot up after the war.

I sweated the national anxiety out in myself, what direction
was I going to go in?, the idea of the novel still hanging over
me as a kind of star but getting further and further distant as
my ignorance in other areas—politics, poetry, sociology, history, painting, etc.—was exposed and I tried powerfully to
educate myself now that as a non-novelist I was being challenged socially and even in print. The dream of being a novelist, the dream that being a novelist had been in this country,
had kept me warm for 20 years; now I was torn from this sus-
taining fantasy by my failure to act and was forced to fend for
my selfesteem in a hardboiled intellectual community (the
literary-political magazines where I published) that had no
sympathy for my little inspirational couplet on What The
American Novel Means To Me. They either thought it was a
puton, because I had written none myself, or a sentimental
indulgence. Therefore whether it was because I temporarily
allied myself with the so-called New Criticism in its more cerebral search for reality—and there were a number who had
wanted to be fictionists (even wrote their one or two novels)
who took this further crook in the country's prose road along
with me—or because basically I did not think "novelistically"
which in all honesty I am forced to doubt or else all my
former covetous years were pitiably unreal—or as I believe
because "truth" no longer seemed to ME to reside in my

beloved American novel as it had in my young manhood—I began in the mid 50s to regard the novel as a usedup medium.

For a person like myself, confessedly given great hope and direction by this medium, justified in all my agonizing human goofs by its very existence because I thought I could one day redeem them through it, the beauty of knowing the novel was there like a loving woman for me to go to when beaten to my knees, it wasn't an easy emotional matter for me to say in my mind, "It doesn't sing for my time the way it once did." But I said it—at least for myself. What had happened, not only to me but I'm certain to others who came from my literary environment, was a fundamental change in our perception of where the significant action lay: the fictional realism on which we had been shaped seemed to lead almost logically to that further realism which existed in the world of fact; we had been so close to the real thing with the STYLE of superrealism that it was now impossible to restrain ourselves from wanting to go over the edge into autobiography, the confessional essay, reportage, because in these forms we could escape from the growing feeling that fiction was artificial compared to using the same novelistic sweep on the actual experience we lived through every day.

In other words the very realistic 30s novel that had originally turned us on made us want to take that giant step further into the smellable, libelous, unfaked dimension of sheer tornpocket reality—my actual goodbye-world flipout in 1955—James Agee actually pounding on his small car in Santa Monica a year before he died and telling a friend of mine who had casually quoted a line from Agee's first and only book of poems, "I wasted it! I should have written only poetry!" sobbing while he banged on the hood with his fists—Elia Kazan looming tightfaced over Paddy Chayefsky and me at The Russian Tea Room saying moodily that he had to see the isolated Clifford Odets, Golden Boy with cancer, who had crept back to New York to sniff the ozone of dead triumphs before perishing on the coast—my remembering while Kazan spoke with disembodied flatness how I had met Odets at 17 at the U. of North Carolina and how he had taken me for a drive in his fast Cadillac (?) and switched me on so that I rapped pre-*On the Road* about speed and how the strange iodine odor came from his antiseptic-smelling body and wiry brillo hair—all these once-reportorial facts now became the TRUER story for those of us whose appetite for what is had been built up to a point no longer satisfied by fiction.

In addition to this feeling of irrelevance that I increasingly had about the novel as a meaningful statement for the late 50s and 60s, the audience for it in America was no longer as loyal and excited as it had been (as *I* had been!) when we were first mentally-emotionally bowled over by its momentum. TV, movies, electronic communications of every sort were cutting into the time that people who were totally alive to their era could spend on prose fiction; if it was STORY you wanted in the old *Saturday Evening Post* sense, you could get that dramatized for you on the Late Late Show while you did a multimedia thing with your companion in bed, and it was only the specialists, critic-teachers, the people in the book trade, who seemed to me to hold out strenuously against admitting that the novel's dash was being taken away from it by the new media. These electronic whispers of tomorrow could in a momentary flash do what Flaubert and Conrad spent their lifetimes trying to achieve with words: "Above all to make you see."

Of course, you can say that the post-Faulkner U.S. novel was no longer sought out for story-values per se but rather for radical insight into existence; that the form provided a framework for an attack from a completely different "existential" or "absurd" quarter than the realistic 30s novel; granted—and also more than granted that extraordinarily talented writers were opening up this form and "making it as limitless as the ocean which can only define itself" (Marguerite Young), writers such as John Barth, Young herself, Ralph Ellison,

William Burroughs, Joseph Heller, Norman Mailer, Hubert Selby, Donald Barthelme, etc., the list is big because there were and are that many highly imaginative writers who have been doing remarkable things with fiction during these last 15 years. (Ironically, as the novel has shed its effectiveness in our society, there has never been since the 20s such a yell of native talent, wild originality, deadly challenge.) But the basic fact I noticed as the deluge of new fictional expression increased and readership became a frantic duty rather than the great thrill it once had been—and the practical impossibility of keeping up with the diversity of new books (new lives!) became obvious—was that the impact of the novel on our beings, on my being, was no longer as crucial as it had been. From my own changing point of view tremendous stateside writers could still appear in what was loosely called a novel—and what form has become looser?—but I felt that the entire role of the American novelist as I had originally heroized it had to be transformed into something entirely different if it was to be as masterful to the imagination of the 60s as it had been to me in the 30s.

In this sense: writing fiction for me and my breed was not an entirely realistic, naturalistic, rational human enterprise in spite of the authentic-seeming imitation of reality on which we were indoctrinated; underneath the accurate surface it was all bathed in dream or myth; we who wanted to mythologize ourselves and America (and they were inseparable) were trying to personally lift the national life into the realm of justice, we were attempting to use the total freedom of our imaginations to rearrange the shitspecked facts of our American experience into their ultimate spiritual payoff. We wanted to "build Jerusalem" (Blake) out of America's "fresh, green breast" (Scott Fitzgerald) and the novel was our transcendent, our more-than-could-ever-be vehicle for fulfillment of both ourselves and the national seed that had begotten us. In other words, OUR novel was a form of imaginative action. If you, the novelist, couldn't make it to the height of your vision in so-called straight or nonliterary life because of one handicap or another, then you did it through your books even better; but the goal was the same as the man of action's, your books were deeds that came out of your mixture of vision and moral commitment (Hemingway, Farrell, Wolfe) and they stood as the seal of where you were humanly at as clearly as if you had sewn your psychoanalysis into the binding. There could be no faking about taking a stand and you were measured every step of the way by readers who took your fictions as acts that influenced the world of the U.S. spirit until they were outdistanced by new and more penetrating fictional commitments. It was a soul-contest of the keenest kind, with the country as beneficiary.

But the effectiveness of such "imaginative action" today seems to have been reduced to mere toenail-picking by the tornado voices of the massmedia. Whether you and I like it or not we have all—novelists as well as readers—become pawns in the newscast of each day's events. "Our" novel can no longer affect these events in even an indirect sense: almost every ounce of my energy (for example) is used in coping with my own life, things happen too fast for me to be affected by the stance of some protagonist in a fiction, I am spun around by each latest threat to my survival, and what was once the charismatic lure of the American novel now becomes for me and countless others an extravagance instead of a necessity. But isn't that what makes artforms change—when life leaves them in the lurch? When concern moves away from them, not by design but by a gut-barometer whereby we seek out what is most vital to us and jettison the rest? Because of my existential impatience with fiction as it related directly to my life—and I concede that this could be a flaw of temperament although it is backed up by my professional work as an editor of new writing—I was and am forced to believe that in varying degrees my experience is true for readers all over the country; and I felt and feel that prose must find a form that can meet this reality and win readers back to the crucial excitement that I experienced when the novel was more than a novel and evoked a mystic response that molded being itself as well as an author's reputation.

But what happens then—I have had to ask myself—to our significant writers who are still either in love or "imprisoned" in a traditional form that is losing its cultural importance in spite of their brilliant personal flights? What happens—I must ask myself again—to that awesome authority of the imagination that encouraged, demanded, people who called themselves novelists to create human beings (like nature itself) and dictate their lives and fate (like gods or supreme justices of the universe)? What happens, further, to that great ton of submerged American experience locked inside themselves, more raw, subtle, potential human riches than the combined knowledge of sociologist-psychiatrist precisely because it was garnered by their blood as well as brain? What happens, in short, to that special mission, what to me for many years was almost a holy mission, of making an imaginary American world that would be more real than the actuality itself?

And where, as a final question, does the legendary U.S. novelist go when except for a handful of individuals* he is no longer a culture-hero in a radically new environment, when his

---

*William Burroughs, Norman Mailer, Joseph Heller, Ken Kesey and possibly a few others (Barth, Sol Yurick?) are novelists who recapture some of the old tribal magic for their followers; but even more significant are the non-novelists like Allen Ginsberg, Tim Leary, Lennie Bruce (before he died), Jimmy Breslin, David Amram, Eldridge Cleaver, Abbie Hoffman, etc., who are setting the current trend of the action-involved Personality who speaks through writing. It seems plain to me, at any rate, that the literary microphone through which you can talk most directly to the most people is no longer fiction even though this doesn't rule out an occasional exploding star. The important point is that it is now the man and not the medium; and what the man who was trained as a novelist, or always wanted to be one, can do through nonfiction today is the whole thrust of the last part of this article.

medium is passing into the void of time, and when he is still stuck with a savage inner need to speak, confess, design, shape, record—the whole once-glorious shmear?

3

There is one drastic way out and even up, as I personally see it now in 1968, and that is for the American novelist to abandon his imitation or caricature of a reality that in sheer voluminosity has dwarfed his importance and to become a communicator directly to society without hiding behind the mask of fiction. (I must make it clear that what follows represents my own need and desire imagined out of the confusion of our time and my unwillingness to accept a literature that is primarily a reflection of our era's helplessness; committed novelists, and some very sharp ones too, will doubtless block me out of consciousness and continue to make an ever wilder art of their materials to match the nuttiness that fevers our days; I will always be a sucker for their spirit and bow to the new images they will offer us, but my compelling feeling that now as never before is the time for writing to become direct action and cause things to happen makes even potentially great novels grow small compared to what I can envision if the novelist puts his power into speaking straight to his audience.)

The American novelistic imagination as I received it with open heart and mind 25 and 30 years ago was really the most fully human expression of this society at that time; and it is the new humanizing of American writing by the boldness of direct communication, the revolutionizing of the writer's relationship to his reader, that seems to me tremendously more needed right now than the pale echo of fiction. Instead of "novelists" I believe we now actually have only literary individuals themselves, men and women struggling with their own destinies as people in relation to other people and with the problems that threaten to swamp us all—emotional, sexual, political, racial, artistic, philosophical, financial—and that these should be stated to the reader as candidly as possible so that he, too, can be brought into the new mutual non-novel of American life and make possible a truly democratic prose of total communication which can lead to new action in society itself.

I believe the ex-novelist, the new communicator that we can already see in the early and various stages of his making (Mailer again, Tom Wolfe, Norman Podhoretz, Dan Wakefield, Willie Morris, Frank Conroy, Jan Cremer, Erje Ayden, Fielding Dawson, Irving Rosenthal, Ned Rorem, Taylor Mead, Frederick, Exley, myself*) should speak intimately to his readers about these fantastic days we are living through but declare his credentials by revealing the concrete details and particular sweat of his own inner life; otherwise he (or she) will not have earned the right to speak openly about everything or be trusted. He should try and tell the blunt truth as in a letter and this includes the risk of discussing other individuals as well—no one should be immune from the effort to clean house, undo bullshit, lay the entire business of being an American right now on the public table without shame. So that the new communicator's statement—about himself, his friends, his women (or men if he's gay), people in public life, the cities, the war, his group therapy, wanting secretly to be a star, wanting to sleep with Mamie Van Doren (or Susan Sontag), still hoping to love and be loved, putting

---

*Here are the books where you can check this out: *The Armies of the Night* plus *Miami and the Siege of Chicago* by Norman Mailer, who is in transition from the novel to the inchoate new form; *The Electric Kool-Aid Acid Test* by Tom Wolfe; *Making It* by Norman Podhoretz; *Between the Lines* by Dan Wakefield; *North Toward Home* by Willie Morris; *Stop-time* by Frank Conroy; *I Jan Cremer* by Jan Cremer; *The Legend of Erje Ayden* by Erje Ayden; *An Emotional Memoir of Franz Kline* by Fielding Dawson; *Sheeper* by Irving Rosenthal; *The Paris Diary of Ned Rorem* by Ned Rorem; *Anonymous Diary of a New York Youth* (Vols. 1, 2 & 3) by Taylor Mead; *A Fan's Notes* by Frederick Exley; *Views of a Nearsighted Cannoneer* by Seymour Krim.

his being directly before the reader as if the page were a telephone and asking for an answer—will be evidence of the reality we are ALL implicated in, without exception, and be in itself a legitimation of this reality as a first step to changing it.

How can we suffer from too much truth? Who isn't heartened to see it when an author respects us enough to tell us where he really lives and by the very nature of his writing asks us to reciprocate? But there is a more significant reason for total leveling than moral straightforwardness in a time famous for its credibility gaps, and that is the power that can return to literature as a daring public act which has to be respected by even those pragmatists who habitually reduce words to playthings. If I write about my own being in relationship to other, real, named, social-security numbered beings and present it to you, the reader, it is inevitable that you too will be pulled into the scene (at least a few hundred of you will know either me or one of my real-life cast of characters) and must take up an involved position about what you're being told and experiencing. You are interacting with me and my interactions with others so closely—assuming I have the ability as well as the stomach for truth—that you have become part of the experience whether you seek it or not. You Are There, now included in the network of my life as I am included in yours, and what you have seen and heard and identified with in my communication will not be put aside like a "story" because it is an extension of the same reality that unites us both; I will have established a sense of community with you about the destiny of both our lives in this uncertain time which becomes as real as if we were communicating in the flesh—and as existentially suspenseful. Reading then becomes a crucial event because something is REALLY HAPPENING in existence and not in "literature" alone; due to what I have written our very lives will touch, the reader is just as much a participant as the writer, your isolation or indifference has been penetrated by reading just as mine has

by writing and the alienation of our mutual situation has
been broken through by my need to make you experience
what I have and share my consciousness.

In other words, I want American prose to again become a
potent force in the life of the individual in this country and
not just his novelty-seeking mind; I want it to be necessary
and important once again—even more important, since I see
its purpose as having changed—as I knew it when it shaped
me; and I want this selfishly because I have devoted my
dreams to this business of words, and my own selfrespect as
mere human refuses to accept that what I once took vows for
can be written off as a secondrate art, which "madeup" and
irrelevant writing often seems like now in the aftermath of
the electronic-visual explosion. But apart from my own investment in literature—and I can't rationalize and say that the
source of my ideas doesn't spring from my own unappeasable imagination as a would-be American novelist who was
once promised the world and shall never forget that
fact—who can deny that once a gifted writer tells it to his
equals exactly "like it is" we are moving into a new dimension
where writing is used to speak directly to being? And where
the talents of reporter and pamphleteer are now usurping
those of novelist to awaken individuals to the fact that we all
share a common bag as probably never before?

It seems plain to me that the man we used to call the
American creative writer is now beginning to express living
history through himself so urgently that he is becoming its
most genuine embodiment. The imagination that once led
him to build a stairway to the stars has been forced into
coping with his own imperiled life on the same quaking
ground that holds us all. Out of necessity he is being pushed
toward a new art of personal survival and as a result he must
move ever further into the centers of action to fight for his
fate; if he left the crucial decisions of our time to The Others
while he concentrated on his "work," as in the old days, he
would be living a lie because he is now too personally a part

of each day's events to pretend they don't shake him and
dominate his existence. His only choice is to insert himself
into these events through his writing, to become an actor
upon them instead of a helpless observer, to try and influence
the making of history itself with his art so that he can save
himself as a man. His driving need for direct participation in
our national life NOW makes the new communicator want
to change America in a pact with his readers, and to begin by
changing his own life in the commitment of laying it on the
line.

For myself time has shown that the vision I saw or read
into the American novel which immediately made me a character in it, the "hero" who wants to be a novelist, could only
be fulfilled if the novel was real and was acted out. Perhaps—in the light of this late recognition of my own need to
personify what to many others existed solely in the imagination—I was scheduled all along not to write novels, as I
always thought, but to try and put their essence into action. If
this is so, I embrace it willingly as the more exciting and now
necessary of the alternatives; for just as I once believed that
art was the highest condition that a person could attain to, I
now believe that if this is true it is the duty of those who conceive such an ideal to use it on society itself and take their literary lives in their hands, if need be, in the dangerous gamble
to make The Word deed. That's where the new prose action
is 30 years after I got hooked—for real, chums, for deadly real.

1968

part 1

intro

The American novel made me, undid me and created out of its mythic reach the faith in a participatory prose experience that has now replaced "fiction" in my imagination with the living actuality of fact. But I had to work to find the words for my growing belief that a truer truth was hiding in the belly of the realistic novel that could challenge not only older ideas about literature but society itself; these words were all I had to extract the new idea that was dominating me and I owe the opportunity to publicly try them out in my own way to a man younger than myself who until then I never knew existed. The five essay-reviews that follow on Frank Harris, Leslie Fiedler, Nelson Algren, Paul Goodman and James Baldwin were all done for Richard Kluger when he was editing the New York Herald Tribune's Book Week *from 1963-66. Kluger became the third editor (the other two were Jerry Tallmer now of the* New York Post *and William Clancy presently a priest in Pittsburgh) to offer me the absolute freedom to swing as hard as I could in a nonunderground publication. When I first got Kluger's letter asking me to do the Harris book—he had fished me out apparently because of the erotic-hipster tone in passages of either of my books,* The Beats *or* Views of a Nearsighted Cannoneer—*my instinct was*

29

*to turn him down; I was (and am) sick unto death of book-
reviewing as such because I have been doing it occasionally
for 20 years as a third-best thing; and in my particular case it
seemed like a fatal retrogression. But Kluger, like every
effective editor, was unbeatable in his enthusiasm; on meeting
he showed me a quick mind, a quick grasp and a polite defer-
ence that moved me; it was flattering to my status-starved
position to be asked to go at high speed for the* Trib *when the*
Times *was officially unaware of my existence and hadn't even
thrown me a one-paragraph review of the* Cannoneer *soul-talk
that had cost me fear's kickback ever since it was published in
1961. I therefore labored for Kluger, demanded and got both
space and billing, but most important he was not afraid to
print my ideas. He knew that I was a butting black sheep in
the New York literary show, neither a star nor a modest first-
ranker without pretension, instead editing a girlie magazine,
aggressive and insistent and voluminously proud without any
uptown credentials except what I forged on my own authority, and yet he backed me without hesitation because he
wanted work that would make his section jump. He couldn't
compete with royalist Francis Brown (his opposite on the*
Times) *in the quiet smolder of money and power; he didn't
have the advertising, the older names, the space, the security;
he needed potential flashbacks and cogent wild men who
could catch attention and he got a number of them, putting
out every week during the almost four years of his tenure (he
was to leave finally in 1966, piqued and neglected) what I
believe was the liveliest book section in the States. From my
point of view I appreciated the opportunity to speak in my
true voice. I wrote for Kluger and the section as a writer and
an ambitious one, not a reviewer, and it was while I was doing
these five pieces that I hazarded my first statements about the
literary artist as agent of history in this era. As for the pieces
themselves: Harris was essentially new to me and I embraced
him because of his vigor and contempt with all his assholism
included; Fiedler and I had clashed in print once before over*

Whitman and I took backbreaking pains with this piece both
to do justice to F.'s unique position in hip-quick American
thinking life and to launch in retaliation my own concepts in
the last quarter of the article; I had tangled with Algren as
well, not in print but at a party, and this assessment allowed
me to say to him what was impossible for me to communicate
in the flesh after he virtually turned to ice during our verbal
fencing-match; Paul Goodman was a bitch for me to write
about because although I have always found him to be a
public nag, he is probably a one-eyed great man—there is the
purity of the true moral teacher about him—and I quit this
assignment at least three times (sweet talked back to it by
Kluger) before walking through my own season of hell or
Goodman's exasperating didactic writing and finishing it—for
which I am glad today; and Jimmy Baldwin, whom everyone
downtown has known slightly for years, myself included, suddenly became a brother who's been away as I wrote when
originally I had no such conscious intention.

frank harris:
the first hipster

Frank Harris, as he threatened, is still haranguing us from that barely paid-for grave in Nice and I'll bet his words will be heard clear and true long after we're carried out also. The gaudiest intellectual bum of the 20th century (he made Maxwell Bodenheim look like a Catholic schoolgirl) has the last word in his 983-page autobiography-geography-sexmanual-Holy Writ and nobody is quite man enough to take it away from him.

Before we get into the meat of his enormous banquet between covers—not so different from the gluttonous London dinners of the 1890s that Harris carves up before your eyes, making you hate English piggishness as he did and as Hollywood never showed us credulous U.S. innocents—the Devil-boy of the Western World should be saluted with a glass of his favorite champagne in one hand, a copy of J. S. Mill's *Political Economy* (an early guidebook of Frank's) in the other, and a naked chick blowing kisses from the sidelines. Harris in the five-volumes-in-one of his last message to this unworthy ditch accomplished precisely what he set out to do, which was to tell as much of the truth about his being and his times as he was *capable* of doing.

I think it is important to establish this immediately because you are going to be reading a lot of contradictory testimony about this rebirth of a monster book completed in 1928, and then slapped into prude's Siberia for 35 years until now, and such literary snipers as Lord Alfred Douglas, Kate Stephens, Hugh Kingsmill and Vincent Brome will be invoked to put the finger on Harris: that he misrepresented Oscar Wilde, contrived the story about Carlyle's impotence, never really met Ralph Waldo Emerson while in America, etc., etc., and the irony is that the J'accusers are probably factually right in two-fifths of their charges but inherently wrong.

Harris, selfknighted in his shy way as "God's spy," had only this final 600,000-word spectacular in which to redeem a lifetime of largely unpaid promises; he was too shrewd, literarily ambitious and convinced of his own greatness to think for a minute that he could blast down the corridors of eternity with anything less than an effort which matched that of his spiritual Big Daddies: Jesus ("The Christian religion as a real inspiration of practical life and conduct is dead, but Christ is a divine master"), William Blake ("Amy Lowell told me I overrated him, poor old schoolmistress!"), Shakespeare, Whitman, Heine, Wagner. Hardsell Harris without a doubt hammed and bulled his way through life whenever he could get away with it, but "literature"—as distinct from the journalism by which he earned, hacked and puffed-up a rich gravy-stained living—was a sacred business to him; and its first rule was devotion to the ultimate truth if only because this was the clinching part of the deal for the immortality he was certain he deserved.

If Harris lied in these five volumes of his last conceivable chance to shove the holy word into the world's teeth, it was because the hipster-conman habits of half a century rubbed off when and where he least wanted them to; and because, as he sensibly confessed, he couldn't always recall the exact date and name involved in some scandal or seduction since he began writing this extraordinary entertainment when he was a

shot 66 and concluded it in bitterness at 73. The old son-
of-a-sea-captain (Royal Navy) had nothing to lose and a halo
to gain by telling his real story, and after wading through a
tangle of charge and countercharge in books and articles
about Harris, it is this writer's conclusion that F. H. meant to
narrate the ungentlemanly truth with more detailed integrity
than had ever been risked before, and then zip his mouth
forever.

Consider briefly, with that in mind, what a fabulous,
tough-romantic, musical-comedy hero Harris was: At the age
of 28, after having shipped alone to the U.S. from Liverpool
at 15 and helped to lay the foundations of the Brooklyn
Bridge, ridden the range in southern Texas with volumes of
Carlyle and J. S. Mill in his saddlebag and been the greatest
college-dropout of his generation—the U's of Kansas, Paris,
Heidelberg and Göttingen—he stormed London à la Balzac
and within two months took over the editorship of the *Evening News* with no newspaper experience whatsoever. After
three years of coolly learning every dirty journalistic trick in
the business and driving his paper's circulation to the point of
profit after he had been faced with an initial deficit of
$200,000 per year, Harris took over in succession the *Fort-
nightly Review* and the *Saturday Review* (not to be confused
with our own brisk little consumer item), making the latter
the "most stimulating publication of its time in the English
language."

Writing for Harris in 1895 were such smallfry as G. B.
Shaw, H. G. Wells, Conrad, Meredith—he had them all; but
right in the middle of this uncanny show of nerve and taste
Harris crusaded off to South Africa to try to stop the
empire-happy Cecil Rhodes ("I knew Zola fairly well, but not
nearly so intimately as I got to know Rhodes") from precipi-
tating an unjust war against the Boers. He failed—what other
sane man representing no combine or official interests other
than himself would even have conceived of success?—but
added the head of Rhodes to a growing gallery of celebrities

that finally makes Elsa Maxwell and Leonard Lyons seem like Dead End kids with their noses pressed against the glass.

Harris soon became the most unashamed namedropper in contemporary literature, and very likely in all of recorded history, as a result of considering himself the equal of every human being who had ever been born with the grudging exception of Jesus and Shakespeare. With such an uncomplicated democratic outlook it was natural for him to go directly to the source when he had a problem with his intellectual income tax, so to speak: If he wanted to find out what was cooking in economic theory he naturally paid a call on Karl Marx and "my German astonished him"; a question about male prowess took him to France and the Hemingway of the 1880s, Guy de Maupassant (whose short stories Harris later cribbed for style); musical problems brought Harris to Munich and a serious dialogue with his newest buddy, Richard Wagner, then understandably distracted because he was tapering off a love affair with King Ludwig; theatrical questions brought about chumminess with Sir Henry Irving, Ellen Terry and Sarah Bernhardt, Sarah much less divine to Frank than Frank; and innate political opportunism—Harris was ready to stand for the House of Commons during his London editing days and probably would have ended up at least Prime Minister if he hadn't publicly defended Kitty O'Shea for being mistress to Parnell—made him tight with Winston Churchill's father, Lord Randolph, who was then being groomed for PM until he suddenly fell apart as the apparent result of an uncured syphilis infection. (Harris has a deadpan quote from Lady Randolph which is worthy of Proust and is even more relevant because it pierces through the band-music of official history to the dirty kitchen of fact: "At first," Mrs. Churchill told Harris after her husband had finally perished at age 46, "when he was practically a maniac and very strong it was bad enough, but as soon as he became weak and idiotic, I didn't mind.")

Overall, Harris is too fishily concerned with "great personages" for our defiant American title-suspiciousness in spite of his really quite decent attitude that he was always trying to help his notable friends overcome their weaknesses. But apart from this touching consideration for those less fortunate, Harris the writer left dozens of brilliantly clear literary snapshots of the most celebrated names of his time caught with their poise down and all seen in a sharply natural, contemporary light.

Because of his fantastic initiative as a catalyst between people and a bridge to events that would otherwise be unlinked, Harris' personal story becomes inseparable from the world's story, circa 1880-1920, which he actually *helped make happen* in spite of his noisily blatant egotism and freakish lack of humor. So completely does this man's multiplicity of private interests become united with the decisive artistic, political and social activities of his era that we are given a scope of significant experience on a history-making level that is like nothing else conceived during this period.

Possessed of the imagination to dramatize himself far more stunningly than the Sir Henry Irvings and Bernhardts who wowed his contemporaries, Harris poetically acted out on the stage of perilous reality the star role of his hero-directed, incomparably individualistic, large-gestured time. Values that have vanished as totally as Teddy Roosevelt's equivalent silent-movie style reemerge to hold the personality of Harris and his age forever preserved in the time-capsule of his book, which is already taking to itself with each passing year the inviolability of a great costume fiction that will never entirely date because of its startling clarity of language and scene. Today, as the human requirements of a dreadfully new world impose themselves upon us with daily, value-revolutionizing pleas—and where society's need for superman-type characters has shrunk to a cartoon compared to the unspectacular necessity for ideological sanity if the human race is merely to survive—Harris' autobiography is released to soar beyond its prideful egotism; his probable fibs or exaggerations are less significant than what we can now see as the complete articulation of a period which he made seem unsurpassably important by the seriousness of his aims.

By tracking to its authentic home each compelling tendency of his time, Harris lived out ideas in their historical context with wholehearted fidelity: 1900-style war took him to Moscow and Capetown and inspired some of his finest narrative writing; loud idealistic principle threw him in a despised British jail (this Irish-born Welshman who looked like "a Jew or a financial blackmailer" outtalked today's Angries in his scorn of British upperclass ignorance and stupidity) and the contemptuous thrust of his behind toward WW I cheerleaders almost got him jailed again in America, where at 60 he was editing the semicrank *Pearsons* magazine. (And characteristically, after the decline of his early London successes which were never duplicated and the dribbling away of a goodsized nestegg which he received for selling the *Saturday Review*, he ran begging letters in *Pearsons* which brought him hundreds of checks from $1 to $50—always hustling a cheap dollar any way he could.)

This particular kind of money-chiseling is not recorded in the What-A-Martyr-I-Am-But-I-Will-Be-Redeemed embarrassments toward the end of Harris' autobiography, and it is in small, ungrand instances like this that one dearly wishes Harris could have had the selfirony to needle himself in the interests of that noble Truth he rants about. Hugh Kingsmill, the English skeptic, is unfortunately all too accurate when he says: "Harris is sentimental, i.e., his ideals and actions don't react on each other. His ideals please his fancy and flatter his vanity, while his actions suit his convenience." While this mighty sharpie was being described by G. B. Shaw as "St. Francis Harris, a martyr to truth" after the autobiography had been violently attacked, Harris suckered crippled *Variety* columnist Frank Scully into writing most of Harris' own bylined biography of Shaw and then kept over 80 percent of the advance for himself. In these last years he dressed and came on like an aging procurer, with his cornball waxed mustache and special-occasion pre-Adler elevator shoes which boosted his 5 ft. 6 in. a strutting two inches.

But it is precisely at this point of almost irresistible ridicule (deserved!) that we are forced to turn up the big ace in Harris' marked literary deck, deliberately saved for last because it has always been used by the lascivious lip-wetters totally ignorant of the purpose and value of literature as the chief fascination of *My Life and Loves*—namely, the overwhelming sexual reality of this book and the muscular aggressiveness, literal and figurative, which brought it to triumphant expression in a period so ashamed of carnal enjoyment that ours today is a positive erotic New Deal compared to it. I use the word "aggressiveness," or even the glib "compensation," because if it hadn't been for our hero-villain's short size, uneven features, nearsightedness—all the unpleasant disappointments of the mirror which he faced early in life like the mensch he was—it is doubtful if literature, let alone custom, would have benefited from such a clean breakthrough as Harris felt ego-compelled to make.

For the majority of men, one of the kicks in reading Harris' play-by-play accounts of seduction is that because of his physical deficiencies he had to work harder than the smoothie swordsmen of his time to succeed. And succeed he did, on a level more arduous and determined than the privileged hotshot who whistles and nets them in like sparrows. Contemporary American literature has absolutely nothing, Henry Miller included, to match the unique seriousness with which Harris approached sexual intercourse and its variety of related pleasures. His straightforward descriptions of some 40 bouts are unpretentious models of sexual realism which show loving appreciation of every conceivable aspect of a woman's body and range of responses.

Because uncompromised writing about this No. 1 area of masculine life was for so long taboo—driving men's literary appetite for sex to the fantasy-world of pornography, the very opposite of Harris' powerful adult objectivity—these passages have the fascination of every original contribution to literature. Although they were written as long as 41 years ago, and sexual frankness in books is now much more commonplace on both a cheap and serious level, Harris' scenes seem newly minted and one is forcefully struck by how naturally they fit contemporary erotic awareness. And the naive idea that Harris "made them up" is surely unrealistic when anyone who gets around today could easily give you the names of 100 restless swingers between New York and L.A. whose turnover of bed-partners is far more impressive, or alarming, than Harris ever claimed.

Rather than be minimized, as editor John F. Gallagher does in his introduction for some surprisingly unconvincing reason—or is it yet another of the degrading strategies to keep the so-called fuzz at bay, and if so what an unfriendly image the law and its enforcers are increasingly taking on during the 60s here in America—the sexual candor of *My Life and Loves* should be praised for bringing into the open what men have always known and what realistic contemporary women are entitled to know. (Unless highly worldly, most U.S. women will likely be resentful of Harris' undeviating biological aggressiveness and, to them, unromantic utilitarianism; but they will relish his mature objectivity about their own sex even more than men will.) However, a reader would be in error to dote on these sections at the expense of the whole, even though as writing they work with crisp effectiveness compared to the disorganized, boring selfjustification that deteriorates Harris' ironman posture toward the end of his marathon. Perhaps, though, this collapse of purpose and narrative into repetitious mouthings of old Harrisian saws and dull holy medals pinned by the great blowhard upon himself is the depressing evidence that gives his life and work its final authenticity.

Here in the sin-will-be-punished last chapter of his earthly story is the aged commandment-breaker heavily in debt, too spent to fight back, barely strong enough to get out of bed and wax his absurd mustache, with the moral nuts of all "civilized" nations out to squelch distribution of his writing and thus deprive him of his bottle of wine with those two-hour Riviera luncheons that made enduring the end bearable. But I prefer remembering this hairy customer at the height of his chutzpah, when his intolerable but undentable conceit was coolly sneering in the face of his mockers: "Christ may go deeper than I do, but keep in mind that I have a wider experience."

Indeed you do, you insufferable hardnose of literature, and may you live forever sticking your rasping book into this world's dishonest business!

1964

waiting for the end: leslie fiedler's bronco ride from pocahontas to marjorie morningstar

Aggressive, cocksure, intellectually sadistic, dogmatic, gossipy, and more keenly involved with contemporary America than probably any of his critical peers, Professor Leslie Fiedler of Montana State University has written a justly bitter book that withholds neither his derisive intelligence nor his superior independence. Misleadingly subtitled "a new work on the crisis in American culture, race and sex," and sub-subtitled "a portrait of 20th-century American literature and its writers," it is instead an incisively personal and unofficial mixture from both these Ph.D. lodes issuing in a single verdict: failure in American life and letters.

With a rare if boisterous courage inspired by his almost total pessimism, Mr. Fiedler faces realities that must cost him dear as a fully committed teacher and novelist-critic who has

43

given his most energetic years to a stance he now questions in the extreme. Passionately involved in prose literature, he now dispassionately foresees the increasing meaninglessness to society of the novel as an artform—one which he himself practices "ironically and desperately" and which from this book you can tell, sadly, still excites his fullest human response.

A professor-writer of the generation of Saul Bellow, Ralph Ellison, Bernard Malamud, Randall Jarrell, Isaac Rosenfeld, Wright Morris—all of them "children of the Depression" who taught or teach in universities in what became a new status-role of U.S. literary life—Fiedler now feels that the wedding of writers to the academy has been a narrowing and probably emasculating experience, however noble the effort to intelligently cloister the raw vision that scorches across all primary American literature.

But it is not even the decay of the novel and disillusionment with the university as a sanctuary for the summoning-up of great work that gives Mr. Fiedler's book its poignancy of wholesale intellectual betrayal. These are only symptoms of a general deterioration of accustomed values so drastic that the end of humankind itself is prefigured with the antinovels of William (*Naked Lunch*) Burroughs, which cast such a hopeless light that it illuminates for Mr. Fiedler the burden of his theme and the title of his dirge. He personally does not believe in any such doomful solution to the increasing corruption of valid culture, purpose and integrity which he sees proliferating in America and the Americanized world. No, his final sinister prediction is that the end will be endless as we are swept forward into a mass-cultural void of such stupefying absurdity that all serious literary communication will cease to matter except as a faint memory.

Before he signs off on this bleak note proclaiming a new, postliterate, essentially idiotic American society—and he has only sharpened with print what other indignant-disgusted minds of his generation and standards have been muttering under their breath—Mr. Fiedler takes the innocent reader on an intellectual bronco ride of such unexpected speed, range, vigor and bewildering transition that one barely has time to get set before the experience is over and you are helped down, dazed and impressed. It is only after recuperation that you are able to measure how much extraordinary ground has been covered—Melville to Mailer, James Fenimore Cooper to Allen Ginsberg, Pocahontas to Marjorie Morningstar—and even though it goes too furiously fast for the normally intelligent head to ingest in one reading, it is a cerebral tour de force without trying.

Mr. Fiedler's mind is the apotheosis of the urban American Jew with a radical literary background who can adeptly spin the world with abstract concepts where others must struggle with long division. But what distinguishes Mr. Fiedler's thinking is that more than 20 years ago he removed himself from the relatively ghettoized East and plunged his conceptualizing intellect into the authentic loam of the American heartland, so that his natural bent to abstraction and spectacular generalization now bears with it the hard ballast of this nation's history and literature as well. His ethnic origin is significant not only in the prototypical quality of mind it brilliantly displays but also in understanding his acute sensitivity to the Indian and Negro as haunters of the white American psyche. If Mr. Fiedler had not been "a Jew among Gentiles, an Easterner among Westerners, a radical among conservatives," it is unlikely that his consciousness-expanding speculations (too often presented as fact) on the unconscious conflict the white man has suffered toward his darkskinned victims would be so pertinent.

Unlike other Jewish intellectuals who looked toward Europe from the mental spires of New York, Fiedler has been a harsh pioneer in pursuing his existential obsession with the racial miseries of American experience to its source, both geographic and historic, and in this sense he is a forerunner of a new generation of young American Jews immersed in the national memory more unquestioningly than he can ever be.

Of course Mr. Fiedler would probably needle them on their folksinging identification with a bluegrass country embraced more from longing than experience, just as he familiarly caricatures the dubious triumph of hyperthyroid Jewish culture in presentday America; hate cards, sick jokes, Mogen David, Eddie Fisher, science-fiction, Mother's Gefilte Fish and the transformation of Huck Finn into Augie March. In an exasperatingly provocative theory which can neither be proved nor disproved, Fiedler accounts for the present affirmation of the Jewish image by the American masses as an act of identification that matches their own sense of exile at home and the increasing contempt shown them abroad. *All* Americans, he tells us with no discernible twinkle, are the Jews of the second half of the 20th century—which makes George Lincoln Rockwell a sulking barmitzvah boy who obviously never received his fountain pen.

The presence of the Indian-Negro-Jew triad in White Protestant American experience, first regarded as evil by Wasps and then after long travail imitated in ironic concession to its vitality—with the three despised groups in turn aping their psychic oppressors in an effort to clutch an American dream that became a nightmare of who's-got-the-identity—is a striking diagnosis that Mr. Fiedler consistently uses to pry open the secrets of national pathology. He voraciously strips every form of native literature to psychodramatize the racial and cultural deceptions which he sees in every ostensibly integral act.

For example, he writes that Ralph Ellison's *Invisible Man* "reminds us disconcertingly of Kafka's K., i.e., seems a second-hand version of the black man in America, based on a European intellectual's version of the alienated Jew"—and although Fiedler gives no weight to the fact that Mr. Ellison is a sharp, complex and wordly mind whose fiat is reality itself rather than Fiedler's brutally confining "black man in America," there is enough glancing truth in the charge to illustrate the keen skepticism of his perception.

But there is also Fiedler's typically generalized language (Kafka's symbolic character K. was clearly a creation and hardly a "version"; Kafka himself was a desperate artist in distinction or addition to being a dime-a-dozen "European intellectual"; there was no concept of the "alienated Jew" until Kafka incarnated the very idea that Fiedler grants a prior existence) which blurs rather than specifies experience. Mr. Fiedler's prose, unlike his dynamic thought, also revels in a welter of teeth-grinding words and phrases like "middlebrow," "mythic," "homoerotic," "symbolic virginal role," "counter-tendency to avant-gardism," "hortatory philo-Semitism," plus a bevy of professorial harumphs which include the various "in any case," "the truth is, of course," "that is to say," and the indispensable "indeed."

But rap Mr. Fiedler as you might for indulging every unattractive liberty that can drive his most willing reader to a near-fit, no verbal carping can undo the slambam immediacy of his highclass muckrake job on American writers. Beginning with "The Death of the Old Men," Faulkner and Hemingway, who ended up by "parodying" themselves—"a slow suicide by the bottle in one case and a quick one by the gun in the other"—he almost lefthandedly butchers Steinbeck, Dashiell Hammett, Raymond Chandler, Sinclair Lewis, but pauses to write a marvelously revealing chapter about the smalltown Midwestern boys who were atheized and devirginized by World War I and Paris and made of their romantic defloration a uniquely American style that was heard around the world. Mr. Fiedler then tunnels into the Depression, naturally praising the comparatively parochial novelists Henry Roth and Daniel Fuchs (as well as the already classic Nathanael West and Henry Miller) while impatiently gutting Thomas Wolfe, John Dos Passos, Theodore Dreiser, etc., with a gratuitous condescension that makes you think they were fink plumbers who flunked out of the Famous Writers School.

And yet this is followed by surely the most perceptive, if

foreshortened, piece of analysis so far written about the enormously lustful and finally murder-hatching seduction of serious writers to Hollywood, although it oddly omits any reference to the most talented fallen angel since F. Scott Fitzgerald—the late Clifford Odets.

Mr. Fiedler occasionally behaves like a latterday Samuel Johnson (and the bluntly conservative West Coast critic-poet, Yvor Winters) as he dictatorially exalts one writer while dismissing or ignoring ten others. Yet there is never a pious or commonplace thought because of his literally orgiastic sense of analogy. He cannot write about literature without calling into play associative ideas from psychoanalysis, anthropology, history, biography, movies, magazines, places, so that you have the humbling sense of being overwhelmed by an intellectual free-lover who shows you what an inexperienced punk you really are.

It is when Mr. Fiedler brings contemporary writing and living up to the present moment, however, that he can really rivet you with his sense of literary-cultural trends, like an inside newsletter—but one perversely dedicated to futility.

The only American war that truly interests even the pacifist young writers, he says, is World War III, which perfectly recalls Gregory Corso's nervy and strangely therapeutic poem of rapturous annihilation, *Bomb*. The only unexplored part of the globe that fascinates the aware young, says Mr. Fiedler, is "that other globe, their own heads," which they are exploring with hallucinogenic superiority; intent upon "the alteration of consciousness" as the foundation for a life-outlook that a former generation of neurotic liberals can find no continuity with—because *their* values were based on middleclass control of unfamiliar thought instead of regarding the mind as an instrument which, if properly primed, can supersede its present vision.

Fiedler pays respect to both William Burroughs and Allen Ginsberg for the Beat breakthrough to at least new possibilities of consciousness and its expression, although he patronizes the equal if earthier contribution of Jack Kerouac. But in the end his skepticism overcomes his journalistic fascination and he sees these two would-be seers as inevitably exploited and exploiting in a time where everyone is on the make— their horror-stories from inner space reduced to mere canapes at some boring mescaline cocktail party of the future.

Mr. Fiedler concludes his book with brave swan-songs to the older poets whose skill and savage integrity have briefly excused America for being—foremost among them Ezra Pound, the recently dead Theodore Roethke and Robert Lowell. However the first impression an impartial reader will take away is one of overall awe for a mind so sleeplessly alert to logging every new literary twitch as evidence for an indictment of life. But it is doubtful if such a reader will get the chance to take away anything because Mr. Fiedler's book is not addressed to the uncommitted, freelance buyer of books; it is an unabashed inside job written for literary and intellectual specialists who share his vocabulary, knowledge and preoccupations. It deliberately excludes the intelligent general public by its unquestioned assumption that what is valuable is by definition antipopular.

In Mr. Fiedler's harsh scale of values, derived from an adult lifetime's involvement in the most exacting modern literature and now applied to the world even more than to writing, the words "debased," "lowbrow fantasy," "middlebrow banality," rightly suggest a toweringly elitist attitude to American insect-life which is the unexpected curse of dedication. What a generation ago was a great and courageous radical-highbrow ideal, the pursuit of God in the secular terms of art and socialism, has now become aggravated into a pained lifestyle removed from its age in any objectively potent and constructive sense; it doubtless yields each lost-causer the satisfaction of the purest integrity, yet seems truly dated when viewed in today's global perspective of unheeding and uncaring millions.

But what is the alternative—submission to the fraudulence, ignorance, selfdeception, corruption of taste and intelligence which the American no-culture has produced? So committed is Fiedler to a Flaubert's Last Stand against the beerdrinking hordes that one discounts in advance any receptivity to a different approach; but so representative is he of a point of view taken to its extreme that it demands contesting when a new historical situation has imposed its imprint on all.

Any cold assessment would ponder the fact that serious literature has been fighting for its public meaning in our time against the gigantic massmedia and, except for a minority whose professional and existential consolation it is, has lost its genuine social significance in the world and largely become the refuge of the victimized or the lip-service of the cultured. Such a literature, one must think, can only perish of irrelevance when the historical moment seems to beg the writer to project his talent out of literature and into the creation of the present.

If Norman Mailer is correct (even a hair's worth) in thinking that his "Superman at the Supermarket" *Esquire* article won the 100,000 votes that permitted John F. Kennedy to defeat Richard Nixon, or if James Baldwin feels as he must that "Letter from a Region in My Mind" in the *New Yorker* was a threat to the lives of his white readers unless they acknowledged his black one, one sees the evidence that writing today can actually initiate history instead of reacting to it.

But the entire conception of the writer as a maker of history realistically depends in this age on the utilization of the massmedia that Mr. Fiedler regards with amused contempt because it is the vulgar antithesis of the literary conscience of the past which he incorporates. His bookish armor to the sweet vulgarity of experience itself today blocks his recognition of the limitless extension and newfound significance of literary power through every form of the mass-communication channels. The possibility of communicating frankly and urgently with a vast number of minds is becoming increasingly apparent to formerly aloof serious writers, since they are the most articulate voices in an unprecedentedly open and therefore determinable human destiny.

Mr. Fiedler could be of tough, active importance to many instead of a standard-bearer for the diehard few if he conceded that literature has been driven into a new power of influence on events themselves—if it can only be extricated from its past, stripped of its dreams of an immortality and posterity that will never come to pass if it doesn't assert itself upon reality now, and directed to an audience whose individual and mass being can never again be separate from the writer's.

1964

nelson a.
and his monsters

The young people's cultural mutiny of the 60s against middle-class authority in the name of the individual conscience has suddenly lifted Nelson Algren from the cliché of being a post-Depression naturalistic novelist into the unexpected purity of a grizzled American guerilla leader. The urban nightmare of the head-stomping *Neon Wilderness* that he vainly projected to the public 15 years ago has now become part of the 1964 Presidential campaign—when will this society's legislators realize that literature is a more trustworthy view of the living truth than even a Louis Harris poll?—just as the underworld that he identified with has now transcended its zoolike novelty and become cynically familiar to the scheming contemporary consciousness.

From jaywalking to pot-smoking to adultery to abortion, the majority of American adults are today habitual lawbreakers who can no longer claim innocence of that experience beyond the law which shaped Algren as its premature voice. Within this radically altered climate, Algren's unpreaching mission to give "recognition" to the publicly unacknowledged life that "multitudes of people have been forced into" has meant more to an Establishment-disgusted generation 20 and

30 years his junior than to his own contemporaries. At the
same time that East Coast intellectual officialdom was impatiently brushing the novelist off as a "rube troubadour, a car-
nival Wobbly"—and the fact that his one New York champion, Maxwell Geismar, alienated numerous open minds by
coarse journalistic demagoguery was no help—Algren's spare,
funky integrity was quietly snaring the imaginations of the
kids with the crooked grin.

A free-feeling rather than a monastic leftist, a *Mad Magazine* clown with the satin stylistic grace of an Elizabethan
lyric poet, a hardedged metropolitan hipster with the gentle
dreams of a flute-player, Algren by his mere tantalizing ema-
nations quietly turned on an underground network uniting
the very brightest individualist-dissident-avantgarde bandits
dotting the landscape; ranging countrywide from Paul Krassner at *The Realist* in Manhattan to the totally engaged columnist Ralph Gleason in San Francisco and including probably the three sharpest of the neolunacy literary jivebombers,
Joseph Heller, Terry Southern and Jack Gelber. A cowboy-
type loner by every inch of evidence, Algren's diffident but
sturdy marginal presence has made him a subterranean American father-figure in a time where all younger farout psyches
are orphaned—an Absurd Father if you will without piety,
pretense or plan who nevertheless seems perfect to his super-
alert bastard brood because they could never respect or believe
in the reality of a well-balanced, well-analyzed, etc.

It is in this uniquely contemporary context that H. E. F.
Donohue's *Conversations with Nelson Algren* takes on the
significance of a cultural (more accurately, *anti*cultural) Happening, the product of informality, honesty, black humor,
involvement, disillusionment, acuteness, bluntness—a kitch-
en-table form of art that thoroughly sustains its T-shirt, egg-
stained charm. Mr. Donohue is a 37-year-old writer (at this
point more earnest than published) who sought Algren out,
persistently cornered him for 13 taped meetings over a two-
year period, and who has the respect for his work to present

these meetings with their sloppy reality intact. Editing was confessedly done to make the manuscript manageable and probably to guard against "libel"—which, as Algren's comments on James Baldwin's homosexuality prove, will one day perish before the fact that truth is harmless and outdated law in itself distorts the human image—yet Mr. Donohue made his cuts with a sensitively rough hand that leaves his questions as nakedly exposed as Algren's answers.

The book is comparable to Horace Traubel's massive *With Walt Whitman in Camden* in several ways: like Traubel, Donohue is the appreciative but salty acolyte who occasionally goads his free-speaking subject to the point of irritation or plain anger. Like Whitman—and the comparison is not intended sentimentally but descriptively—Algren is outwardly uninhibited, colloquial and talks like a White Tower counterman rather than a book. Donohue, to his credit, is a tenacious answer-getter, and the reader soon discovers that Nelson Algren Abraham was born in Detroit in 1909, the youngest of three children in a lowermiddleclass family. His father, a machinist with a credulous, one dimensional view of experience for which Algren had honest contempt, moved the family to Chicago when the pre-pre-Beat novelist was three, and it was on the hustling streets of that "spiritual Sahara" that he patched together his generously ragged point of view.

The "Abraham" which Algren legally dropped from his name when he entered the Army in 1942 is significant to our understanding of his maverick stance from a number of angles. Apparently a three-quarters American Jew, Algren was named after a bizarre Swedish grandfather christened Nels Ahlgren who became a convert to Judaism and renamed himself Isaac Ben Abraham. An Old Testament fanatic, Ben Abraham immigrated to the United States before the Civil War, became a "Jew's Jew, a rabbi's rabbi," a Zionist and a socialist, then "a con-man adopting any faith that would send him all over the world." He deserted his family to follow his half-missionary, half-freeloading destiny and died when

Algren was in high school, both a pauper and a nihilist: "There is no truth, there is no religion."

Algren tells Donohue that he always felt much closer to this courageous crank philosopher than to his passive father or his mother's family of American Legion-loving, reactionary German Jews. You can immediately see the similar strain of independence between grandfather and grandson as Algren offhandedly makes the connection, and yet hiding in the wings unspoken is the anomalous position the author holds in relation to American Jewry as a result of his peculiar ethnic position. He has never been welcomed or at home in the intellectual American Jewish Establishment from *Commentary* to Brandeis University, has never been linked with such Chicago-Jewish literary stars as Saul Bellow and Isaac Rosenfeld, has indeed evaded all typical Jewish novelistic entrapment of subjectmatter and tea-sipping wisdom for the less predictable possibilities of the nonkosher world. To be candid, it is conceivable that Algren was ashamed of or in conflict about the Jewish millstone wearily complicating ("I didn't think Nelson Algren Abraham could get on a theater marquee") a blonder viking image that was also his legitimate birthright: the air of almost indifference with which he lightly sketches his family background could imply an ambivalence which doubtless went into the making of the writer and gives Algren's comments a teasing simplicity that is moving by its omission rather than its explicitness.

As he later in the *Conversations* refers to Hemingway as "a great nocturnal" writer and hardly the jolly Santa Claus of his late Abercrombie and Fitch period, so Algren himself reveals a darker presence than his casual street-style allows for, almost as if it had to struggle through a bookie's criterion of good taste to assert itself. Donohue leads Algren across the days when he worked his way through the U. of Illinois, graduated with a meaningless degree in journalism into the pit of the Depression, then grifted and hoboed through the Southwest until he wrote *Somebody in Boots* in 1935 on a $100 advance from the Vanguard Press. From then until 1940, when he published *Never Come Morning*, Algren was a buddy of Richard Wright's on the Illinois Writer's Project (WPA) and busied himself between the racetrack and spasmodic pro-Communist causes that were typical of the politically activist literary zeitgeist before the war.

Algren makes clear that he was never a Communist because of the party's bureaucratic regimentation and his own anarchistic waywardness, but his respect for acquaintances who fought or died in the Abraham Lincoln Brigade in the Spanish Civil War is unqualified and unhesitant. Unlike other devious and suspiciously complicated memoirs of this period, Algren is straight (and stubborn) as a gun in recounting his experience. Even today when his homemade leftist economic reflexes—revealing the stamp of the 30s and the echo of the *New Masses*—divide the world into American imperialist Bad Guys vs. defenseless small-nation Good Guys, he displays a willingness to go to the edge of the roof for his beliefs that redeems by example what it fuzzes away by unconcern with strategy and close distinctions.

But if Algren were a formal and elaborate radical thinker, he would have as much emotional immediacy for the new Joan Baez-Bob Dylan generation of unrehearsed, unpretty, uncosmeticized blurting expression as Thorstein Veblen— which is to say none. As Donohue's questioning makes clear, Algren's symbolic stature on the hip-rebel scoreboard comes from his undoctrinaire reliance on his senses: pitching the concrete details of a scene he has lived through with a bare wit and an uncommon common man's language that nails down a shared reality with inner freedom of imagination. As he tells Donohue about his three years at war as a medic, the outward events are not truly weird but the liberation of the eye that ticks them off in cockeyed perspective is a measurement of an extremely quick speedup of comic-moral perception which uses jazz-cinema abbreviation instead of creaking platitudes.

Algren was 36 when he got out of the Army in 1945; return-
ing to a $10-a-month room in that "backslum loudmouth of
cities" he wrote the graffiti-stained valentine *Chicago: City on
the Make, The Man with the Golden Arm*, and, ultimately,
A Walk on the Wild Side. The failure of these books to
"reach" the middle class left Algren with a sense of the impotence of literature to affect American society which embitters
him to this day. With the innocent zest of a freshman, Donohue puts an edge on Algren's pessimism by walking him
through the farce of peddling *Golden Arm* to Hollywood.

First John Garfield ("a friendly little guy who could only
repeat the phrases he had heard others say") died in a girl-
friend's sack before he could play Frankie Machine, then Herr
Otto Preminger took over the project and at the introductory
meeting confronted Algren with this winner: "How come you
know such terrible people to write about?" Their relationship
lasted exactly three now-immortal days, with Algren accurately mugging Preminger's popish highhandedness for Donohue but inaccurately disparaging him as a talentless, money-
sexed manipulator.

"He can't act, he can't use a camera, he can't write a story,"
Algren says convincingly while everyone in U.S. film knows
that Preminger's cockiness springs in part from the fact that
he can do each of these and more—a wicked parlay for a
Malibu greenhorn like Algren to thrust his defiant sincerity
at, especially when controlled by a cynical intelligence that
regards pure passion as a childish indecency. Algren's unwillingness to maturely cope with the trim worldly minds who
apparently cashed in on his work in both Hollywood (the
screen version of *Golden Arm* netted him a big $15,000,
reminiscent of Pietro di Donato's even more royal screwing
with *Christ in Concrete*) and Manhattan is sharply challenged by Donohue. He says that Algren's display of soul in
the pursuit of money is a hypocrisy when the rules of the
game are obviously bidding, trading, sweet-talking and
mutually selfish compromise. In an awkwardly moving

answer, Algren strips down to his basic caustic values and maintains that, yes, he is not above "selling it," but he is so constructed that if he had gotten on more smoothly with hustlers like Preminger and a former literary agent who duped him he is certain he could not be the same person who wrote *Golden Arm* and *Wild Side*. He is refreshingly pessimistic ("There is no way of being a creative writer in America without being a loser"), proud of his worth ("I'm a platinum saxophone"), straightforwardly bitchy ("If James Jones, a fourth-rate writer, is worth three-quarters of a million on the market then I must be worth Fort Knox"), but as he defends himself against Donohue's jabs it becomes clear that beneath his crisp one-liners he has paid high dues for having been an outsider for 30 writing years.

Money saturates his conversation ("Even a million dollars ain't enough") as a status substitute for not getting what he calls the *reward* for books he hoped would be wanted by his uncaring countrymen and which he is now certain were not. At 55 he feels (wrongly) that he has had no influence on his time and that he would be a sucker to spend five painful years on a big book when he has lost belief in the possibility of any significant response to a serious novel. The negativism of Algren's statements cuts through the grease of most public declarations about the novelist's role, to the point that, like any committed view of the truth, it becomes exciting precisely because of its unsynthetic blackness. But so sealed is Algren within the confines of his own battered literary bathosphere that he is oblivious to the stingingly defined symbolic, moral and personal position he holds in many minds because of the consistency of his anti-Establishment stand. Probably no one in current U.S. literary life has been so effortlessly feisty, undeodorized, prickly and sourly suspicious of sham as this "one-man lie detector" whose inner current has kept the climate of rebellion charged. It is therefore painful to read about his God's-a-lie loss of literary faith, his compulsion for "self-respect" via capturing large sums of money, and the cranky rearguard action he is carrying on against younger writers: Baldwin, Kerouac, Jones and particularly Mailer.

Since Algren is an obviously alert and pouncing reader of other writers—his forthcoming book on Hemingway should be as penetratingly inside as Beckett's unique little study of Proust—it is easy enough for him to caricature weaknesses in the prose of his juniors. But as a necessarily cagey, defensive campaigner all these risky years he is temperamentally unused to the implications of a strategy alien to his own. Norman Mailer is a creative illustration. The butt of Algren's funny but nearly feline portrait of "Norman Manlifellow" in *Who Lost an American?*, Mailer nevertheless indicates directions of positive action that are sharply applicable to Algren's present stalemate.

When the older writer modestly tells Donohue that he "wouldn't mind running for office" if only to get the confidence of public response which he misses as a literary specter in a pragmatic culture, he is instinctively reaching for the dynamite Mailer held in his hands when he boldly declared his intention to run for mayor of New York in 1961. Behind this act at its purest can be seen the major intuition that the way the serious writer in America can break the trap of cultural impotence is to take his vision into society and prove the practical reality of the literary imagination.

Literature *in action* has become a necessity to a growing minority of writers highly conscious of the wasteland between personal insight and public effectiveness. If the most sensitive and perceptive young American writers have been the victims of a society which denies the writer power while flattering his ego—and the casualties of this divorce from genuine influence in the world are probably higher than in any recent U.S. literary generation—such consolations as the word "art" no longer kid the artist and one now sees a new generation of writers, poets, painters, actors and lowbudget moviemakers subjecting their role in this society to a drastic redesign.

The nightmare of sheer survival in a culture of such mur-

derous indifference to the individual being has made them
coldly aggressive about converting art into electric shock to
awaken the conscience of a puppetlike, things-oriented, mass-
minded enemy. Any one of them will tell you that it is not
the Communists or the Negroes who are the bitterest antago-
nists of presentday America; it is America's artists who hate
her the most because they love beauty, and what its ideal sym-
bolizes, and they feel that the land of their fathers has turned
them out with its commercialism, callousness, opportunism,
unimaginativeness, stupidity and dishonesty. A number of
young writers and artists (Albee, Feiffer, Southern, Ginsberg)
have fought this through their talent alone, which has
rewarded them with a sardonic celebrity that appeases nothing of what sent them into action. Others like Mailer have
attempted to transform the imaginative vision of art into an
influence on mass-communications and political events in
order to combat the powerplay whereby individual creative
works have no social effect upon men comparable to the
cheapest cigarette advertising.

Yet the power of art is becoming increasingly trained at the
common man's eyeballs and should it metamorphize out of
moral necessity into the politics of reality—besides being its
soul—final homage must be paid to the monsterland that
forced its truest lovers to learn the genius inspired by hatred.
Nelson Algren was among the most devoted of America's
vomiting sweethearts long before they became the only true
model of health.

1964

calling in a
deficiency expert

Not since the 30s has there been such a slaughter-job on the country we live in as the one being performed today in new American writing. From James Purdy to William Burroughs, Allen Ginsberg to Edward Albee, Terry Southern to Hubert Selby, the contempt and murder directed toward our glittering synthetic-heap of a culture approaches the monstrous. Rarely has the human spirit in any recent historical period reacted with such violence to what by a growing consensus is thought to be an antihuman and psychopathic society. That it should happen in the contemporary world's first formal, selfcongratulating democracy only adds more misery to the fact; yet at exactly the same time that a new generation of writers is confirming in their work the comment of the tragic Ezra Pound, who recently said in Italy that the once-heroic U.S.A. had become a complete "insane asylum," we observe official America telling us that the future will be a sensible utopia of material well-being, shorter work-hours, longer life and (what incredible nerve!) spiritual health.

It is the barefaced contradiction between the experience set down by our writers and the cheerful abstractions offered by members of the so-called Establishment that hopelessly confuses one's sense of reality, being, functioning, the whole psychic balance. Is it possible that this country's artists can sound the fire-alarm of a national nervous breakdown on the human level and be met with an assured optimistic voice on the government, financial and technological levels? It must be either falsehood or pathology when people living within the same society, sharing a common fate, can have such different public pronouncements to make about being alive in America today. Who's crazy—we or they? Our writers have too much honest hatred of the indignity and meaninglessness of their environment to kid themselves with lines like "the great society," while the White House-scientific architects of our future are too intoxicated envisioning solutions to mass quantitative problems to concern themselves with the desperate condition of the American soul.

And yet this "soul," as Paul Goodman has made embarrassingly clear in four small books since he drew blood with *Growing Up Absurd* (1960), must be the foundation for a society in which people can live with some degree of sanity and the possibility of fulfillment, or else deteriorate further into comas of alienation and powerlessness. In *People or Personnel*, Goodman is concerned with the reformer's task of trying to recreate a dying national morale by advocating methods of decentralization and localization—in order to humanize The Machine and redeem work from cynicism and absurdity. He puts his argument very succinctly in the first chapter: "Decentralization is not the lack of order or planning, but a kind of coordination that relies on different motives from top-down direction, standard rules, and extrinsic rewards like salary and status, to provide integration and cohesiveness." The rest of the book is essentially a quick blueprint of how the country could convert both economy and government into a semidecentralized state that would reestablish the mutuality of communities, in place of an urban sea of statistical victims, and give people an authentic relationship to their labor and each other as a result. For instance, he proposes neighborhood police forces, greater geographical dispersal of huge physical plants like GM, combating the chain-grocery system with independent community grocers, etc.

Although Goodman is very reasonable, clear and practical in his suggestions for scaling this monster of an industrial-governmental complex down to human size—so that we can "diminish power and grandiosity" and substitute for it a self-redeeming initiative on simple neighborhood terms—I doubt that all but a handful of his readers will be as hot about the fine-print details of decentralization as the author is. Like any man consumed by a vision, Goodman can be stubbornly insistent about taking a single thread of thought to quaint and intricate lengths; also, he can't resist lecturing his sophisticated audience as if it were a CCNY nightschool class in civics, a habit which makes one's little ego squirm; and despite his incorruptible principles of egalitarianism and maximum freedom for each individual, as a writer he can be a noble bully who takes the flavor out of reading because of his know-it-all omniscience, overly sententious and quirky manner, and intellectual selfsatisfaction at scoring such an impressive number of hits on the opposition.

These qualities are irritants, yes, but then Goodman has become nothing less than a national irritant in the last five years precisely because he is indifferent to critics like me; he has had the selfdedication to apply his ideas to a public reality that can no longer afford to deny their pertinence because they have been proved in action. If anyone still doubts that the temper of the 60s is wide open to shocking change, unprecedented in our experience, consider that for 25 years Goodman as speaker, essayist, anarcho-syndicalist, poet, novelist, psychotherapist, playwright, community-planner, literary critic, teacher and utopian had an audience for his multiverse roles that numbered in the hundreds. To the crowd that worshiped Ernest Hemingway or Tennessee Williams or even Murray Kempton, Goodman, if he was known at all, was tagged as a crank New York basement radical doomed to

scratch his loser's pen for amateurish little magazines and
50-cent anarchist press pamphlets while the real world swept
by.

Who then had the prophetic ability to reckon on the Beat
phenomenon, the first of the spontaneous "decentral-
ized-anarchist" outbursts of this period? The Negro revolt?
The independent pacifist movement? The militant homosexual groups and the Legalize Marijuana agitation? And finally,
the student Free Speech insurrection at the University of California at Berkeley, where this same Paul Goodman was
invited to speak as moral-intellectual hero to several thousand
(no more hundreds!) undergraduates who had read and
affirmed *Growing Up Absurd*, *Compulsory Mis-Education*
and *The Community of Scholars*? It certainly could not have
surprised Goodman that the students at Berkeley flourished
IBM cards as a symbol of their protest against totalitarian
efficiency; his insight into the deep-freeze of organized depersonalization was probably sharper than that of anyone in the
country and realized earlier.

But who over 40 would have dreamed—as Goodman apparently always did during those lean prophet-in-the-urban-wilder-
ness years—that ordinary American college kids could absorb
mature libertarian ideas and become a political force that
would cause their most honest teachers to become *followers*
and shuck the dated garments of superiority? David McReynolds, the executive secretary of the pacifist War Resistor's
League who also spoke at the Berkeley explosion, hazarded the
educated guess four years ago that the greatest lever of contemporary history—replacing Marx's proletariat as a potential
revolutionary body of far greater consequence for our time—
would be the serious youth of today. Should this come to pass
in even the most embryonic form during the next decade (and
from the hardboiled student talk of fighting for a New Morality that accompanied the California blowoff, it would be a very
unimaginative adult who thought *his* typically compromised
values made such an eventuality unlikely), then Paul Good-

man's major intuition into the interior being of the betrayed American teenager (*Growing Up Absurd*) will take on a historical consequence that can't yet be fully appreciated. Let it only be said that once again Goodman has planted seeds of thought ahead of events themselves.

Although *People or Personnel* is not the most universal of Goodman's recent tracts—it actually seems addressed to social planners and suffers from the kind of shorthand "insiderism" that will probably make it mean more to his Fellows at the Institute for Policy Studies in Washington than to non professional readers it shows no lessening of his urgency to apply a radical intelligence to the conventional mess of our society. It is, however, deliberately more moderate and pridefully empirical than his last three books: almost as if the 54-year-old Goodman now wanted to convince such power-figures as the Secretary of Commerce of the practicality of his visionary stand ("so long as people are transformed into personnel—management-personnel, labor-personnel, professional-personnel—we cannot expect organizations to be internally humanized by their persons, for there are no persons") and let his bohemian disciples of a new basement era bide their time until his next assault.

But this desire, in fact need, to be *publicly effective* brings us to the secret weapon that Goodman has been holding ever since he mounted the national stage as an unexpected player in the big show. Although he has become a father figure to an entirely new breed of nonviolent, non-Communist revolutionaries who have a deeper stake in the future of this society—and a greater chance of drastically changing it—than any previous vanguard of youth in the more "stable" past; although he has distinguished himself (along with Harold Rosenberg) as the most constructive voice of a distinct Jewish radical-intellectual tradition forged in the Depression, tested in *Commentary* and *Partisan Review,* and now unashamedly given to a change-or-perish American society at large; and although Goodman stands cleanly on these hard-won achieve-

ments where others from his roots as anxious to change the
world have cracked under the pressure or finked out in the fat
of middleage, we still cannot understand his ultimate significance unless we see him as an *artist*.

Even though Goodman has taught, lectured, debated and
used every conceivable medium of contemporary intellectual
life to express his beliefs, the clue to his central motivation
was given in his own words: "I am a man of letters in the old
sense, one who thinks that the literary process itself, the criticism of life, adds a new and indispensable element." Goodman may be "oldfashioned" in his classic conception that the
mere act of articulation holds experience up to the light of
judgment and by this perspective finds it wanting; but by the
same token what is imperfect or false to the agonizing sense
of justice possessed by the literary artist must be ameliorated
by his effort or his suffering will be infinite.

If you conceive of Goodman as operating under this burden
of moral and esthetic conscience, it is not difficult to take the
next step and see his total variety of expression as an effort to
put art into *action* against an American society that will vic-
timize the pure poet but yield to poetic *ideas* couched in practical terms it cannot refuse: efficiency, beauty, utility, economy, thrift, health, the amelioration of unnecessary physical
or mental pain—all the concepts Goodman preaches with
understandable confidence because they are indisputable. I
therefore believe it is illuminating to see him as a strategic
artist who has trained himself in the workable techniques of
constructive activity—because they are viable in society
whereas destructive expression, *however more valid as art*, is
always punished by each generation's hypocrisy. But one
should never forget that beneath his busy-brained involvement lies a heart that is the very "fiery furnace" of which
William Blake spoke and out of which a Dostoevsky wrote.

Let me explain specifically what I mean. As a vulnerable
artist beneath his arsenal of facts and figures, but one who
realized early the impotence that the contemporary angel of

truth and beauty suffers in the vise of a power-oriented American society, Goodman out of selfdefense felt the necessity to impose his ideal vision on a brute social structure that by its very being was his enemy and wanted to crush him. Thus, just to survive he had to convert the purity of his artistic sensibility into aggressive political and moral activity; yet his essential being remained and is still that of an artist, but one who is now so closely bound with the fate of society itself that he eludes all formal mediums and typifies a new emerging personality created by the realities of our situation in America.

Like a growing minority of other vows-taking artists forced by the contradictions of our culture to forsake their consuming esthetic religion, Goodman wants the values of art to be effective in ways which *directly* affect society now and permit the artist-in-action to influence the direction of contemporary events. The traditional martyrdom of the artist, to be swooned over by a Sarah Lawrence girl 25 years from now, has become a cliché to this new spiritual Irgun; rather than be hung on a wall, they want society itself to be the work of art and future Beethovens—or Charlie Parkers!—to occupy the White House while generals and politicians become the new untouchables. Yet the risks involved in such a desperate bid for total justice are enormous, since art by its transcendent nature stands for all the freedom that can be imagined; and by calculating his effectiveness within the framework of social action, a Paul Goodman must of necessity reduce and target his imagination in order to achieve his urgent goal—influencing men's minds to bring about change.

Because of his commitment to art as moral action, Goodman cannot cultivate the full dimension of imaginative and moral truth vented, for example, by Hubert Selby (*Last Exit to Brooklyn*) or William Burroughs (*Naked Lunch*), who, while they write "fiction," brutally illustrate Goodman's themes of urban alienation, distortion and depersonalization. Since their style is by liberal intellectual standards "destruc-

tive" and "antisocial"—although a man like Goodman understands perfectly the superior morality in these ostensibly sub-
moral works—he himself could not afford to jeopardize his
immediate effectiveness in half a dozen political-moral areas
with such uncompromising, disdainfully unexplained, authentically disgusting parables of American Man's fouling of the
earth.

But what happens then to Goodman the artist? Does his
esthetic freedom shrink as his polemical power increases? And
does that mean that the individual who influences ideas in the
immediate sense must sacrifice his role as witness in the ultimate Day of Judgment that has always been part of the pure
artist's faith? As literature, it seems clear that a good part of
Goodman's hasty pamphleteering will date overnight whereas
more grimly neutral works like Burroughs' and Selby's will
become icons for our time. Yet for those of us who embrace
the new moral imperative to impose the vision of art on reality itself—indeed think its full implications are as yet unima-
gined, historically necessary, and truly revolutionary—Goodman remains a unique example of how the genuine, paradise-
ravished artist (the very one that MGM and Irving Stone have
sentimentally mucked into millions) will one day become
the acknowledged legislator at this society's gaping core.

Uncle Sam, you bum—beware of angels who have grown
teeth!

1965

the troubles i've seen

Baldwin's first book of short stories sums up work from 1948 to the present and if you were among those who thought that *Another Country* was a strained and uneven effort, I believe *Going to Meet the Man* will impress you. Baldwin should be proud. As these stories testify, he has almost always tried to dig into the humbling soil of the experience of the Negro, the expatriate, the homosexual, and come out with uneasy and disturbing truths that linger a good while after you come to the end of a story. Technically, the stories reveal an integrity to their experience that surprised and enlightened me after the embarrassing botch of *Another Country*; one forgets how hard Baldwin has worked to establish *his* sound, that particular signature of long and patient sentences that never hurry a moment when it should be sweetly tasted and have enough selfconfidence in their leisureliness to envelop the reader instead of lightly touching him.

Baldwin's writing, depending so much on the straightforward humane statement rather than on irony, wit or the savage comic imagination of a Ralph Ellison, occasionally falls into platitude; but Baldwin is intuitive and courageous enough to know that this is where his chief strength lies—common experience uncommonly probed—so that while he occasionally expects the flat statement to do more literary work than it humanly can, I am still impressed by his maturity and understanding as a man. He knows life in a way that I can only call enlightened by Negro wisdom; it is the same older, deeper, seamier, finally larger grasp of suffering and reality that I have heard in the great Negro singers and have observed in certain subtly seasoned black acquaintances.

Let it be said quickly that this reviewer is well aware of the pitfalls of this kind of generalization and there is an ample share of American Negro art around to prove that mere superior "humanity" is not enough in the long run to make a commanding artist. But in Baldwin's instance I am certain that much of his inspiration and insight comes from a long river of Negro experience that has been journeyed in blood and has amazed all of us in the voices of such singers as Bessie Smith, Joe Turner, Mahalia Jackson, indeed Billy Eckstine, all of whom can pour beauty into our ears only because they've had to lift stones into song; the gravity of their effort has a physical reality that can be imitated by whites, never duplicated. Baldwin is not unlike them. In a sense, he is a singer in print, just as he is a preacher in print, and both these qualities obviously go back to the Harlem church days that he wrote about in *Go Tell It on the Mountain* (1953) and find their echoes in the first two stories in this collection, "The Rockpile" and "The Outing."

I would like to take the preacher-singer analogy a little further: Baldwin's power as a writer depends almost totally on his rhythmic, often semimesmerizing use of language. His individual scenes rarely have the striking imaginativeness or surrealistic jolt of Ellison's—his chief rival as a so-called major American Negro writer—but the words creep into your inner ear with a subtle and persistent persuasiveness that does its work at deep levels of receptivity. Baldwin in this sense is something of a witch-doctor; this added spiritual resonance of his language is what often makes his statements more memorable than their actual content. In his longest story in the present book, "This Morning, This Evening, So Soon," about a successful American Negro singer in Paris who has to come home and face his obsessional nightmare about being humiliated or worse, the cadences of the Baldwin prose are as smooth and natural as the waters of a brook. He lulls us into the experience where on other occasions he has shrieked like a dervish, but the final result is the same—a honeyed skill with words and their evocative psychic consequences that is evidence not only of conscious artistry but of that deeper intuitive sense which is the legitimate inheritance of the Negro's grim odd-man-out experience in America.

One hears in his prose the murmuring and quiet groaning of countless other Negro lives, the clank of slave-chains as well as the jump of jazz, and it is this constant ambiance of blackness that pulls Baldwin's work out of the merely effective and gives it the power to really speak which has won him his controversial white readership. This brings us to a less noble point; I have heard white writers and intellectuals put Baldwin down as a "white liberal's Negro," a synthetic creation inspired and tenderly nursed into being by the guilt of liberal American Jews and Protestants. He has been characterized, and not just by one or two envious literary losers, as a fairly shrewd operator who has played on this enormous white masochism for his own selfadvancement and exhibitionistic ends. He has further been accused, in Mailer's three-bagger of a phrase, of not "smashing the perfumed dome of his experience" and letting the real gritty story of his life come out in all of its smelly underwear.

It is natural, of course, that anyone who rises to unusual heights as a literary personality—especially a black American and someone as gregarious and attractive as Baldwin happens to be—will be regarded with great suspicion by others who lack his flair and see it mainly as selfseeking or solemn camp for the whites. But such reasoning in my view is as blind and cheaply superficial as the overenthusiasm of middlebrow college graduates who have never coped with Ellison's *Invisible*

Man or Richard Wright's *Black Boy* and think American
Negro writing was initiated by Baldwin. The fact that Baldwin is a writer who can dramatically project his vision in basic
colors and capture a wide audience because of the intensity
and directness of his beam should be appreciated for what it
is; no other black writer of 40 in this country has been able to
awaken a white response comparable to Baldwin's because no
other black writer has hit the same clear notes on the national
white heart, or what passes for such. Whether these notes are
lasting, whether Baldwin is a phenomenon closer to journalism or theater than literature in its knottiest and ultimate
sense, are questions that beg the issue: in the here-and-now
Baldwin has achieved his present distinction on the basis of
what he has given, and by this criterion he has *given* more
openly and directly and regardless of what tricky motivations
are ascribed to him, than anyone else. There can be no other
reason for his singular position than the fact that he has rung
a big American bell which has tremendous reverberations for
many people caught in the black-white impasse.

The possibility that Baldwin may have used his message up
seems to me legitimate—although this book of stories is not
repetitive or monotonous, two charges that make partial
sense in some of his other work—but for the young literary
turks, like Tom Wolfe, to throw Claude Brown or LeRoi
Jones at Baldwin and suggest that the older streetfighter is a
sissy because he came out of a different turf is much too slick
and easy. The craft and feeling that went into this book, with
the exception of the title story, "Going to Meet the Man," an
unconvincing slice of agit-prop, was hard won; it is true that
Baldwin's tone, at least in the present book, is somewhat
milder and more muted than the bullets Brown and Jones are
ostensibly spitting out, but since when did one or two writers'
virtues replace equally valid concerns from another direction—a subtler kind of obsession, a more subjective handling
of Negro experience? For the sake of argument it might well
be that Baldwin has passed his peak as the most eloquent

Negro prose voice of this time and place; perhaps eloquence is
no longer what is needed, as I'm fairly sure LeRoi Jones
would say, springing his blade, but to scratch off a writer of
Baldwin's exceptional power before he has had a chance to
permit his potential its fullest range is a revealing indication
of how bitchy and pop-arty the literary picture has become in
the last few seasons.

In a sense Baldwin himself is to blame for the fact that his
rather flashy personality has interfered with a cold appreciation of his unusual ability as a simple writer; since he had to
make many of his most effective writing moves through his
personality—not unlike Whitman, D. H. Lawrence, Henry
Miller, even Henry James, to drop a few respectable
names—his meanest critics can spot the egg on the man himself between the lines of the work. But why put a higher
demand on Baldwin than on any of his white counterparts
and why all the false piety? It is hard to imagine any Negro
artist (let alone most whites) in this country who is not mad
for fame as a vindication of his or her very being in the Holly-
woodized environment that molded and then excluded the
spades; a ghetto Negro as brilliant as Einstein or as pure as
Christ would still be nothing less than human if he wanted
above all to be known to the world as someone who survived
an inhuman situation and was going to make certain that you
who put him there knew his name.

Baldwin's pride of being, it seems to me, is nothing more
than normal; if his public personality smacks slightly of the
knock-'em-dead-sweetie Sammy Davis Jr. kind of performer
rather than T. S. Eliot, if he has gotten nailed right into the
niche of international celebrity a la Noel Coward or Maria
Callas rather than some bookish notion of the selfeffacing literary saint—and I believe he has his share of this too—don't
blame Baldwin for being human but rather blame our world
and its new swarm of literary publicists, journalists, agents,
gofers, editorial call-boys and gushing parasites who sell
"talent" to the masses for their own psychological jollies and

commercial ends, and encourage writers to behave like movie stars. William Faulkner's daughter once said unemotionally in my presence that her father was literally the scorned "town bum"; anyone who loves American writing knows that our great writers have been and to some highly dangerous but unavoidable degree must always remain the town drunk, panty-fetishist, psychotic, exhibitionist, junkie, lesbian—the existential pretzel always struggling to be straight and gouging out his or her most authoritative work within this tension.

But American writing is big business today, with huge scores to be made out of book-club and subsidiary rights and large "packages" to be cut up by movie and paperback foxes who have hundreds of thousands of dollars riding on words that might as well be advertising copy from their point of view. The writer who succeeds in this kind of environment becomes a Valuable Property for reasons that have nothing to do with literature and everything to do with worldly power, the market, the "product," the fortunes of coattail-hangers, the reputations of restaurants the writer timidly patronizes or people he inefficiently sleeps with. Overnight the man who has felt himself a freak and struggled for survival through his work becomes a Presence In The World, to be guarded and flattered by the growing numbers who live off him. The disparity between his inner life and his outer would be enough to drive such an exquisite barometer crazy if he didn't already think he was and snort at midnight at the even more cruelly absurd spectacle set in motion around him.

Therefore, while I believe Baldwin's celebrity was justly deserved, it was undoubtedly also exploited, and in a nasty, uniquely contemporary way taken away from *him* by the ego-snatchers of mass-communications and civil rights causes; they hoisted his name and "image" on high for reasons that first must have been warming, as they would to any serious insecure writer who slaved for years in a tiny world far from the big one, but then the resentment and remorse at having one's private self manipulated for the most selfish motives of others must have produced a lump of murder in his throat and driven him both away from the United States and further into himself.

What happens to the psyche of the person encased within the publicly manhandled image is something that only a candid literary celebrity of this time will be able to tell us; his name might even be Jimmy Baldwin. But until he does tell us in such a way that it lays to rest whatever pains of jealousy cause us to misread the image for the man, it is up to us to try to distinguish the valid words that speak to our intelligence and feelings—and mark Baldwin as a writer—from the commodity he has become in the hands of others. If he humanly or even kittenishly played into these hands at the beginning of his career, one can logically assume that they now suffocate him and that the struggle against his "friends" in this second half of his life as an American writer will be as tough as his resistance to his enemies (beginning with his father, which you can clearly see in *Go Tell It on the Mountain*) was earlier.

Baldwin is now in a unique position, with roots and threads that reach from the funkiest gutters of American Negro experience to the plushest cosmopolitan centers of power and sophistication, and his opportunities to tell us about life he has lived and we have not have never been greater; I also believe that given his unusual intelligence and flaming pride he will disassociate himself from that image in which, ironically, we see and measure ourselves rather than Baldwin, in order that he can be free in a more subtle way than the majority of "his people" have had to worry about.

If only by the unanticipated problems that confront him and no one else, Baldwin is still the New Negro in more ways than one and still coping with it; this new book is gentle, not soft.

1965

part 2

part 2

intro

James Jones and Norman Mailer preoccupied me for 10 years
in an immediate way, so much so that the opening article on
each (I have three pieces on Mailer and three on Jones) dips
back before the 1961 starting point that I have set for myself
in the rest of this book. My preoccupation was personal and
yet impersonal: as I have written in the Cannoneer, I had
wanted to be a novelist with a national capacity when I first
began to write seriously and these two men, one a year older
than I and the other a year younger, had done just that. My
relations with each have been interestingly unsatisfactory as a
result, although they always turn me on because I have a dose
of hero-worship for what they have done; I have never envied
them for more than an involuntary moment nor have I
wanted to write novels for some time now, but I have measured myself against each in the fullest sense; and both men
along with Alan Kapelner of our mutual generation (and
James T. Farrell of the older one) have by their almost
unconscious behavior taught me root-truths about the boldness necessary for being an American writer of consequence. I
have learned from everyone, but I hold these four special:
each can be a parody of himself, as I myself can, but each can
best and educate me in some specific area of perception, guts

81

or imagination which is why each is constantly fascinating. I am not interested in those I can be superior to because then I have to repress the most fecund part of my personality out of shame. Jones and Mailer have been so close to our time in America that you can almost reach out and touch them which I have tried to do in these slightly compulsive closeups. Kapelner (too little known) is seasoned, unique, resourceful, beautifully cocky toward existence and humble to individuals he respects, a writer lying in wait for readers, practically undiscovered in the overpopulated wilderness of the U.S. 60s.

a comment on our lunacy in america

By the time you read this the news will be out that *Some Came Running*, James Jones's second book, is a dud, a huge crate of matter (1266 pages) that rarely gets off the ground and leaves even the most sympathetic reader with a sense of flat disappointment. In some quarters Jones will be hanged high because he hasn't made the reception of the book easier by remarks like: "I'm fully satisfied [with *Some Came Running*] but I hesitate to call it great on the grounds of immodesty." The fact that a young writer like Jones can let himself go with such straightfaced blather, after having barely served an apprenticeship, is probably a comment on our peculiar lunacy in America. We need and worship overnight heroes, force them to believe in the myth of themselves by our hot attentiveness, and then when they swallow it all and try to live up to it we indifferently turn our backs and go after the newest celebrity.

I believe Jones is the not unwilling victim of a cynical, barbaric, probably psychotic cultural atmosphere which has encouraged him to try and be a literary Gargantua instead of letting him prosper quietly and grow with time. No doubt our hero is partly to blame, because there is no denying his ambition, his grim, expressionless plugging through pages and pages of unleavened type that make the reader finally beg for relief. The book is monotonous: an almost unrelieved and drearily uniform telephone directory about a number of people who flourished in a small town in Illinois from 1947 to 1950, between two wars. The sexual, financial and emotional (so-called) lives of some 20 characters are put on the line with a headfirst, relentless, savagely dull attack. After miles of documentation, Death, Taxes, Disease, and Disillusion come out the winners, but the edge of any tragic moral has long since been blunted and made almost meaningless in the sluggish bowels of the performance itself.

Mr. Jones doesn't believe in suggestion, in subtle or distinguished or even decent English, or in letting the reader use his own imagination. Everything is spelled out in a thorough and uninspired way, with the words finally becoming as impersonal as numbers, as if the author were making an inventory in some vast warehouse stuck out in a desolate part of the Midwest. People ultimately become as common and uninteresting as canned goods or raincoats as they pass through Jones's writing machine; by the time the reader nears the end he literally does not care if the characters live or die—getting through the book has become the sole, overpowering obsession (perhaps not only for the reader, said he significantly).

The fact that one has to say all this—especially someone who guttily enjoyed and was powerfully moved by *From Here to Eternity*, in spite of its stagy plot manipulations—is a sad thing. It shows how futile an unimaginative and overearnest conception of "writing a novel" can be today; it also shows the almost agonizing pressure on Jones to create something that would "surpass" his first book. He all but breaks his back in this effort, and yet one would have wished that even after six years of labor, and the many small deaths and even larger ones of the writing, his advisers would have persuaded him to put it away. Nothing irrecoverable would have been lost. A legend would have been saved.

There is no doubt in one's mind that Jones is a serious, perhaps "overserious" (seeing humor as frivolity) human being,
and in his own estimation a fanatically dedicated writer.
Some of the most penetrating passages in the book are when
Dave Hirsh, the central character who dies unconvincingly
and needlessly at the end (but luckily before the reader),
speaks about the artist's need to "expose and self-incriminate
himself." Jones's immersion into the motives of what he calls
the "artist"—Hirsh is a novelist trying to produce a book after
a barren period—seem to me honest and excitingly unsparing,
a worthy footnote to themes that haunted Thomas Mann.
Jones is not afraid to face himself, which immediately distinguishes him.

But he is afraid or unable to give up the unnecessary machi-
nery of the traditional novel in his ambition to be big, granitic,
monumental—the mostest. The mechanical contrivance of
the changes of points of view, plus the stretching and bending
of the accommodatingly fingerable story to give the material
narrative shape, strike one as either esthetic cheating or a limp
reliance on 19th-century techniques—as being "novelistic," in
other words, in the most transparent and obvious sense. It is
hard to understand how Jones can reconcile the truth of his
insights with the bloated untruth of his fictional method. One
has the instinct that if he just kept to his particular understanding of truth, his particular cache, and gave up every
temptation to fictionalize it according to elephant-heavy
devices or "scenes," he would write in much closer contact to
his living experience.

Jones's mentor, Mrs. Lowney Handy, is quoted in *News-
week* as saying that this novel shows that "Jim can become
what Dickens was in England, Tolstoy in Russia, Stendhal in
France." You can see what the author was up against with
this kind of encouragement. But what is really interesting,
and of value in trying to understand why *Some Came Running* becomes so oppressive and tedious, is the steadfast pro-
vinciality of Mrs. Handy's examples. We do not need another

Dickens, Stendhal or even Tolstoy. They were great prosewriters produced by their environment, which had an entirely different sense of form, of rhythm, of time-sense, of the particular desperation of the animal, than our own.

You will notice that Mrs. Handy makes no mention of such Bolshevik contemporaries as Proust, Joyce or Kafka; this is because concretely—where the work of art always reveals itself, beneath the classy platitudes and generalizations of partisans, literary agents and critics—they are too perplexingly undead, and have too many headcracking implications put up against "Jim." One need hardly mention that these three characters, let alone such secondraters as D. H. Lawrence, Céline, Henry Miller or E. E. Cummings, are of the 20th century, which is top-blowingly more fragmented, aformal, untypical, and less graspable in both its life and art than the stereotypes of "greatness" that Mrs. Handy points to in the conveniently distant 19th century.

It is just this predictable, stereotyped German clock called "fiction" that Jones has used as the device for his materials; it makes his book unimaginative and prefrozen, and worst of all for a writer of his intellectual honesty, false—because it relies on furniture, no doubt subscribed to by Mrs. Handy, that is museum-pieceish, since real esthetic life (actual thrill, surprise, illumination, indeed "tragedy," or, closer at hand, terror) has fled elsewhere.

Let us concede it (a point your host and a couple of others have been braying about in print for 10 or so years): traditional fiction-writing today is *artificial* writing, and except for purposes of entertainment, its place in our laps is becoming increasingly meaningless, and the strain on the eye not worth it. It has been replaced, slowly and unofficially, by "imaginative truth writing"—a genre as creative as fiction used to be, which uses the staples of the older art (characterization, dialogue, narrative) when it needs or wants them, but expands it into deeper worlds, or realer worlds, of contemporary reality.

It seems to me Mr. Jones must make a choice. Does he

want to be a Great Novelist or a genuine, lowercase, modern-slob imaginative writer, groveling down in the unsifted pay dirt with the other geniuses? There's more contemporary reality in such a decision, more important but less visible drama than in killing off your leading character in a "madeup" story. Paper murders and paper books, even of a billion words, are less real than the carving of mature, maniacally thoughtful works that keep the integrity of actual personal experience intact through overblown times like these. Your move, Mrs. Handy.

1958

hungry mental lion

Mailer's beating in the uptown New York press on this book [*Advertisements for Myself*] is one of the more, maybe even the most, grotesque and illegal unrealities of a time so screwy that a majority of not only people but also book-reviewers obviously don't know if they're coming or going. Seen with the eye of history—that eye which Mailer imposes and ignites in a person with his own avaricious historical vision—this 532 pages of great odds and ends is a deeply disturbing, stunning, existential goose; it gives the reader a perspective on Mailer's enormous grapple with the destiny of his own botched age and reveals the man and writer to be superior to his faults by the sheer extent of his range (unmatched in his league, the under-40 writers) and the nonkidding deadliness of his perceptions. Mailer is no pushover even when he's going through the defensive, spoiled-boy, cocky act; indulgent he is, given to posturing and partially unpleasant nastiness in his italicized personal introductions to early stories, chunks of novels, short articles thrown off with reckless flair and go-for-broke raids on the universe; his manner sometimes smells of corny I-stand-alone melodramatics, a combination of Douglas MacArthur, Humphrey Bogart, Hemingway plus maybe Poe, and it jars the finer teeth when Mailer yields to this reverse

selfpity which extrudes as arrogance; but beneath this obsessive profile-consciousness we are given the lifelike portrait of
an individual so intensely aware of his and other existences
that one can only marvel that a man can participate so completely and unlimitedly in the hot centers of the life of his
time.

Mailer is PMishly topical, but wins his thought back from
journalism, like Koestler and Auden in the late 30s, because
he brings a baroque novelistic imagination to newspaper headlines and plants his own personal time-bomb in the sheaves of
journalistic drippings. Nothing he writes, or almost nothing, is
dated and trivial even though his spontaneous and often
offhand manner of working would seem to make for waste
and regret; what redeems his pieces, makes them not only
alive but vast in implication, is that he brings to them large
concepts—such as the unprovable but bang! shattering idea
that White Protestant repression in America is leading to
total cancer—which only the *intellectual imagination* of a
novelistic mind could conceive and express. The forbidding
climate of formal ideas that existed on the American literary
scene for the last 15 years, which made many prosewriters
shrink with inferiority because they weren't New Critics, logical positivists, psychiatrists, any official legal fortress of truth,
has all come back to imaginative literature as it had to via
Mailer's intuitive utilization of large ideological concepts with
the touch and conviction of the novelist. For this if for nothing else he is exciting, right, making more use of the available
than any of the other highbrow intellectuals who fell impo-
tently gelded between the two mountains of Literature, on
one side, and Ideas on the other; Mailer, the primitive
"quick" of animal life very much in him (the word is his as
applied to others he admires) has sculpted a new unity or at
least a tentative unity out of what 10 years ago were thought
to be impossibles, has used his dramatic senses to make real
his ideas which are the flower of his being. All of this is life-
giving to other writers, points beautiful directions out of ster-

ile alienated-man hangups, restores and furthers the use of the imagination to the accompaniment of reason—the two will no longer snarl at each other from across the room and for that we are indebted to Mailer's uncanny *creative* use of ideas.

But now to the form and shape of the book: obviously the book is a heroic improvisation, in keeping with Mailer's need to publish, to keep his fine un-Italian hand very much in the changing literary picture and not let it develop without him, but his grand bid is both cunningly and convincingly made into an imaginative and timely (Mailer right on the beat again!) package by the running commentary of personal confession which starts off each item. These inside stories about how each article or story or novel of the past 18 years came to be written are undeniably human, juicy, satisfying each reader-voyeur's love of bedroom bathroom uncensored talk; they are newly candid and except for the Famous Writer jazz which occasionally exudes from Mailer like bad perfume they are fascinating with a minimum of bullshit. Mailer is wrong, however, to think they are a completely original technique; plebian Paddy Chayefsky used the same subjective-honesty approach to precede each of his published TV plays and did it with unusual competence (as he does practically everything). What makes Mailer's confessions more interesting, however, is the unapologetic boldness, frankness and terse intelligence with which he discusses his inner life, bouts with marijuana and seconal, fear, exhaustion, vanity, the entire variety of high desperate kicks and anxieties which every live adult on the scene experiences today but rarely concedes because there is no precedent for it. Mailer establishes the precedent without shame or qualification, which is a manly gas; and rather than such experience being unique or "pathological" or whatever the square middleclass-moralistic labels hung on it—which was done by the *Time* and *New York Post* crybaby reviewers—such a variety of inner paranoias and labyrinthine semisuicides and redemptions is merely the rockand-

rolling rhythm that ravages a majority of today's elite minds
and sensibilities. Mailer has turned the inside out, which
reflects an increasing tendency on the part of all serious writers
to extend the printable to that most pregnant area of all at the
moment—the self. It goes without saying that he does this
with the class we expect from him, the boldness, the dignity,
and occasionally some of the romantic selfdramatization
which always both stains and puts a velvet fever-glow on his
experience. But for the massmedia reviewers to suggest that
this inevitable 1959-necessary exploration of self smacks of the
dated Fitzgeraldian "crackup," as several implied or did say, is
either density or lying; it reinforces phony taboos and categor-
ies which writers like Mailer and others are knocking themselves out to destroy and thus allow more open possibility for
both existence and literature; and it unfortunately once again
draws the lines hard and bitterly between honest writers and
padded fakes, with the "well-balanced" inhumans of the popular press and magazine world robotlike speaking out on cue
church-words which apply to nothing but phantom ideals of
the past that are repressively nowhere today.

Mailer's technical job in this book—to return to the concrete fact of the book as an art-grenade—was to resurrect and
then set his old pieces (essays, short stories, newspaper columns) in the arc of his autobiographical necklace; this he
does with daring and unexpectedness, rarely letting the reader
down and also discharging from his tough sour stomach much
of the spleen which the recent indigestible years have accumu-
lated; as a simple formal accomplishment the book is highly
novel and provocative (quite apart from the worth of individual pieces which will be discussed in a moment) because he
has found a form suitable to his own kaleidoscopic sense of
the world and one which instinctively matches the present
mood of others as well. For reasons which are probably too
intestinal to trace to their source, the span of present concen-
tration on the part of the liveliest minds around is not as
extensive as it is intense; the blinking lights of reality are too

abrupt and various right now in America to allow for long-range, calm, unshifting, unnervous, sober application; thus the form which exigency determined for Mailer—namely that he had a lot of pieces and hip snips and murderous hunks which he wanted to collect plus the fact that as a very conscious name writer a book of his was due—is almost symbolic of the forms of experience which contemporary necessity is imposing on his readers. Should this be at all obscure, put it this way: Mailer's living imagination found a form out of necessity which corresponds to the nervous beat of his readers, and although the novelty of the book wasn't apparently premeditated by Mailer over the course of many years, the very pressures which prey upon him also prey on those who will dig this book. It is therefore a Venutian marriage of restlessness, ambitions, egos, anxieties, rebellions—with Mailer both matching and shaping the temper of his changing time. Thus you can read his book straight through and be both entertained, horrified, annoyed and sent; or you can browse in it, read parts of it over the phone or in bars, have the fun and freedom of moving around in its pages without crucifying yourself for losing the thread of continuity amidst the abrupt stops and starts of your own life. All of this is not to be taken too lightly; reading today must give people kicks or freedom or they will not bother with it; and Mailer has improvised just such a free-associational form, like an intellectual House of All Nations, where you can pick the subject-bitch you want to ball with most and be conducted from boudoir to boudoir by an electric, suave and machiavellian host.

So much for the form, which will have reverberations on the literary scene because it is not choking and has the morbid gaiety and swiftness suitable to a crucial, wide-open time; the content which determined this extraordinary window-display is equally fresh, but (mostly) invites our big respect as well. Mailer begins by unloosing some of the short fiction he wrote at Harvard, and even in those early works we get a sense of the unusual assimilative powers of the writer,

the quick facile learning ability, and also the silken gift of
being able to make the leads and hints of other writers his
own in brief time. Before he was 17 Mailer tells us he wanted
to become a "major writer"; even at this age his will was
demonic, his eye for subjectmatter shrewd and hardboiled,
and his sense of the beautiful or profound already conditioned by a knowledge of "who has the power," as he writes
about his ex-pal James Jones in a brilliant gossipy chapter on
his contemporaries; in other words he is a worldly man,
acutely aware of fame, money, the material realities which
determine the struggle for both personal success and historical
change; all of this requires a practical as well as a visionary
mind and Mailer refined these qualities in deliberate fashion
(it would seem) after he was magnetized by the example of
André Malraux. There is little doubt that Mailer is not so
much a hero-worshiper as a hero-directed man; Malraux and
recently Picasso gave twinges to his own inner compass which
were then steeled by will and application. But even in his
early fiction, where Mailer freely and maturely acknowledges
the influences of Faulkner, Farrell, Hemingway (who still
sticks in the belly of his pride), we see an extremely precocious sensitivity to what he was later to label (there is an over-
reliance on Big European Thought tags in Mailer) the Existential Plight of the modern individual; yet even at an early
age Mailer had the impressive adult ability of organizing his
fictional concepts and carrying them out.

Even before he went to war—the war he will always carry
with him, that hardened him in its image, that provided for
him the vaster image of the 20th century as a battlefield
where he must outgeneral the Eisenhowers as well as the literary Japs—Mailer was thinking in terms of a war novel; crafty
mind was apparently unceasing; thus his war novel was quite
real but its reality was trained for by the professional writer's
conversion of experience into organized impacts that could
win the day. Mailer and war were made for each other, personality and history fused and heightened each. What

immediately distinguished Mailer after the big national major-writer-U.S.-dream-come-true success of *The Naked and the Dead* was plunging into the "bombarded cellars of my unconscious," as he puts it, to write the unsuccessful *Barbary Shore*. Mailer by this ambitious failure proved, but only in retrospect, that he was a singular independent ballbuster to reckon with—veering away from an easy repeat of his original ("Should I have written *The Naked and the Dead Go to Japan* as a followup?") to follow his tunneling vision, erratically lit as it might be. Chapters of *Barbary Shore* reprinted in this book do not redeem it as complete accomplishment of a writing kind, although Mailer sees it as the awkward beginning of his philosophy of Hip ("It has in its high fevers a kind of insane insight into the psychic mysteries of . . . narcissists, children, Lesbians, hysterics, revolutionarics") and the inseminator of all his devilish later work. Be that as it may, we see here the broadening of a talent and mind which is doubtlessly selfwilled in certain ways but on the evidence transcends brute ambition or lifts it to the point where the world of real people and events is as much evident as Mailer's passion to "change the consciousness" of his time. Here is cold bombing ambition, in other words, extravagant lust for great power—but also the ability to back it up with an objective and perspicacious view of the world. Such qualities rarely go together; when they do they are wisely feared, respected and positions are assumed in relation to them; all this should be clearly said to disabuse certain minds of the luxury in not taking Mailer seriously. It is obvious that he is both serious and formidable, and the selfhurting or boyish clown that occasionally performs in print (and in other nightclubs) for relaxation or easy applause is hardly the measure of the man-mind.

As Mailer's showcase develops past *Barbary Shore* certain qualities implicit in the writer at the beginning become more prominent; stride has been hit; his writing style, often grey or inconspicuous and undistinguished-mechanistic at the begin-

ning (with eerily oldman-wise exceptions like *The Man Who
Studied Yoga*), picks up true natural elegance and metaphori-
cal power which spins the very world before your eyes. There
is a magician at work in *The White Negro* who is a real black
dazzler, but the words are not used to show off anything
except the even more fascinating ideas: here the writer is at
his peak as he is again in the two chapters we see of *Advertisements for Myself on the Way Out,* the tentative inclusive
title of the long novel he claims will take at least 10 years to
do and then be unprintable in the Random House world.
What we see in this kind of prose is an almost Proustian
refinement compared to Mailer at the beginning, a struggling
with the most minuscule detail which he nevertheless keeps
fresh and hot by the power of his attraction to the underground, the violent, the orgasm, the X of masculinity,
the—modern scene as we have come to know it. Occasionally
Mailer's verbal style will become decorative, and therefore
weak, without reason—even debase his meanings, as when he
writes "I watered my cup" for his firstperson hero's urinating
in an athletic protector. This kind of flowery euphemism
takes away from the reality of the scene he's painting and
throws attention back on the clever and graceful narrator
rather than the thing narrated. But then the whole problem
of narration is one of Mailer's biggest but most secret problems, not exposed in his pages the way he exposes his life but
running like a needle of doubt through his explicitly novelistic (not philosophic at this point) thinking.

The problem can be reduced to this: Mailer prefers the
third person, he tells us, as a novelistic point of view, but
finds now that he can only write with full force and freedom
through the first. The first is an approximation of self, of the
writer as person, and yet Mailer's heroes, narrators, alteregos,
romantic selfidealizations have become centered on the mythical hip Irishman who Mailer once conceivably wanted to be
but couldn't. The problem of the American-Jewish novelist in
creating fictional personages whom *he* can believe in, and who

are not dynamited into fragments by the author's bugging consciousness of his own Jewishness, is not an easy one to manipulate; several American-Jewish novelists have been sunk by it, for to the subjective-overburdened Jew he is a special creature and he wonders from within the submarine of himself whether he is psychically entitled or able to create gentile types as validly as the Jewish self and selves he knows; Mailer's firstperson identification with the swinging Irish tough-guy-romeo-hipster type whom he either admired in his boyhood or in his mental Hollywood is at best a tentative solution, abstractly swallowable in the samples he is showing us of his new outlaw novel, but perhaps not entirely real in the ultimate sense. One winces a little for Mailer the man to see him lave upon his new pages the details of a sinning Catholic upbringing because they have the inverse quality of a loving fantasy. All of this would go down much easier if Mailer wrote in the third person; this way it seems uncomfortably close to a denial of his own Jewishness (or is your reviewer being narrowly Bronxy in using naturalistic criteria for Mailer's new supernaturalistic, multiple identity, cosmic-gambling fictions?), an escape from that nasty fact perhaps, and a glorification of a reality he can never actually *be*—glorification ultimately meaning falsification. The problem is too arguable to be answered here but in a writer as often personal and demonic as Mailer it is necessary to raise the curtain on why he has chosen to write a vast firstperson saga (qualify that to part of one, since Mailer is chameleonlike and could cross us up in the course of his book) in the persona of the Irish fighter-cocksman whom practically every New York Jewish boy of Mailer's and my generation once dreamed of being.

But to do him justice: Mailer is a serpentine, several-headed, surprisingly unclassifiable writer, science-fictionally invisibling beyond even telling criticism that would embarrass a lesser trickster; nothing that preceded him quite prepares the reader for the Mailer experience, either the new voluptuously purring prose or the radical thought that follows its own

curves with bowman grace and equal killing accuracy; he is by
every available signpost an "original" (jigsawed together by
the anomalous contours of the modern story) engaged in a
superior contest with Time and History—yet encrusted with
wiseguyisms, superficiality and petty brutalities; but always
redeeming them by the seemingly intellectually-michaelangel-
esque span of his vision, which is not satisfied with anything
less than total engagement with human life in this century
and domination, if possible, over every aspect of it that cannot
match his insight and greater demands from existence. He
says at the opening of his book that he has been running for
President these last several years; I believe he is to be taken
literally; he means that his being is no longer satisfied with the
conventional novelistic role, that his restless ambition and
sense of high existential adventure refuse to be stymied any
longer by the dull images of either traditional literature or
government, and that he is a hungry mental lion let loose upon
the sidewalks of the dog-stained contemporary world. Such
concepts as he holds are not rhetorical; they are a meant challenge; contained in them is a vision of life which goes beyond
Mailer himself, because rebellious, offbeat men and women by
the thousands feel the same way but lack the inner eye to
define it and the grand operatic selfconfidence to voice it.
"There was a part of his mind that drove him to do things he
feared and detested," writes Mailer of a character in *The
Naked and the Dead*—obviously sucking the insight out of
himself. He lives now, shedding day by day the mask of a
character in his fictions (except for the mythical Irishman),
going ever further in defying his fear and detestation; as they
have increased in dimension so has his daring and scope. In
this book seen as a whole he comes completely, Destiny-
baitingly out into the open, enjoying the role of guiltless assas-
sin, shaming his fellow petty-humanitarians by their silence in
the face of his highly imaginative sense of evil. It is an exciting and significant breakthrough to a reader-writer like myself.
    Smart as he is, though, Mailer can still be taught; and the

advice he gives to brother-novelist Chandler Brossard in his nervily candid chapter on his competitors—namely that Brossard will write a big book only when the rest of the world becomes as real to him as he is to himself (although Brossard would wittily argue that he is unreal to himself!)—can and should be applied to Mailer. His unleashed hipster ego, so proudly defiant, is only the mirror of numberless others taken to a more glistening power; brave as he is, his bravery is only ultimately significant in turning on his more timid contemporaries to an equal surmounting of the fraying chiches of capitalist society, authority and puritan-induced masochism, which hold the Gulliver of Self strapped to the ground; in short, Norman's leadership could be consumed in the heat of his own private flight when the much more awesome release of the ego-energy in a million I's lies ready and waiting for the Edison who throws the switch. In the meantime Mailer glows like the very radium that he once characterized Allen Ginsberg's *Howl* as being as hard as: there is a powerful and unconsolable mensch among us, and it makes life heroic and purposeful for a generation that really needs him now as it doesn't *need* 98 percent of its writers.

1960

a private letter to
james jones

Dear Jim,

I don't know if I'll be able to finish this letter about you and your book at this sitting, but at least I'll be able to get it under way. I finished *The Thin Red Line* approximately a month and three quarters ago, Jim, but so consuming have been the details of my job—and so imbued with a sense of responsibility toward your book was I—that the combination of fatigue and work and the nagging feeling of being unable to do justice to the book under those conditions prevented me from trying to set down my thoughts. Nevertheless, now I'll try. The novel is tremendously readable, to take it on the first level that will affect a majority of its readers. Your style—to which I will return again, because in your case style certainly is the man—is a remarkable combination of power and precision in this book, so that the reader instinctively knows that the man writing these words means what he says and this gives the reader confidence. There is an authority to your combinations of words that allows the reader to relax, as he does not do with a good many unrestrained writers who either exaggerate or don't give the impression that they clearly understand what they are talking about. As I was reading the book I kept recalling an aphorism by Ambrose Bierce which your writing here fits to a T: "Good writing is clear thinking made visible."

You always give the guarantee that you know what you're talking about in *Thin Red Line*, and it makes us hang on your words because for many of us you are taking our minds and beings into areas of experience that we do not know firsthand, and it is extremely comforting in this increasingly bewildering life to trust the individual, or author, who is leading you by the hand. This feeling of trust is a very important thing; it is almost as if you, Jim Jones, are a father-figure in the course of your book, but a genuine one, without either pomp, ceremony or title. I can't emphasize strongly enough this particular sense of assurance that the reader receives from you. It is as if you are clearsighted and clearminded enough to blow away the haze that surrounds so much of experience, and we are enormously grateful to you because you have cleared the air in perhaps the most crucial area of contemporary life—namely war, and even more important, war as it affects an average or normal citizen of the United States. I learned more about the nittygritty of the Second World War from your book than from any other American work I have read about the war, including Joe Heller's brilliant *Catch-22*. From the opening chapter, with the men packed like equipment into the transport ship, to the very last, where the survivors of C Company are getting ready to go to New Georgia, I got a steady, inch-by-inch immersion into the actual experience of the war. I was fascinated by the informational side of this huge experience but not as I might have gotten it from a fact book; the simple fact that a novelist of deep understanding had taken me into this experience made even the most trivial information about the common American soldier doubly and triply interesting, because the details became charged with significance that would have been lost if a less observant and humane man had written about this major historical event. Thus, Jim, every ounce of detail about how the

soldiers acted, under fire and out, from our friend who stole
the gold fillings from the mouths of dead Japs to the chap
who discovered the cache of MGs and got permission to steal
them, made me and (in time) thousands of others live the
experience as though we were there. I doubt that any of us
will forget your overwhelming basic point: that modern war is
a heroless game of numbers, with even the illusion of free will
having been taken away from the human ciphers imprisoned
for the course of the game. This central point is made with
such ferocious simplicity that it is inevitable that everyone
who reads your book will come away from it bearing your
view that modern warfare is in itself totalitarian, anti-
individualistic, undemocratic, impersonal and that the
so-called human being becomes merely a piece of functioning
meat with a number pinned on him. It will be hard for me to
forget this vision, or the character of Welsh—who reacts to it
in the only logical way. With madness and gin.

It is, to repeat, the great simplicity with which you bring
this to the reader's consciousness that makes it branded in
the memory for good. In this sense not only have you written
a thoroughly engrossing story, which most "serious" novelists
cannot always write, you have also shaken the reader to his
spiritual boots concerning any romantic ideal that he might
still hold about the masculine, chivalrous side of war. The
scenes of the actual fighting were extraordinary to me, especially the one where the medic goes out to help the hopelessly
wounded man, is in turn killed, and then Welsh runs out and
they have that strange encounter before Welsh finds the syr-
ettes. Once again, due to your talent, to put it as unemotionally as I can, I felt I was there and knew what it was all about
whereas before I had no inkling of the fantastic reality.

In the course of putting forth your "argument," giving
shape to the experience which constitutes the body of the
book, you use a method which I would like to raise some
questions about at this point. Most of the soldiers you treat
are concerned about fairly elemental, often basically simple

things; through your novelistic imagination and proportionate
execution you make them highly convincing, we become
absorbed in their concerns as if they were our own, but I
wonder if at times you don't oversimplify the thoughts and
preoccupations that run through some of their minds. Understand my lack of knowledge in this area—you know your
material, I don't, and if you believe that you have done ultimate justice to what the majority of men think of and feel in
this situation, then I must go along with you. But on the basis
of my experience, which is all any man can go by, I felt that
on occasion (p. 227 for example, when Bell thinks about
making love to Marty as the sole incentive for surviving)
there was a reduction of motivation to the most primitive
drives. Perhaps men in war are stripped to their balls, so to
speak, and only that reality counts. But I, who must judge by
my civilian mentality, on occasion thought that you brushed
aside too absolutely the shades of feeling and motive that
must go on among men of even mediocre intelligence. In
other words, Jim, I'm suggesting that perhaps even men at
war have more complex and articulate reactions to that
experience than you have allowed for. I know that within the
book there are varied reactions, and I feel intuitively certain
that you have come closer to the actuality than any other
American writer, but I still feel a slight qualification which
stubbornly persists—namely, that there is a biological sameness to the reactions of all the soldiers in your book that
sometimes has a laboratory predictability about it. I realize
that men at war are limited by their situation, and have relin-
quished much of their outward freedom, that they are conditioned by the reality they must wake to each new day, but I
wonder if at times you stress the physical and "animalistic"
terrors at the expense of the more complicated ones. I'm well
aware that there are plenty of subtle, person-to-person
moments in the book—the homosexual awkwardness between
the two soldiers, for example, after the fistfight—but the
impersonality of the treatment at this point made the scene

subordinate to the overall experience rather than something I strongly identified with. I felt it, but at a distance.

I don't gainsay the strength that comes from your rather monumental simplicity of method, if I may call it that (I realize that it is a vision as well as a "technique" and that the two are indivisible). It is only, again, that I have to integrate it with my own knowledge of experience, and on that basis I felt that you showed me the common denominator of the war more often than its differentiating aspects. In this sense I was reminded generally, but not specifically, of Tolstoy's method in *War and Peace*, where he also takes a huge canvas and simplifies it with extraordinary humanness; it may be that both of you, working with such broad areas of action and such a large cast of characters, have to typify the reality by bringing to light the most representative and homeliest details. The huge cast determines, in part, the point of view toward the material. That which unites all the men caught in the experience is more significant than that which separates or disunites them; perhaps they can't be conceived as anything but members of a monolithic body which is more important than their individual silhouettes against the horizon. I felt, however, that an occasional portrayal of more explicit complexity of motivation would have raised one or two of them above the war—certainly a man like yourself was comparatively detached, complex and untypical in his thinking even while slogging through the mud when you were in action—and if only for the contrast involved I would have responded to a slight alteration of the tone and outlook for even a brief moment. But, again, make no misunderstanding of my reaction: it was all so goddamned convincing—your untheatrical and dead-center ability to show the average fighting man in action—and, as I told your editor Burroughs [Mitchell], I don't think it has any precedent in our fiction. Stephen Crane's *Red Badge* might be the closest, to my memory, but with all respect it is military child's play compared to the extent of your picture.

For me, there wasn't a boring sentence in the book except

for a couple of paragraphs when you were describing the military strategy in such minute detail that my mind could not hold it all in effective relationship of part to part, but this could very conceivably be my own limitation about containing large numbers of specific details in my mind at one time. However, my instinct is that some other readers must have had a struggle with the material at this point, when your knowledge and drive toward explaining military tactics in extensive detail suddenly gets the better of your novelistic wisdom and takes over. Burroughs told me that some of these passages were cut, as I recall. Even so, they sacrifice novelistic flow at this point to either educate the reader or give vent to your own fascination with this aspect of the war, and the upshot is that momentarily you lose the average reader until you get it fully out of your system. Once again, this is only my supposition on the basis of my own reaction and the limitations of my patience. But I refer to the wisdom in Henry James's phrase "the platitude of mere statement," wherein he clearly and sanely points out that when the writer ceases to dramatize, and lectures or educates by direct expositional prose, he is in danger of becoming a schoolteacher.

I would like now to get into your "technique," in which I see great practical virtue and also an avoidance, deliberate or unconcerned, of one of the great breakthroughs in modern storytelling which men like Joyce and Faulkner have brought home to us: immediacy of rendering experience as opposed to what might loosely be called the crowsnest method. I'll spell out what I mean. Your fictional presentation in *Thin Red Line*, which is handled with complete authority and naturalness, is to observe the entire experience from an omniscient point of view. You enter the minds of your major and even your minor characters when you wish to, then withdraw when you wish to, describing all of it from a "godlike" impersonal point of view. I found myself compelled to turn the page because of the ease and believability with which you accomplished this. I am appreciative of the art involved, as well as that quality which art by itself can never fake, namely your embarrassingly real human understanding, and I would have literally gone along with you for 1000 pages let alone 495. That is because you are a superb storyteller at your best. At the same time the technique you have developed often walks very close to a historical report; I find this cool factual style absorbing, frankly, because it tells me things I formerly didn't know. But its danger is that the writer must depend on his personal charm of style when he is conveying information rather than in the intensive dramatization of his scene, where the actors carry the ball. I would like to return to James's remark, "the platitude of mere statement." It means, as I have always read it, the *telling* of fact, or the recapitulation of the action, as opposed to the more difficult job of constantly dramatizing so that the action speaks for itself. I find you a persuasive enough writer—always interesting in each successive sentence in this book because of your uncanny sense of the concrete—to go along with you even when you confine yourself only to description of the action for longish passages. Your personal style of delivery, which is unique without being flamboyant, rivets my attention because of the clarity of your vision. Not one word is wasted. It is clean and yet full. At the same time, when you tell what happens as opposed to showing what happens, the characterizations can lose their specific reality for me, or at least I don't believe in them as wholeheartedly as I do when your scene speaks for itself. I refer to a description of yours about someone "being built like a Greek god," which is so commonplace and general that I can't visualize it. ("Above all I want to make you *see*," Conrad is supposed to have said.) Again, you write "He was a big, bluff, open sort of man," which with the best will in the world strikes me as being uninventive and a convenient thumbnail description of a character so broadly conceived that he remains undifferentiated in my mind from a mere human blob. Once again, don't misunderstand me: so powerful is your theme that, like the Pacific over which your soldiers travel, it can sustain any small chips of throwaway writing (which I think this was) and keep them afloat without trouble. But I feel I know when the invention is synthetic and when it is real; and further feel that telling the story from an omniscient point of view—rather than showing it all in the manner of, say, *As I Lay Dying*—permits you to be facile in occasional characterization because you are not held down by the rigors of a pure dramatic framework. Of course, I see the advantages of your overall plan: you can give an outline and perspective to a huge experience that might have been presented with more constant immediacy only to obscure the significance of the whole. This is your mind at work, and I think it is a broad and fascinating mind, perhaps more finally interesting in its directness than Faulkner's in his convolutedness. But the danger of having your characters subordinate to the overall plan is that they can come dangerously close to being stereotypes, to being generalized "everymen" in spite of the pains you take to give them distinguishing details and characteristics. In this sense, they are perhaps not so much realistic, in treatment, as having the illusion of reality, which is, maybe, what you consciously wanted. And yet every now and then this illusion—even on your own terms—is broken for me due to the omniscient manner of your narration, which allows you, as creator, to paint in a character here or there whom I can never grasp hold of in an ultimately convincing sense.

In a word, I think the dangers of the would-be Olympian, omniscient narrative technique are that the picture of life, which should speak for itself, is replaced by the author's words on occasion; he is telling us that such-and-such a character exists, whereas it is much more convincing to us if we are *shown* him in the act of existence and make up our own minds about its significance. The other, the telling, is very much like the editorializing which you took such pains to avoid in the theme of your story: as you once told me, this is an antiwar book unlike any other because it does not propagandize in the slightest, but lets the experience speak for itself. And I agree, which is why the book had such an almost bodily effect on me. But in occasional moments of the writing I felt the editorial hand showing in your technique and at such moments I was conscious of you as a deliberate illusionist rather than the artist who was submitting himself to a reality greater than his own. The difference between control and manipulation is probably a very subtle one; but on the couple of occasions where I was not "convinced" I was conscious of you manipulating the story, I thought I saw your hand, and this broke the spell. These moments happened, by the way, when I intuitively felt that you were grafting a story or anecdote, or even an Army cliché, that you had heard onto a certain soldier in order to make him more lifelike; but instead of making him more lifelike this struck me as exploiting the material instead of creating from it, which I felt was the case—sheer, sheer creation—in the great scenes of the book.

I mention what I think are imperfections, Jim, merely to bear honest witness (or try to) to the entire experience. The book as a whole is to me the most authentic imaginative work that I have read by an American about the war. It placed me there in a central way that, literally, makes up for the fact that I wasn't there in the flesh. You have brought home the bacon, so to speak, like a hunter of old and like no one else has done.

On the basis of this you are our outrider, our most forward troop, and thus you have a unique place in our literature and in our awareness of the meaning of modern experience. What's perhaps more important, I think you will keep developing as a writer (although after this contribution you could safely rest for a very long time) and to what rare places you will penetrate I believe only you can tell. It is an unusual position you now hold, completely unique, without comparison to the other novelists of our generation because you see life so separately, you are so much your own man, your own spirit. My own feeling is that *Thin Red Line* has already created a special place for itself that cannot be undone. As Burroughs said, it will stand like a rock and become the standard by which other war books are measured. Its size is beyond the reach of most of us, its even tone in the midst of murderous folly is hard for more conventional folk to comprehend, its originality of viewpoint (your greatest gift to me in all you write) could be conceived by no one else and yet, when we see it, we know immediately how human it all is.

Seymour
May 5, 1963

an open letter to norman mailer

Dear Norman:

When yours truly was editing that serious soul-and-pussy journal *Nugget* (and how can I ever forget we paid you $750 for 10 of your "short hairs" when we should have gotten at least a miniature prose erection at that price?) Jim Jones encouraged me to send him a straight letter about *The Thin Red Line.* "No prettying up of your thoughts, fuckface, let's hear what that hush-hush private machine really thinks about what I used to call my comic war novel." I sent him three thousand of my most conscientious, honest, slightly sentimental, modestly critical, literary good-guy words and never heard from him again.* That's what makes Joos philosophical, goddammit; if the Joneses of this world (not the LeRois, he's another horoscope) treated the Krims right, Joos wouldn't be prey to wonder, eventually become smart and deep by their wonder, and end up with psychoanalysts and Hitler to cool their big fat overloaded heads.

---

*I finally received an answer almost four years after my original letter.

But since you and I are both greying J-boys, and since I
know our jousting but first cousin contact will stay alive
because we share the same basic coloring (Bronx crazycat?)
and can't resist occasionally peering in the mirror provided by
the other, I have no hesitation about getting the social clap
telling you what I think of your latest book *Cannibals and
Christians*.

Let me begin by saying it's a characteristic middle-period
Mailer, which means big and freewheeling, unique, unfin-
ished, smarter than hell in patches, noble, unrealistic, loudmouthed, tough as a murderer and coarsely playful as a freshman pantyraider, tending in about one-third of its 400 pages
toward the doomful science-fiction which seems to be as natural to the disillusioned technician in your imagination as it
was to older intellectuals like Huxley and Orwell. The book,
as I see and experience it, is also likely to be the last one of its
kind that you're going to unveil for the next several years; if
I'm wrong, the burden of awareness at any rate will be on
you; because apart from *An American Dream*, which from
your view was probably existential roulette and to us fascinating not so much for lit. reasons (some of your slickest writing
varnishing a paper-thin Tokyo highrise fantasy) but in recognition of your selftherapeutic race to make the *Esquire* deadlines, this is the third collection of pieces you have brought
out since starting with *Advertisements for Myself* (1959).
The form that was so freshly invented by that book—the
most stimulating intellectual smorgasbord in New York, main
courses from all over the world with good solid meat as well
as fine spicing, a closed-circuit Mailer spectacular with each
flaming dessert—is now beginning to repeat itself and become
routine instead of creative. Stop and think: since *The Deer
Park* came out a decade ago in 1955 you have been publishing
your books in newspapers and magazines and then collecting
them between covers.

That's 11 years of making babies in public.

In order to make each of these collections seem entirely

linked together, not just a dumping-ground for pieces that have amassed along the way, you developed in *Advertisements* those highly inside, personal, revealing bridges to each selection which did more than just set the scene; they gave each piece a new significance because you showed so much of your complex Halloween psyche in front and then planted the formal hunk of writing right in the center of your pants-down confessions. The introductions in that earlier book, still a classic crackerjack box which is almost a kid's pleasure to stick a blind hand into, had a rich texture and newly-discovered urgency for you which has been thinning down through *The Presidential Papers* to the comparatively slack afterdinner speaking of the present book.

I will get to the angry muscular subjectmatter of *Cannibals* in a moment and drop the way it's put together, at least for now, but I think it's clear to readers who have followed every dart and twist of your work—and likely to you too—that the form is now too mechanically rehearsed after the platinum light of inspiration in *Advertisements*. Now the intros that are supposed to bind the pieces together, and make a whole book, seem as transparently cooked up as TV commercials; even though I'm aware of a gently selfmocking change of tone in the way you write them, which indicates to me your condescension to a method that is beginning to lose its spine for you. And the collected articles themselves, in spite of all your practiced artfulness and deliberate attempt at verbal hypnosis ("trust me," you soothe the reader during a chapter break, "indulge me"), hang piece by separate piece instead of making that continuous shimmering path to the top of the truth that I think you wanted.

But right at this point, where I must cut short my esthetic pickiness (do I have the niggling lace soul of an interior decorator trying to tidy up Big Boy Vulcan's shop?) and get to your ideas, is precisely where you are faced with a spectrum of hard choices that probably keep you more sleepless than the rest of us: (1) Should you continue writing long but finally

shirttail magazine pieces that momentarily quench the need
of what you would call (I've never liked the pomp in the
word) a major book? (2) Are you too impatient and extroverted by now—is the entire New York scene too
fragmented-discontinuous-nutty in the most symptomatic
sense—to hole up for five or so years and do your writing out
of the spotlight demanded by your greyhound ego? (3) Is the
drive for immediate social and literary POWER, rejected by
the temperate and quite shrewd old Chinese man who pe-
riodically sits at your controls (p. 255 of this book), ready to
be channeled into a proustian TVA or is it your destiny to
spontaneously "shoot all over the shithouse wall" as you've
phrased it?

I'm fairly certain you live on intimate terms with these
choices, at a more suffering level than outsiders realize, and
that you will cope with your literary being in the most imaginative way you can conceive; but in the meantime don't let
any of my earlier words give the impression that the extent of
your commitment and accomplishment is lost on me or any
of your several hundred (thousand? million?) snarling literary
rivals. There is no one in our mutual generation of U.S. writers—to get inside *Cannibals and Christians* through the side
door of your recent characteristic work—who has written
prose about coliseum-size public events that comes close to
"Superman Comes to the Supermarket" (the Democratic
nomination of Kennedy in 1960), "Ten Thousand Words a
Minute" (Patterson-Liston in Chicago in 1962), and "In the
Red Light" (Goldwater gets the Republican nod in 1964),
your big gorgeous political piece in the new collecton.

It is original work like this that made the occasionally hardnosed poet James Dickey, new Library of Congress consult-
ant, recently say without an ounce of the usual throat-clearing
that you're a "great journalist." While I know this doesn't
soften a cosmic conspirator of your interplanetary ambitions—in fact you're probably p.o.'d because he didn't say you
were a great novelist as well—what Dickey was putting on the

record for most of our contemporaries is that your mixture of novelistic feel-smell-nuance, slashing political nerve, and total personal engagement created a new kind of confrontation in American journalism. The fact that you played all your space music without inhibition in this once-restricted area of magazine journalism is going to be a mind-opener for others, and without detracting anything from the way in which you asserted your soaring balls, it is also significantly of our time; in the last five years we have seen comparable assaults by Baldwin, Capote, Tom Wolfe, Breslin, Pynchon, Markfield, Mark Harris, to break traditional journalism's control of fact by means of a free nonfictional prose that uses every resource of the best fiction.

With reality itself in so loose and disheveled a state of undress and new fittings, aggressively serious writers like yourself have instinctively gone into the "real" world (funny word if I ever heard one for what's Out There) and tried to shape the flux itself as they once would a novel. In fact there is a good argument to be made that the Great American Novel today is society itself, and its author is the man who can give squirmy living material the harness of meaning and purpose that once only went into a book—never the street, which is fast becoming a big new unexplored page for some of our saltiest anti-Establishment writers to work in (yourself, LeRoi Jones, Ginsberg, Lennie Bruce, etc.)

In your case, as evidenced by *The Presidential Papers* and now *Cannibals and Christians*, I don't think the apocalyptic street-preaching is just a temporary smothering of the novelistic role; part of the extraordinary fix you're in is that you combine the personae of prophet, politician, novelist, showman, mystic, journalist, sociologist, lit. critic (some of your best prose, fink!) and dada limerick-writer, and they interact all over the place. For example: in the present book you are the scourge of faceless contemporary architecture, minority whip inveighing against the deteriorating national fibre, City in the Sky planner, and Dr. Sigmund Havelock Jonas Salk Mailer

diagnosing "the plague"—namely violence beneath both the
Christian (fading Wasp) and Cannibal (Faulkner's Snopeses
taking over) exteriors, labor unions becoming sterile, medicine overburdened by wonder drugs, marine life disrupted, old
neighborhoods destroyed, totalitarianism imposed from above,
and on and on.

If proof of your impact is needed—which it isn't—accept
the fact that I personally am made to feel frivolous and irre-
sponsible when I listen to your thundering condemnation of
the plastic condom that America may well have become.
Frankly, you have the updated rabbinical power to make the
majority of us feel like adult debutantes for having such a selfishly limited range of concern when measured against your
own. But the price, as I once heard Susan Sontag say at a
Columbia Writer's Conference, is that you have to become shrill to be heard above the din when you get in your
angry prophet's bag; the same might be said for Allen Ginsberg, who has exploded categorization in much the same way
as yourself and also finds the nation a surrealist nightmare
peopled with immoral phantoms and all the other horror
shows of the American undermind. I'm aware that Ginsberg
has not involved himself as flamboyantly as you in Washington D.C. center-of-power issues (although he asks in a recent
poem: "Why is it that the little prince of the FBI has
remained unmarried all these years?") and is not built close
enough to the ground to have courted bullies—and borrowed
their techniques—in the gut-sense that you have. His public
courage is extreme but more aerial, as I compare you both.

Actually, no one among our neo-Beat, Hip, Pop, Black
Comedy gang of 40-and-over bitter idealists has really stood
up so chestily and spoken as directly as yourself about the
cheapened cartoon that Americanism has become during this
disillusioning time. Nor has any of us expressed himself in
such selfconfident battledress about basic issues like God (a
relative?), time, consciousness, cancer, and all the rest of the
topics in your new worldsaving handbook. The broad scope

and intensity of your concern staggers and diminishes me, Norman. As a writer it personally challenges and stings my ego to its foundations, and I know I speak for closemouthed friends as well. Although I see you using leads in your new book that stretch from Gide (your imaginary interviews) to Sartre (your capsulization of *Being and Nothingness*) to Bill Manville (cha cha cha) to Henry Miller, D.H. Lawrence and the handiest literary moth of the moment—although I see the spires of Spengler and feel the foundations of Marx jutting from your prose, your imagination, your ambition—I can have nothing but amazement touched with envy at the way you have put your world together, made it work, and kept it as surprising as it is serious.

But strictly as worker to worker, on a shoptalk basis, I risk the charge of oneupmanship and caution you hard about that sweet tooth in your head that tempts you to intellectual gluttony. The very cancer that represents to you a symbol of decay running amok seems at times to symbolize your own intellectual voracity; you gobble ideas the way fat people do food. Since you deal with abstract notions in such an imaginative and offbeat way, full of startling tarzan-leaps coupled with the most mature kind of manipulation of ideas, my caution is made in spite of appreciation for how you handle it; nevertheless by riding your pet theories too exclusively in essays, reviews, hocus-pocus theatricals for grandly sounding off without rebuttal, you lose the real opposition of other characters to keep your kosher as an artist.

The dialogic device you use in the 130 pages of imaginary interviews in *Cannibals* is really a thin man, no matter how nattily disguised, and what the reader is actually presented with is a monologue by Mailer on Soul, Spirit, Why Picasso Is Good for Norman's Tired Eyesight, etc. For the most part I enjoyed it as still another class performance on that portable stage you tote around, but I was depressed by the obvious fact that I was listening to you talk to yourself no matter how you camouflaged it, or tried to. Compared to the elastic snap of your work at its most professional it was also loose, padded, selfindulgent (?), and finally monotonous to me even though the ideas were fascinating when you first presented them.

To touch the nerve, the danger as I see it is that you can hypnotize yourself into becoming an exotic crank or selfinfatuated astrologer via these loose forms rather than the superwriter (and you know when you have been there) who pits himself Houdini-like against an objective situation and uses all his ingenuity to speak his devilish piece through the restrictions of the situation. You flirt with air as a writer, in my opinion, when you permit yourself to talk metaphysics without a concrete opposing voice spitting and scratching at your imagination—whether one you have created yourself in the form of a fictional character or a real one like Sonny Liston or Gov. Scranton in your inspired reportage. When you just talk and don't act out your ideas in print (*show* me a man eating a plateful of bull-testicles so I can test your speculation about virility by my honest stomach and not my deceivable mind) it tends to balloon your thoughts into an uncheckable faroff ether and becomes a display of mental spacemanship that can produce sudden dazzle, but then be forgotten like a pot-fantasy.

But even as I say this to you, the first fighting, unequivocal American Jewish writing hero since Clifford Odets, in my 1930s-stamped way of reacting, I know that writers do what they can much more than what they (and other shmucks for them!) choose; and when they can do as much for the contemporary anxiety-choked reader as yourself that's no less than having a Christmas Orgy in the White House, or any other rich chocolate-covered psychedelic image you can dream up. But old Krim can't help being a moralizing editorial writer for one last thought and remind you that men as purely gifted as Saroyan and Henry Miller lost much of their most loyal audience over the years by subjectively willing to remain monologists rather than reality-edited dramatic writers, stars rather than telescopes, egos instead of superegos. I know you will steer it as you can in the traffic-swift tunnel of your being and wish you the protection of the God you say you believe in to consolidate your extraordinarily challenging talent at its most potential height and might; even though the writer in me will competitively burn during raw moments—because you have embarrassingly shown us all up (I actually mean down) to ourselves—the best part of the man will be rooting that you achieve what you already deserve.

All good wishes & keen radiations,

Sy

P.S. Just saw the movie version of *An American Dream* and came out holding my nose with one hand and my asshole with the other (since you put great faith in anal expressions). I have a stinkbomb to throw myself so get your sensitive sniffer prepared: If manly integrity is the big issue—and you've had your fun with Salinger, saying his last two books "seem to have been written by highschool girls"—why is it that he refuses to sell his work to the Hollywood circumcisers and you didn't even con them into script adviser or something on this before collecting the $200,000? You come on mucho strong, N.M., and it seems to make sense at the time because of your locomotive weight, but your followthrough is often a vanishing cream and at this late date it has to reflect suspiciously on your values and work. If you are bold or possessed enough to write like God's spy how can you not stand by that work with even a dollar-sacrifice; doesn't it occur to you that a fraudulently cheap piece of salami like this with your name above it is a cynical insult to your writing, its vision of America, and to those of us who want to believe in a hip Santa Claus?

1967

maverick
head-kick

James Jones is a trudger, a plodder, an American farmer or
miner at the typewriter trying to do "honest work" in the face
of what he often wrongly thinks is bullshit, phoniness, the
avantgarde conspiracy, and one has to admire the unadorned
plainness of both his soul and his method because we live in a
time when selfdoubt lathered up into selfadvertisement has
stripped the oldfashioned notion of straightforwardness and
simple grit from most talked-about current writing and
replaced it with sensational bids, prophetic lunges and much
flashier ideas than Jones is either capable of or permits himself and therefore almost as an act of stubborn revenge ("He
is the most stubborn man I have met in Paris or probably ever
met"—Leslie Garrett) Jones now in his fifth novel *Go to
the Widow-Maker* practically wallows belchingly fartingly
unimaginatively but thoroughly in a prosaic story of how he
disguised as a playwright met the woman he married and as
an act of nose-thumb at the gossipcolumn world he both
enjoys for selfish reasons and despises for moral ones he brutally and enjoyably gives a round-by-round description of their
fucking-sucking habits and the number of people the lady

121

screwed before their own great coupling and along the way
almost as if he had a map in hand Jones takes you over the
terrain of his life ten years ago from the Midwest to New
York (a New York seen from a smartass farmer's view but certainly not the New York where people like ourselves live crisis
year in and out) and then down to the West Indies where the
Jones-playwright character gives an endless textbook description of what it's like to skindive and swim underwater in a
realistic but rather simpleminded, sturdy, greatly detailed
chunk of the book which proves once again even as the dis-
proportionate length of time and space he spends on his
man-type athleticism mounts that he is at heart indifferent to
standards, indifferent to his reader's boredom, intent with a
rareness that occasionally shines through the uninspired list-
ing of every street-name and make of car and type of underwater watch and what we had for dinner to tell *his* story, not
yours, not mine, and while the normally bright reader will
fidget and then do a slow exasperating burn for the duration
of this slowfreight travelogue-fuckalogue there is no doubt in
my mind now that Jones has removed himself from "the
novel," from "writing," from consideration with other "writers," and instead like Prew in *From Here to Eternity* he is
using words rather than boxing-gloves or a bugle to declare his
awkward independence from every school of art and thought
that he can't understand or refuses to understand in order to
assert some raw, rank but finally uncheckable and unbreak-
able maverick essence which is very important in the long run
of the American future if there is to be one, and to the world
if there is to be one, and while he muffles and covers this
essential pilot-light with carpets of words and endless almost
pointless descriptions of trivia that come right out of a nightschool composition class you have to burrow beneath the colorless surface or catch the music behind it to see and feel that
Jones in his materialistic, naive, one-armed, heartless, toneless,
simplistic, selfcentered, literal way is trying his best to keep
the world alive by going his own way, that is his message, that

selfishness carried to the most extreme length becomes a good
if it is fought for every inch of the route against prevailing
codes from friends, family, state and ideology, the "I" must
not give in because there is nothing else says Jones all through
this book in the almost deliberately perverse, nonliterary,
I-suit-myself style in which he tells his puffedup story, so that
finally if you see the story as an excuse for the expression of
an acutely primitive individualism that is blind to the most
tumultuous colors of literature you will not judge it ultimately as a work of art because it is a selfindulgence on that
level and yet it has at its core that philosophical element of
"Here is my world you poor follow-the-leader nebishes, look
at it the way a man who has to think for himself sees it, my
belly-button probably knows more about the basics of life
than your eye," and if you receive that authentic, proud, seriously individualistic head-kick from Jones you get to the root
of where he's at, which sets him apart as a "writer" and to me
redeems the fact that he is not a born writer but a laboriously
schooled one (the schoolmarm figures in the book, an honest
and cruel but necessary thing for Jones to finally get out of his
system) who learned how to write his thug-novels in order to
say something exactly like what Faulkner had in mind with
his by-then generalized and overblown rhetoric when he told
the Nobel Prize people "Man will prevail," except Jones is
saying it less romantically and with deliberate, sloblike
woodshed style in order to shove his finger up the crack of
conformist life and letters and declare his separateness (he
thinks) in a world of losers, affluent smoothies, loudmouthed
"radicals" who make more noise and do less good than nuns,
etc., and I for one am proud for Jones's you-can-hurt-
me-but-you-can't-kill-me point of view because it has taught
me something I never really knew before about the length
and strength of Wasp integrity when it exists in this
country (I see it of course in Selby and in my friend Michael
St. John, the publisher of *Nugget*, don't judge a man by his
cover) and therefore Jones to my mind is not to be seen as a

writer first—although like every strong personality on the scene he privately thinks from a sentence in this book that he's a "great" writer, whatever that cornball Hollywood concept means in a time where every decent man knows he doesn't have the exact definitions to know who he is and what he is and where he's really going and can only always reach for these definitions during a lifetime—but as a unique force who literally comes out of the particular gut of this country, as opposed to other countries, yet applies to everyone to some degree because his insane independence cut away from the crap in which it is often wrapped is a marvelous gift to the future, a hope for my selfish future as an American prick hated unjustly and superficially by my opposite numbers in other countries because they don't know that beneath the hysteria and external imperialism of this country it has anonymous people who have more rugged dignity than a tree, and most important if history decrees that this society has had it the idea driving Jones as it did as fiercely to E. E. Cummings that there is nothing more beautiful and inevitable than a scared solitary human being standing up ever saltier for all his undefined rights is one of the great ideas that came out of this mess of U.S. "democracy" now being mocked, probably justly, and that is something that should be inherited if we crash down and Jones with his crafty Army sergeant bigeyes about being a "celebrity" (there's a necessary new one every minute as he should have realized after reading the humiliating reviews of this book) and making his Big Crap Game money like Robbins and Wouk and voicing defensive and uninformed remarks from his artificial headquarters in Paris about "faggot" writers who can handicap him nine fingers and write him into the bends as far as sheer virtuosity goes, Jones and what he stands for must go into time yet to come as the best of this country must because it hasn't all been a waste.

1967

ubiquitous mailer
vs.
monolithic me

1

I sit with Mailer's *The Armies of the Night* to the left of my typewriter and *Miami and the Siege of Chicago* standing straight up beyond the roller so that it can look me right in the eye but I know that the books will be incidental to what I must say. These are Mailer's latest writings and as an engaged literary man I must deal with them, especially with the inspired journalistic-novelistic *Armies* which acts out themes that have been obsessing me for the last several years about the literary artist being in the center of actual history and shaping it with his voice, but the books have also become an extension of Mailer's presence in New York life and it is this that is smothering me, raking me, bringing to the surface raw competitive feelings which have nothing to do with literature as an end in itself.

For example: I had a good chance of getting planked one night about three weeks ago, I was looking forward to it because the girl was darkeyed, salty and keen, quick to judge and flaring in opinion but this seemed merely to open up wider the potential excitement of rocketing with her, when she started to rave about Mailer's *Barbary Shore*. *Barbary Shore!* The novel is 17 years old and I have never done it justice; it struck me as a failure when I read three-fifths of it in 1951, a potentially fascinating probe into the shadowland of ex-communism but novelistically a fallen weight, and now this hip young literary snatch was carrying on about it in a way that would have offended Mailer himself. I lost my trick of the evening because of the stone I turned to after this Mailer-infected preacherette thrust him at me like the sacrament and now I must reread *Barbary Shore* myself to discover, beyond my ego, the worth of the book. Without wanting to I will become a Mailer scholar because I can't move in Manhattan life today without having him imposed on me, and my own honor as a "man" demands that I break my behind to be just (or at least to try) even when my gorge is packed and rising.

I have almost always been cool and appreciative of Mailer, for a decade now, and have felt detached and unruffled when brother bigtown editors and writers have told me of his being everything from a superficial and flashy writer, an overrated fighter, a potential suicide to a loudmouth, a prick, a maniac (literally), every conceivable rasping putdown with which we block off those who threaten us. We are all imperiled egos on the make in New York, the bigger the emotions we hold the more we suffer by being cramped and squeezed out of our ideal shape by someone else's filling the available space at the top, and I have listened to such comments meditatively; in my own smaller public orbit I have also been called crazy, arrogant beyond belief, a tiny talent who whacks off publicly, etc., it seems that any writer or individual who is hard to classify today must breast the worst tongs of the psychiatric vocabulary by which others try to wrench you into place in a world without a scheme.

So I have never been seriously shaken by any of the comments I've heard about Mailer, except to take momentary pleasure at some of the knocks because of inevitable feelings of envy brought on by his domination of the foreground; yet these malicious tidbits of satisfaction at another's putting his foot in the turd have never lasted long because of my respect for Mailer's powers of recuperation, like those of the now-dead poet Delmore Schwartz, and when we were closer and there was real trouble such as the stabbing of his second wife Adele I stood by in court with his then young protegé Lester Blakiston ready to do what I could, which was nothing. (I recall the midnight that the news of the stabbing hit the airwaves, he was about to run for Mayor of New York, I was to be "publicity campaign manager"—according to a grinning flower thrown me by Norman at a party—and then, suddenly, we were all at a cocktail scene at the Village Vanguard the next afternoon for a new Vance Bourjaily novel and at that very hour Mailer was being hustled from the courthouse to Bellevue for observation; I had been through the same pride-stripping machine in 1955 and as I sipped the martini in the dimly lit Vanguard where Mailer would have been cavorting and heard and saw 40-odd people totally absorbed in the New Moment, Mailer's name on no one's lips within my hearing, I realized how quick the reversals of "power" are and how quietly satisfied some would-be lit. stars in the drinking mob were because Mr. Brassballs Mailer was getting what was coming to him.)

But now I can no longer be cool, appreciative, observant, philosophical, certain of my own identity in the face of Norman—no, for the life of me I can't help feeling uptight myself. When my sister recently came to town from St. Louis she plied me with questions about Mailer ("Is he really as intense as he appears on TV?") and her brother-in-law, a New York lawyer, told the livingroom at large what a competent businesswoman Mailer's mother was and as a clincher, "HE's obviously a brilliant man." Here is what's left of my family, decent media-washed people who with possibly one exception don't read Mailer, who stand for everything he presumably does not—with the crucial Jewish middleclass exception of "success"—telling me how brilliant he is! I am now at the age (46) where I resent this until my nerves sing; yes, I want them to understand my brilliance as well, to allow my literary pride to breathe, to try and understand the remarkable effort I put into my own work and what it signifies. Of course I don't really expect them to "understand" (sympathize with?) these things, but don't they have eyes and ears and can't they see or project their imaginations into what it must be like for me, or even A me, to sit still under this kind of pressagentry? Because it is not Mailer the author they're creaming about nor was it the writer sans a whole shimmer of extraliterary goodies that turned on the young clit I wanted to make it with.

No. It is Mailer the Individual who has now sizzled over Manhattan in a way that I imagine he always wanted (hell! that 95% of us would have wanted) and if he survives the current suffocating prevalence of his personality will probably no longer want, and it is just this Mailer—the multiplied image of a man with every person outside of what they think is the charmed field of force adding his or her own frustrated hope for excitement to N.M.'s own need—that is suddenly, bewilderingly, finally, driving me to the wall. I DON'T WANT to walk around the city constantly being Mailerized by my friends (and even dim acquaintances) who use me as a bridge—D. D.: "I hear Norman is acting impossible again, have you seen him?"; S. M.: "I saw two of his wives [Adele and Beverly] at a party when we were playing that small theater in Provincetown but I didn't see him, if you had been there you could have introduced me"; B. R.: "Could you give me the Great Man's phone number, daddy, my kid cousin from the West Coast is here with big eyes to meet him and a Ph.D. thesis on his work?"—because it brings into the open the throwback emotions of defensiveness that reduce me when I've got to stand fully tall and that hammer me into selfprotection, frustration, anger, when I need every ounce of the freedom that is my savings bond as a human being.

Human being! It is this essence, my identity in the world as a person, that is hurled into a tight knot by all the talk that swirls around me concerning Mailer-this and Mailer-that and which now triggers every protesting hope of my own birthright. If this is an indication of my own insecurity as a man, of my own marginal position on the New York status scale, of every wound and hangup of my own which Mailer now brings to a head because of his aggressive ubiquitousness in the literary-sexual-intellectual-avantgarde Manhattan environment where I must live my life, so be it. I will cancel nothing out of my possible motives in resenting Norman's imprisoning effect on me because I want to know too, I'll whitewash no conceivable unpleasant impulse—envy, jealousy, wishing I had the same gift and the same attention, the applause, charisma (it was Mailer himself who first told me the meaning of that chic word so representative of our period in a bantering exchange we had in 1961), frontpage reviews, "in" national reputation, I'm scraping the brain sac to try and come clean here—and yet I truly feel it is none of these things in themselves and not even the total that punishes my spirit and makes it necessary for me to declare myself. Believe me, I can put up with overwhelming fame or notoriety in my business and not let it eat away at my days and work; and of course YOU HAVE TO PUT UP WITH IT if you don't own it yourself, so that as a writer ages he has to come to terms with the actuality of the landscape he exists on or he will be driven mad with envy and frustration; it is not Norman's "fame" that bugs me but the quality and type of it, because it is not based on works alone (Ellison, Nabokov, Lowell) but rather on an imperialistic personality that gobbles up territory that I want for myself.

This is no accident: when Mailer said 10 years ago that he wanted "to hit the longest ball in American letters" the appetite of his personal ambition was defiantly announced to everyone (honorably, it seems to me, instead of the secret insanities that keep others going), and yet it is the grandiosity and collegiateness of this conception of writing-as-personal-superiority that is at the root of his effect on other wordmen, myself included. This last sentence stinks slightly of moralism, as if I were above the compulsions of "grandiosity" and "collegiateness" and since it is particularly suspect or could seem hypocritical in a case like mine—when I have used the "I" as assertively and with as much apparently cheeky chutzpah (according to the young director Leo Garen, at this writing one of Norman's sidekicks) as anyone using words in New York today—it is worth exploring further. When I say that Mailer's use of writing for Personal Competitiveness, Personal Power and the Proclamation of Personal Superiority is a pain in the ass to other literary strivers on the scene I am not exonerating myself from probably having such needs.

No one is writing today with any impact who doesn't load his lines with every inch of his private needs, either directly or some other way, and how can you have had an American life with its emphasis on sports, money, politics and the other sex without having had competition and the itch for power reamed right into you from the start? But I am saying that Mailer's naked and often proud emphasis on competition, being the best, beating you in the arm-wrestle or any of the half-dozen games he used to initiate, comes no doubt out of a heightened boy-fever within himself but it is also the reaction of a man so VULNERABLE to the sweeping powerdrives of this society, vulnerable to the point of determining to get on top of them at almost any price, that you can only understand What Makes Norman Run by your own perception of the enormous contradictions in this wealthy, earnest, corrupt, endearing, irrational, glamor-oriented bad dream of a society.

Mailer the guy, the individual whose insatiable needs, successes, grandstand plays and endless performances have penetrated my life whether I will it or not by the unsolicited remarks of my friends, other writers ('Doc' Humes: "Did you know your prose is closer to Mailer's than anyone else around?"), fellow newspapermen (Pete Hamill, Al Aronowitz, Charlotte Curtis, Jack Newfield), women I would like to sleep with, my fragmented family, etc., this Mailer can only be understood by the novelist whose precise and tormented intuitions have exposed so much that is paradoxical in this country. Understanding that, that the fantasy-rich novelist is necessary to understanding the behavior of the man, understand also how the man now uses each sidepocket of his novelistic imagination to extend the presence of himself in a world he no longer trusts to literature alone. The resources of the highly creative writer in Mailer are now almost exclusively at the service of the man, his writing (and films, plays, statements) at this moment takes second place to the gyrating real-life novel he has been living out through his use of all the available media, and it is this EXTENSION of Mailer's being in the very airwaves that invades MY being to the point where I must consciously fend him off, hide my resentment at his everywhereness, adopt a strategy in relation to the inevitable drop of his name, devote time and energy to coping with his invisible presence which is unlike my picture of myself and yet is real, God knows, burningly, frustratingly real.

And yet it has got to be made plain that this has nothing to do with Mailer's prose, which I enjoy, admire, reread for gut pleasure (especially the firstperson gold that runs from *Advertisements for Myself* to *Armies of the Night*) and would find literally painful to be without, although the Germanic bloat of the last section of *Armies* seems to me to vitiate the buoyant originality and superb deftness of the first three-quarters. No, Mailer the writer is most often a positive credit to the life of this time and his excitement, surprises, wit and brilliant ease of expression aerate my brain like the keenest menthol. Not only am I indebted to Mailer for his writing, the gift of one man's life to another, but I personally received nothing from him but open generosity and the most silken perception when I was painfully putting together my first collection, *Views of a Nearsighted Cannoneer,* to which

Mailer contributed a passionate small foreword. Therefore in a poignant way it is not Mailer as he actually is that for my own selfrespect and breathing-room in the world I must rebut, because what he is as a writer and active nerve of our time can only heighten the quality of prose and perception around him and make consciousness a more exhilarating experience for me and my contemporaries, it is rather the uses to which his drive is being put because of the aggravated needs that are blasting him: those unwanted American super-hungers and skyscraper anxieties which as an author he can articulate with surgical touch and control but as a cat on the scene has to act out for immediate and bigger and bolder and deafening rewards.

Stay with me in case you think I'm primarily interested in puritanizing Mailer here: I have no illusions that we'll go back to a period of "pure literature" in the decade ahead but every hope that the writer-in-action will become an increasingly significant figure in the hub of U.S. life, not merely as a "celebrity" but as an active influence in the interpretation and even creation of events themselves, using his imaginative involvement and independent voice as the highest articulate measure of everything that happens in this country. If ever there was a time and a need for the literary imagination to prove its greatness in a madhouse period like ours that time is now, and Mailer's swiveling engagement with every day-to-day eruption seems to me right and necessary for dealing with the landslide of phenomena that confronts consciousness. Putting aside his flamboyance, he takes it all on like the gamest of stalwarts, is faked out by none of the tracer-bullets of a multiple reality that fires in upon him from all angles, and copes like a standup dock boss until he is drenched in psychic sweat and exhaustion—only to renew his taunts and jeers at the impossible load an hour later. His stamina in the face of the contradictions and incongruities that contort us and our society is unique, a startling example for us not to throw up our hands in recoil or drop out but rather to direct our moral grenades at the conditions that have made us what we are—and because of this he has excitingly glamorized the role of literary activism for the 60s.

But Mailer is, when you look at it closely, a transitional figure in "the Movement," not a true steady flame of the moral activism that has come to ripeness in this time, although (when you look back) he was a singularly shtarke maverick who stepped out of a premature, certified, middle-class success at the start of his career to pursue his wild ghost absolutely wherever it took him. Yet everywhere he traveled literarily or polemically after *The Naked and the Dead* he trailed the specifically American banner of a man who has been a public winner ("Mailer hated to put in time with losers" he tells us chestily in *Armies*) and with it that even more telling dividend, the person with an image, a glow, the radiation of adult magic, which is more effective in the daily life we live here than the depth of one's work—a hundred times more effective. Images usually come to people because of spectacular or well-advertised achievement, but in the insecure heart of this country they stand for more than the event or even the lifestyle (Marilyn Monroe, Toots Shor) that bestowed the image; they become additions to Being itself, as though one's very substance were giantized through an electronic magnifying glass to the entire land and every other human being susceptible to this image then walked around with your face and soul in his head. The man or woman with an image becomes a psychological phantom who hovers over the secret life of others; he is their invisible companion, the embodiment of their need and the target of their competitiveness, the standard by which they act and judge themselves. So that, for example, when Nat Hentoff tells Mailer in *The Village Voice* (as he recently did) "Yes, you are the best and most honest writer in America," it is probably as gratifying to Hentoff to feel free enough to finally say this as it is reassuring to Mailer to hear it.

Such an act means—if I can interpret from my own cat-

footing experience in this minefield—that Hentoff now feels
so secure as a public presence himself (deservedly) that he
can honor Mailer's image without any loss to his own; and by
complimenting Mailer to the far point of his literary taste he
shares in Mailer's most recent success, becomes part of it by
perceiving it with generosity, and defuses his own hostility to
a possible competitor by absorbing him—absorbing the image
into his own security of status instead of fighting it, an often
sincerely unconscious strategy that makes life simpler as you
penetrate further into the boobytrapped thicket of celebrity,
fame, ego-moves and above all trying to live at minimal peace
with oneself in a time increasingly haunted by the images of
others.

And I say this as a man who has obviously been haunted by
the image of another.

2

I was not immune to the power of Mailer's name when I
first met him in 1959; but as I've suggested, names have
different power to each of us depending on whether or not
they sum up an area of fantasy that has been coveted in our
separate heads. To my own imagination, or projection of
myself into the limitless continent of possibility, Mailer was
fascinating to meet in the flesh because he had engaged the
American world as sulfurously and totally as I had always conceived of myself as doing but never had with anything like his
breadth and vision. Even closer to home, he had done it as a
New York Jewish novelist who had crashed out of the
parochial Brooklyn-Washington Heights-tea-and-wisdom orbit
which was our mutual ethnic hashmark into the splendid
chaos of everyone's U.S.A., and based on my own inability to
honestly transcend myself in writing—that is, whatever I
wrote in those days had to emphatically come from my personal experience or I disowned it—I admired him doubly for
being free enough from the overwhelming experience of self
to lose it in the faith of his own creations.

He, in turn, was surprised and impressed by my stubborn commitment to my own subjectivity when we discussed it briefly once after my *Cannoneer* book came out in 1961. But it was I who measured Mailer much more closely than he did me because he had PULLED IT OFF, I was hypnotized by the fleshly presence in front of me of what I thought of as my own dream-vision of myself, and I related tenderly and uncompetitively to it. I was glad that Mailer existed, as I think down deep we are of every human evidence of heroism, because it gives hope and credence to our own projection of ourselves; as Mailer already knew, he had become the focal point of other people's frustrated sense of themselves and he peered out from behind the external neon face of his presence to make shrewd inner judgments that his fans were unaware of. My point is that Mailer soon learned after the public success of *The Naked and the Dead* that he was the tempting apple of certain people's inner eye; even austere literary types who could legitimately criticize the book for its reliance on the spadework done by previous American novelists (Melville, Dos Passos, Farrell) were impressed by his achievement at 25; and then more than impressed by the extraliterary vibrations that bounced off Mailer, a seemingly juicy combination of celebrity, money, good looks, swift, boldness; and within this network of projection, magic, goodwilled (and not so goodwilled) envy, identification and symbolic leadership, being the recipient of every hidden genital emotion that his eager congratulators poured onto him, Mailer was in a position to see some of the slime of contemporary inner life denied to those who were not in his unique situation. The same could be said of Ginsberg, Dylan, Tim Leary, Joan Baez (although "slime" doesn't exist for that sweet dove) or any of our present-scene Dream People but I doubt from their public statements that they have observed the reactions to themselves with the careful third eye of Mailer and probably Baldwin and Capote as well; the business of the novelist and now the novelized New Journalist is people pure and unsimple, and the opportunities for insight into the most private reactions of others can be profound when you yourself are both the writer and the throne, the articulator-definer and also the charge itself that animates the room and produces the psychic undress which feeds your mind and then your pen.

I'm certain Mailer saw into me with this builtin fame fluoroscope parts of my mental anatomy that I could never see for myself, because when I introspected I did so on a solipsistic turf relating only to itself, not itself in relation to a broader, bigger field of operations where the very size of your mental frame and its shape is more apparent to others than to you. Norman was often amused but thoughtful (always thoughtful unless he was stoned or turned on by the spurt of the moment to climb it like a steeplejack and roughhandle anyone in his way) at my sober insistence on being my self, using only the "I," as a literary credo; but by inference and silence he suggested a wider area of possibility than the one I allowed into the intense but comparatively narrow strip of experience I was guarding like an Israeli machinegunner. Yet neither of us really gave that much to the other—I don't want to mislead—he because there were always voracious ears offered to his lively mouth when he chose to rap and because he had long before decided on his inner scoreboard how much to reserve and when and where to give, a scheme which often went up in smoke because of the combustion of the chance moment but a general strategy nonetheless; I because I had to preserve my integrity or consistency in the face of his aggressive charm while at the same time relaxing my literary spine all the way so that it could be responsive to the faintest touch of new sensation that Mailer was capable of delivering. But unfortunately my friendship with him was never balanced because although I was as singleminded about my own cause as Norman was about his when I was alone, or with my own collection of friends, it immediately changed when we met in a group or anywhere in public where there were more than just the two of us; when that happened he assumed (and I didn't contest it) the central role that was his right based on actual holdings in the world—performance, rank, notoriety, money, applause-volume, all the goodies—while the major part of my possessions were invisible and tangible ONLY to that comparative minority who knew my work and intentions. As for the rest, the majority, especially that flashy fringe cinched together from Madison Square Garden, Broadway, off-Broadway, TV, the outer rim of Mailer's fluctuating expansiveness—we shared another hard core of raunchy Provincetown-East Village friends which I'll get to shortly—I was considered just another vaguely known ego-hustler who had attached himself to the Mailer fount in order to find a substitute identity and mystique absent in his own bleak life.

I therefore had to walk a tightrope between my own selfrespect and my fascination with Norman and recognize that as cutting as I might be as to why others wanted his friendship, I also was a pushover for tight association with that particularly mindblowing seal of American success which has been confirmed by the media and all the other mirrors that multiply the godhood of the Chosen One in our society. This hardly means that we don't genuinely like the star of our choice when we get to know him (her); in fact we're so prone to begin with that we can easily LOVE the chosen one at the modest lowering of an eyelid (what dignity!), the beginning of a smile in our direction (what humanity!), a kind word—any crumb that we can gobble up, because to love the Star is to love what has been rated the best of our time, to feel that lucky you are participating in the most precious moments available to your generation. But, of course, how much of this love is selfcongratulation, convincing yourself of your own reality and worth by finding it in close contact with another harassed human, but one whose "reality" and "worth" can't be doubted WITHOUT DOUBTING ALL because it is attested to by every playback machine in our culture? I feel I can now say from the pit of my sensitive gut that the drives which circulate around the concept of the "celebrity," both being one and its effect on the inner lives of

others, are more crucially revealing of what men and women
in our time are really made of than any other phenomenon of
the 6os: because if it were not for the conspiracy of his court
(you, me) who admire the attention and power that the
celebrity wields he would not possess it; the celebrity is finally
made by others into the unique figure he is in our world
because he represents the hidden desire of each person who
wants to protect and serve the celebrity as the eventual possibility of their own lives.

My own relationship to this "possibility" when I was seeing
Mailer was ambivalent: although I was fascinated by fame as
an American of this time and place, where the very idea to a
people living on the edge of confusion and unreality sometimes seems like the only security that the primitive ego in all
of us can understand—"fame" then becomes such an extension of personal recognition and approval that the private miseries of the artist, or American-in-extremis, seem to his imagination justifiable or bearable only by his measurable impact
on masses of people—I only wanted it on my own terms (I
thought) and as a result of the individuality of my own
vision. If it were to come to me as the result of pounding my
own beat to the point where I broke through to a new china
of imaginative truth, fine, I would glory in it like every American whose heart and head have been shaped since childhood
by stars, stars, beautiful stars, to quote L. Bruce in another
connection; but I had nothing but contempt in those days for
anyone in literature who would deliberately seek it (contempt
has now been replaced by a crooked smile of understanding)
when the stakes seemed so different from showbusiness or any
other outlet of hardboiled selfadvancement. In relation to
Mailer, which was eerily special because of the closeness of
our age, background, the Jewish thing, jazzedup urban experience, etc., and with people like Saroyan, James Jones, Willem
(Bill) De Kooning, Joan Blondell and Anthony Quinn both
before and coequal with Mailer, I was as interested in observing "fame" as owning it; smelling it, absorbing it, seeing its

effect on myself and others as well as the way it was handled (tough outer confidence and outspokenness!) by the men and women who had worked so hard for it.

I appreciated their candor and indifference to livingroom approval ABOVE ALL because it meant deeper and more slashing communication in areas where the majority of people, however bright, are soul-cautious; they haven't been confirmed in their bones that they ARE the living truth as measured by the ecstatic spasms of others and the music of the cash register, no matter what gorgeous dreams for the future swell the air in their heads. But I also found in each case that a point scored in head-to-head flow, when you were seduced into opening up your most private bag by the candid assertions coming from the opposite chair, could suddenly be choked off by an arbitrary shrug, a pout, a putdown, intelligence and sincerity and the running tap of eager warmth coming from yourself could be cruelly stopped cold by the slightest ruffle in the celebrity's inner weather. In the case of Mailer this was always tempered by a kind of guilt, a violent tenderness in his awareness—never quite articulated but always present—of the impossibility of personal justice in this world, or even in the livingroom where he was then pontificating, given the anarchic forces that drove being. Mailer tried very hard to be sympatico and straight in the early stages of a social situation—very plain was his sense of appropriateness, consideration, adult realism, that quiet yet considerable quality of understanding so evident in his novella *The Man Who Studied Yoga* and so sobering to those who think of him primarily as a fireworks-salesman—but there was usually a turning point in my presence (around the third drink?) when the showboat cowboy in Mailer would start to ride high, bucking and broncking, particularly in the special company of our mutual funky friends.

These mff's were a gang of post-Beat kicks-oriented writer-fighters and wildassed gallants from P-town, the East Village and Washington (D.C.)—Bill Ward, Danny Banqo, underground moviemaker Rick Carrier, Lester Blakiston, Dick Dabney, Bill Walker—who admired Mailer as a guy who could more or less write like a bitch, drink like a cop, put his index finger up the System and still crack the headlines and bank the bread, a natural Jack Armstrong to raunchy scufflers who found bourgeois success as meaningless as an orange julius and needed a new White Nigger hope that coincided with their own roaring dissatisfactions. Mailer armwrestled, shadowboxed, sucked the pot, downed his Bellows, exploded energetically (I've seen him lift up a woman and windmill her around his head without sweat to either party) and generally had a ball in the shoulderpunching warmth of his barracksroom camaraderie; but he was also always conscious of being the dean of an after-hours school of tough talk and flowing booze, with fights, momentary flipouts, psychic confrontations, girlstealing, crazy tensions, sometimes even murder threats finishing off one of these "existential" evenings. These were my friends, too, as was Norman, so my description is hardly a value judgment. In the early to mid 60s we all had urban Huck Finn eyes for this hardliving scene which crackled with real action, insight on the move, the faint presence of danger, the full presence of respect and sudden love—"You're beautiful!" said by one guy (or one chick) to another without shame after a telling small deed or gesture—when you earned it.

Part of the reason Mailer swung so well in this environment (more earthily than at the Flashy New York Upperworld parties which were always on his calendar but not as exclusively as they became after the advent of Lady Jean Campbell, his third wife, and appreciation from a grander new crowd of tailored winners: sports, theater, politics, journalism) was that he covered the human waterfront for this crew of literary outlaws. He had achievement and money as well as the physical gameness that was a trademark for the P-town–East Village battalion and it was the combination of Establishment SUBSTANCE side by side with bohemian piracy that made him such a hot pistol in our setup. But I was always aware that if Mailer had not written a bestselling war (MAN's) novel and broken through to the gossipcolumn kingdom of The American Dream his friends and mine would not have felt they were swinging with a mythopoeic male who embodied all the contradictory colors that they themselves wanted to flaunt in this society. It was public certification that they lacked and public confirmation that Mailer possessed and even though they, along with Norman, mocked the sitting-duck Establishment and hated it for its sham their very sources of selfapproval seemed to need some of its bad blessing—especially as regarded their SEMAN (or names, spelled backward) which in our country today has become the symbol of a potent soul. Norman was of course the biggest name in our group, which conferred glamor on all the rest of us in the eyes of impressed outsiders; and although I could live with that as a fact of life even though I had always felt, and always will feel, every inch an equal to Mailer, I had to lock up these feelings in this quickly perceiving community of ours out of respect for the values of others.

If a loner like myself wanted the sense of SHARING and warmth generated in this freeform gang that floated north to Provincetown in the summer and south to the Village or D.C. in the fall (our emblem was the chaotic, surprisingly sharp, $-disastrous Provincetown Review, still going on no regular schedule, which was the first to print Hubert (Last Exit) Selby's toughest story plus Susan Sontag, Rosalyn Drexler, Alfred Chester, etc.) I had to see Norman with group eyes: namely, that it would have been phony for me to challenge his leadership when it was acknowledged as unchallengable by my friends' burning sensitivity to that very American World on which he had scored a vital shot and at times seemed to have even "conquered" on his own terms. What ultimately became clear was that in the total society we all now participate in through the howling of the media and our own echoing inner voice if I or anyone wanted the "grace"

that surrounded Norman he would have to make headlines
for himself, match Mailer in trying to "hit the longest ball,"
"reach out and GRAB what he wants" (Jimmy Breslin)—
become a hotshot competitor, in other words, in that eternal
100-yard dash which is either a necessary effort of adult life
everywhere or a local disease that comes from living in our own
unique 200 million-strong highschool. I had the highschool in
me too, let there be no mistake, I also had college and graduate school; I was a stinkfinger kid and a Herr Professor in one
suit; in fact I was a Civil War, updated, between ambition and
soul, leadership and indifference, pride and prose, winning a
popularity contest and glorying in my artistic apartheid, and
there it stayed—unresolved, unspoken, Mailer once or twice
clenching his fists when he smelled my own Presidential
thoughts, me sneering coldly when he led "the team" on a
drunken march to a High Wasp Truro restaurant where we
were cooled off in the lounge (obviously) and even Norman
the Awful couldn't bend them for so much as a fugging sand-
wich for the troops. Score one for my side. But nothing was
settled for me by such microscopic oneupmanship except my
stinging confidence that I had correctly targeted the problems
as far as they pertained to me, that I knew the choices, that I
was playing the good old American Postponement Game in
my head instead of declaring myself in the race or out, in front
or behind, genius or jelly; N.M. with good justification could
have said I was sweating out one of his archtypal existential
chessplays and except for that fact that I don't want to breathe
comfortably inside the kid's metaphor (he's a year younger
than I), I'd rather make my own in the high thin Mexico
City air of my own quest, I'll say this—S.K. had to move,
physically, emotionally, outwardly, frankly, and stop polishing
that dime he stood on like a miser.

3

In the last four years Mailer and I have seen very little of
each other: another Bourjaily novel therefore cocktail party at

The Plaza, a Barney Rosset spread on University & 11th St. for Michael McClure's *The Beard* where we just looked for a long beat at each other unspeaking but cool. Our "group" or gang, and the second word says it better, has fragmented into and out of jail, hospital, nomadism, marriage and a new generation of hipsweet kids unlike ourselves—no longer as tight or slashing-bright as a unit—and I now operate in my New York world in Jay (The Celebrity Checker) Landesman's phrase as a "semi-name." (And below 14th St. on my local East Village battleground as in fact a name: "You've at least got a name," *Provincetown Review* editor Bill Ward told me pensively in a verbal beer-sweep down at the south end of the St. Adrian Co.'s long bar the other night; "When you go to a party anywhere in New York at least one person there will know your name," a modest window-dressing fag told me wistfully at a sparse uptown Christmas gathering in the season just passed. He meant it as a darling compliment, not knowing that once started there is no security for you until the ENTIRE party stops as if shot at the sound of your ——.)

When I moved off that dime I used my personality more consciously, expansively, deliberately, strongly on the public scene than I ever had up until then—writing for the dead but unforgotten *New York Herald Tribune*, advocating a style and point of view through editing (*Swank, Nugget, Show, Evergreen, Provincetown Review, New York Element*, etc.) and pushing work (Hubert Selby, Jan Cremer, Tom Wolfe, Leslie Garrett, Erje Ayden, Fielding Dawson, etc.) I believed in, teaching my faith in "creative nonfiction" from Columbia University down to a workshop in a deserted courthouse on the Lower East Side. I did nothing different in kind than I had in the 10 years before, but I was (and am!) acutely aware that in the society we live in—this U.S. earthship hurtling toward a new world—my intentions and would-be nobility of stance mean nothing compared to what I can impose on the scene around me. As frankly as I can put it, my sex life (I've been a bachelor for 17 years), my financial life, my relationships with friends, lovers, potential buyers of my talent on every level of American and even international life, depend on the impact I must make on the society I hear buzzing away each time my telephone rings. On the most hardnosed level I count for nothing out there except what I APPEAR TO BE TODAY in the status-clocking eyes of others: this is what 20 years of, from my view, intense, independent and risk-taking literary work and advocacy have boiled down to on the image-dominated marketplace (include in that marketplace the haughtiest universities, foundations, Knopf-type publishing houses, all danglers of the New Dollar while intellectuals sing and beg for their new green supper).

Within this superpopcommercial world that has mushroomed around me my own newly conscious "flair"—not stinting on color, boldness, selling yourself hard while keeping your words loose with each new performance—is my shield, apparently, when as much as anyone I've ever met or read about I wanted not flair but "truth" inscribed on it, "art" blazoned across its middle, "dedication" heralded at the top, "honor" quietly tucked in at the bottom, "integrity" bolting it together, etc. But in a new era with superstars rocketing across the sky of the mind, with the media blasting the faces of my friends across the globe and back, where am I to seek the purity I thought was my mission, where can I, the man, hide from the storm of unasked-for envy, career lust, the weakening or breaking of selfconfidence that each new emolument to the latest star heaps on all the rest of us—where except by staking out MY OWN territory and dirty-fighting for it like every other American savage of my generation? I am too exposed to everything as writer, guy, parched lover, genuine victim of the epic anxiety of democracy which drowns you with its flood of possibility and opens every pore to the slightest rustle on the ego-threatening wind, to find shelter anywhere unless I create it for myself by the power of my presence on this scene. Indeed I can sense myself as I write this pushing out a jaw that was once clean and memorable and now through the habit of defensive aggressiveness has become blunt and thickened, I can intuit the traps and pits of "celebrity hell" that were once moviecolumn hilarity to me becoming stronger as I nibble at the edge of the very name-fame trip I once stoically observed (and already know how the "secondrate" name burns in the glare of the "firstrate" one), I can see stretched out on the track of my imagination a future of desperate jockeying for billing on the marquee of literature which pays off in cash-prominence-veneration when I wanted Flaubertian sainthood, poverty be thou the bride, a religious quest in prose where Art was God and I pursued it like a driven priest.

But what kind of a nonabsurd holy man am I to be in the midst of a cultural orgasm wher friends and contemporaries (Calder Willingham, James Baldwin, William Styron, James Jones, Herbert Gold) pull down advances in excess of a 100 or $200,000 on a single book, where Norman's *Barbary Shore* (which I have now reread and admire in patches but find a sealed crypt as a whole) is symbolic catnip that brings hippie pubis to its byline instead of a difficult headtrip that demands debate and thoughtful examination? In this unreal, inflating, sell-the-sizzle-and-not-the-steak scene how can I live, function, breathe freely without being forced out of selfdefense to hustle for that stardom myself, to drive the sweetest of my instincts to make that unsweet impact, to insulate myself against the victories of others by scoring for Seymour Krim and holding my own against an electronic wave that can smash your spirit no matter how high your inner flights? As a matter of fact, how do millions of us live with any niceness when neighbors, friends, even enemies, are churning up the turf and we eat clod as we watch their speed and curse ourselves down for tameness, highmindedness and lack of the competitive instinct?

Listen: I know we also are responsible to an American society with "real" problems of freedom, change, the necessary dignity owed to each citizen, an ideologically shriveled labor movement, a strident New Left, the technological revo-

lution on every side—but it is the so-called soul of the man or
woman underneath that I care about because I have to suffer
it in my mortal way just as you do. And that soul if I'm any
judge is now an ulcer of frustration in The Age Of The Glorified One no matter how straight your vision and tough your
hide: face it, we live, hell, we CREATE with each passing
minute a world that pays more attention to the myth-person
who makes the deed than the deed itself. ("I'm THE Ronnie
Tavel," said a young pop-camp playwright to me over the
phone two weeks ago, giggling at his parody of himself but
meaning it all the same, calling to find an agent.)

Can I, then, in my daily luncheonette-going, friend-seeing,
check-writing, street-by-bar-by-cab New York life allow myself
to be fucked up, put down, put uptight, made to writhe or joke
or mask it at table when I hear Norman's name mentioned?
Should I permit myself to bear that imprisonment to my own
life-force and personality without fighting back with all of the
brute weapons of success that Mailer has mortared my town
with and which are now potentially available to me even if I
once scorned them (truly?). Of course when I am alone in
my small pad, right at this moment, I feel no resentment, no
competitiveness, no feelings of being humbled, I wish Norman
nothing but the best—conquer the world, baby! I mean it.
Because here I have my yellow paper, my oldfashioned
Corona, the dream, I'm King Shit here and the equal of any
mind or soul in action anyplace on the planet. But in two
inevitable hours I'll be hungry and walk down 10th St. to
Second Ave. and then up the block to Sonny's Pizza and
there over meatballs and spaghetti I'll run into Jerry Roth or
somebody from The Poetry Project at nearby St. Marks
Church (where I teach) and he'll say, "F'Chrissake Krim why
don't you get someone who's with it to guest-lecture, yeah
some cat like Mailer . . ." and even though he'll wink because
he perhaps senses my availability to pain I'll feel the metal
harden in my blood, I'll wrack my head for a quick comeback
and fail, and once again as in a script before my eyes I'll see

my energy and imagination and every rich thing I believe I am or can be freeze so hard you could bounce a handball off it.

You see what I'm really asking is whether one man's public triumph—which abstractly I approve of, welcome, see as a sign of hope when it has been made out of the materials of truth—is to be another's heartache in this homeland of mine which puts such a premium on being IT that it even cripples those of us who should know better. I don't, I swear to you, want to write books like Norman Mailer. I don't want to write in his style; I've got my own, thanks. I don't want Mailer's social life, his Brooklyn Heights home with its crowsnest, his part-ownership of middleweight Joe Shaw and *The Village Voice*, his royalties, films, prizes, the works—I HONESTLY DO NOT WANT THEM. But I also don't want my friends, colleagues, women to bug me with his name, his doings, whether he frowned at Casey's (the West Village celebrity hangout) when he went over to Barney Rosset's table to speak to Harold Pinter, was he at his P-town house or in town over Easter?, this, that, the galling other. Slowly, unalterably, determinedly, to save my image of myself to myself, to relate to people I love WITH love and without hangups, to be the free man I know I am at my best and not a tense crank, TO GET NORMAN OUT OF MY GODDAMNED HEAD I must own a piece of this world more solidly than I ever have before, I can't rationalize it, I have no other choice. I ask you: Isn't that what's necessary to get the good tail, win respect from my media-impressed relatives (I was orphaned young and pine for it), be looked up to by the newspapermen and women I sentimentally cherish, have clout out on the 10th Streets and in the pizzerias of my time?

And yet if I lived in a less tight climate—out of the city, shacked, familied, not dependent on the underground bars and parties where we solo artists nakedly seek our opposite numbers to stave away the empty-bed blues—heart and head tell me that the task I was put here to plug at lies in a differ-

ent direction for a conviction like mine. I want no less than
to see the literary artist become inseparable from the leadership of history, I want to see him influence events by address-
ing his work to the people who make them, I want to see him
take hold of the channels of communication marrying his
vision to the news to recreate the meaning of reality in the
interests of a New Day. My idealism, in other words, which is
massive and genuine, has contempt for the Writer As Glamor
Boy; I want the Writer As Saviour, if you will, and let him
perish in the attempt if need be. But even as I say this and
mean it I know as well as you that my words here are not primarily about literature. I am dealing with the agenbite of
being, emotional survival, living your 40s inside the heightened Manhattan crucible, all the loner necessities that must
be coped with at every hour when I am not at my desk with
the literary bag snugly over my head. And it is here that
Norman, buzzing, perverse, challenging, decent to me with
only occasional snot, Norman whom I have felt a brother to
in the past, it is at these eight or more hours a day away from
the role of writer-editor that I have learned to hate the sound
of his overspoken name on the lips of our mutual friends, on
the kazoos of our mutual generation.

Item: Did Mailer ever stop to think that his gigantic personal needs for being indiscriminately admired would help
smear up a standardless period, seed an unbidden resentment
and defensiveness and equal yen for the most whorish show-
biz lights in others who once thought they were content to
work in the stacks all their lives and wear the good odor of
library must like Spinoza and (N.M.'s beloved) Marx and
Joyce before them?

Item: Did he ever imagine that his "longest ball," which he
wanted to hit out of the private ache and need for dominance
of his gut, would be a metaphor of romantic U.S. greed that
would fly beyond his own smoking brain into the brains of
men and women who are sharing his generational time—and

further, across the sea, where narroweyed America-watchers
are sardonically handicapping our future?

Item: Did he know or care that someone named Seymour
Krim would be on the receiving end of this nonstop grandstand play and that this Seymour Krim would find his own
existence brought to a crisis by Mailer's own lust for making
stardom out of literature, money out of truth, personal power
out of principle?

In other words, did Mailer ever see the implications of
being Norman, which reach far beyond himself?

Whether he did or didn't—and my more than educated
guess is that he didn't, couldn't, wouldn't—it is still beautifully true that Mailer has defined me to myself, forced me
and a horde of other under-50 writers to fight for our identi-
ties and rewards in every sense, in a way I would have dodged
without him. Much as it stings to look in the mirror he has
handed me out of the grit-and-sand of his own unashamed
ego, I see how sensitive I am to recognition (I who was above
it), cash (I who solemnly transcended it), how I crave the
leverage of broad public muscle, influence, fulfilling myself in
every conceivable public sense before I'm wiped out. Norman
has brought these things out of me like a one-man Turkish
bath and I suppose I can be grateful to him for having had a
superior "animal sense of who has the power" (as he has written about James Jones) in order to shake me loose from a
frozen image of The Writer and rub my shrinking nose in the
competitive stink that so richly steams from the lockerroom
of our generation. Norman, sweetheart, you have without a
doubt slicked me down and toughened me up so that I can go
my own way as ruthlessly and wholeheartedly as you have
gone yours!

But even as I know that I now mean to have my share of
the most striking notoriety, money, pussy, fun English shoes,
TV interviews, the entire swinging menu while I still try in
my inner temple to make THIS writer the significant figure in

America's destiny that I believe our wordmen should be
today—even as I attempt to mount a two-winged campaign
that embraces my private career and also that of the artist in
relation to this juggernaut which has never felt his full vision
as a force in its day-by-day decisions—I know that what
Mailer has done to me I WILL DO TO OTHERS whom I
have never seen or heard of. If I succeed in becoming the
public force that I must now become to protect myself from
the Mailers of my time, what insane itch for the new name-
fame powerplay will I implant in others, what jealousies and
outraged thinskinned needs for capping me will I arouse in
their all too human beings? Will my outward "success" be
their failure unto themselves, will my stardom eclipse their
inner faith, is this the only route we U.S. writers (born idealists who cynically learn that they must take care of themselves
first) can follow to the end of our compulsive lives?

To tell the truth, as I see it, the best thing that could
happen to me would be if I FAIL to make that booming
public impact, if I eat my heart out in the shadows and if I
follow my vision with total immunity to applause and try by
example to show what the writer-in-action can do to counter-
infect our history and change it by the new utilitarianism of
his art. But as a man alive now, flung headlong into each day
with only 170 pounds to confront the weight of the world, I
don't have that ultimate cool, resistance, certainty, ability to
stride through fire to the pools of the spirit up ahead. I have
no armor when I have to walk down Norman's streets and in
spite of my knowledge and forboding of what I am doing, of
the final futility of deifying my "I," the One, the Me, the pal-
triness of living for oneself in a scene of many, the pettiness
of selfprotection compared to the grandeur that lies in selfless
service to a concept bigger than oneself, the example to the
young and unborn that I and every articulate American have
or should have on our consciences, I can't help myself. I must
therefore fight in this local Manhattan environment that
Norman (more than anyone else) has created to protect what

is mine, my words, my women, my status, my own greatness, and like a primitive with echoes in his mind of a civilization more beautiful which he can never entirely demonstrate because of the eat-or-be-eaten realities of his own life I must announce myself as another New Sonofabitch who dreams of peace—but only dreams. Thank you, Mr. Mailer, for everything!

1969

i talk with
alan kapelner

KRIM: . . . I want to get to what you mean when you say you want your literary men to make statements? Do you mean direct statements, or do you mean symbolic statements, or—
KAPELNER: Well, statements in terms of one's time, saying something about the world you live in, whether it's in terms of love or hate, or pity, or complete venom. I think that Camus made a powerful statement in *The Stranger* and in *The Plague*. I think one of the most powerful statements Sartre has made has been in *Nausea*. I don't think he realized it, and maybe that's why it wasn't so "fixed" in terms of his other work. This is what I call a statement. The *Underground Notes* of Dostoevsky; Raskolnikov as an individual is an immense statement for the fellows of his time. See, what I think is wrong in writing today is that everyone writes as if sex is it, sex is everything. And . . . that everything is in a room. It's a girl and a guy in a room; a man and a wife in a room. Well, I don't look upon this as a statement. I think this is a very personal way of writing. Some of the work is excellent, but I personally can't go beyond the excellence.
KRIM: What was the statement you were making or trying to make in your first book, *Lonely Boy Blues*?

153

KAPELNER: Well, in short, and possibly also in essence, it's just the failed men and women, greedy, hungering to resurrect themselves in their children. To relive their lives in their children, never realizing they're destroying their children. Now this is all over the world today, and this is why we have the children saying the elders are terrible, bad, no goddamn good, they stink. I'm convinced this is what I was attempting to say in *Lonely Boy Blues*.

KRIM: What was the statement you were after in *All the Naked Heroes*?

KAPELNER: That's a very difficult thing. See, in *All the Naked Heroes* I wasn't too certain. *Heroes* was improvised from beginning to end. I didn't know what was coming next. Two brothers, one with the total inability to face a crisis, another brother with the ability to go beyond the crisis on the basis of possibly the crisis doing him a hell of a lot of good. I'm not too sure, as the guy who wrote the book, if that is a statement as I previously tried to describe it.

KRIM: I'm getting to a problem that I want to pursue. You said, and I agree with you, that the literary art that is most interesting is that which makes a statement. At the same time, you also know the dangers—we saw them in the Marxist 30s over here—of propagandistic art which is all statement and no art.

KAPELNER: Yeah, but those fellows were hired men. They were hired not on a basis of financially being paid, they were hired on a basis of being tied to a locomotive. You know Lenin said, "The locomotive of history." They were passengers on that train. There was no stopping for them. Someone once said, maybe it was Koestler, that they were Artists in Uniform. Well, that's what they were. I'm without uniform. I am with uniform, my own uniform, but those fellows of that period, the women of that period, were very idealistic. I never went along with the idealism.

KRIM: Alan, I want to cut into your thoughts and approach the problem from a different direction. You said earlier that what you want in a writer is a statement, finally.

KAPELNER: Not what I want in a writer, what I'd like to see in a writer.

KRIM: I get the distinction and acknowledge it. Do you think that writers who become too hipped on making statements lose some of the subtlety of their art?

KAPELNER: No, not if the writer is a good man and has eyes, ears, a feeling for sound, smell. I don't see why he should. I think we're getting hung up on the word "statement." Maybe it should be put in terms of a man speaking to his time. That doesn't mean he'd be hung up on anything. I think he's a free man once he gets that way, providing that no one is impinging upon his emotions, no outfit of any kind, no hip group or political group. Does that sound right?

KRIM: Yes. But let me go back. Because when I asked you specifically about your own books you honestly said that you didn't know if they contained the kind of statement—

KAPELNER: Well, I think that *Lonely Boy Blues* contains a statement. By God, I believe it contains a very big statement. It was only years later that fellows like Dan Wakefield said, "Gee, you did it so long ago, and now people are getting on that sort of thing without even knowing of *Lonely Boy Blues*." *All the Naked Heroes* was a pile-up, a conglomeration that piled up into moods, emotions, which made for a kind of a pyramid. Now whether it's a statement as I see it, I can't be too sure. I may have failed because of the looseness of the improvisation.

KRIM: Every writer improvises, it seems to me, even just to find the imagery for his statement. If you're a novelist or a dramatist, you do it with people and scenes and characters, and so on, and you usually don't know the precise arrangements your mind is going to make during the act of writing, isn't that correct?

KAPELNER: Yes.

KRIM: But yet you seemed to say before, a little wistfully, that you were improvising and you improvised yourself away from your statement.

KAPELNER: No, I didn't mean it that way at all. I think we

are getting stuck with that specific word "statement." You
know, it just occurred to me that the marvelous writers who
were of their time and saying something to their time and if
possible going beyond their time, were the political and social
animals and the sexual animals, I think of these three elements, politics, sociality, sex. You see, when you go back and
look at people, say, from the Greeks on, you'll always find the
best men were very political and very social. They were political animals, social animals, and God knows we have very few
of them when you think of the great mass of writers, and just
the few who had that quality.

KRIM: Let me ask you this: I know that your inclinations
among presentday writers run to men like Malraux, Camus,
Sartre. Now how do you deal with a man like Céline, who
was a rightist and who I'm sure you'll admit was a brilliant
writer, but was outside of your tradition of the explicit political and social animal?

KAPELNER: Céline, like Genet, like Burroughs, like a few
others I can't recall at the moment, and even in a sense like
Oscar Wilde, I don't know if these men are important to
their time. I always looked upon them as the exotic flowers of
literature. Céline I think is a very fair example. Genet is an
excellent example of this. I can't for the life of me find them
uninteresting. But I can't put them alongside of men
involved, *committed*, I think that could be the word more
than a "statement," committed to their time.

KRIM: What makes you say that Camus or Malraux are more
committed to their time than Céline or Genet?

KAPELNER: I am only basing what I say on their work. You
see, Genet is more interested in the homosexual apparatus,
and on that basis alone he's an exotic flower; and Burroughs'
interest is in the hung-up scene, the dope scene, whatever the
scene might be, but all based on the needs of either enthusiasm or retreat. These are the exotics. They're not speaking
to a time at large. They're speaking to a certain sector of

people, they are obviously very significant to these people, and sometimes quite significant to me.

KRIM: In other words, if I can translate this into my own terms, you think that they're too private in their preoccupations.

KAPELNER: And also precious.

KRIM: Don't you think the soil of the contemporary world is conducive to that kind of work? More so perhaps than ever before?

KAPELNER: Yes, but this doesn't put them in the state of largeness. They're so narrow, they're confined, they're working from within their own cells. They're cell-addicted, cell-oriented, and the others are not—they're walkers, talkers, they move around. Genet doesn't move around. Burroughs doesn't move around. Céline never moved around. Of course, being a Jew, I dislike Céline on other levels.

KRIM: Proust, you'll admit, was a large writer, and yet he worked out of a specialized "cell" as well.

KAPELNER: Well—and this might sound awfully precious, possibly—if a man *sings,* if he's a singer, like Joyce was a singer, and he's a composite, or he contains, or he's an eater, a devourer of sights, scenes, smells, and it pours out of him like a crazy, weird, but yet very super-real song, he is not going to be confined, he is not going to be in a cell, in short he's a free man, 'cause he's singing all that. The others are not free, those you've named. Proust is a special case entirely. Right now I can't put my finger on why I think he's—I *know*—he's a special case. But he's a far superior man than the Burroughses and the Célines and the Genets. Proust has a certain kind of power, a neurotic, lonely power, you know. There's something very sickly about Proust. But he's a very, very special sort of case.

KRIM: You say, and you mean it, that you want your writer or artist to be a free man. And yet think back on the men who have made the biggest marks on literature. Most of them were neurotics or compulsives, even those who stood for freedom were "sick" compared to the majority.

KAPELNER: Neuroses and psychoses have nothing to do with freeness. A man could be free and be psychotic or neurotic and so I don't understand that point you make.

KRIM: Let me say it again.

KAPELNER: Let me say something right now. Maybe this is it . . . freeness in the terms that he has made his own philosophy, his own psychology, his own feelings, his own song, or even his own lack of song. That he is not an annex to any main chancellory or main corridor of society. That he's his own man. In that, I think a man is free.

KRIM: In other words, you're asking for originality?

KAPELNER: Yes, yes. I think one of the great troubles today is that literature has gone into a Hollywood syndrome. And even the so-called good writers have gone into this syndrome. They're writing the same song, the same scene, the same *chazarei*. The same junk.

KRIM: Alan, your first book *Lonely Boy Blues* came out in what year?

KAPELNER: 45

KRIM: 1945. Your next novel came out in—

KAPELNER: 60.

KRIM: What took up those 15 years?

KAPELNER: Well, after *Blues* I didn't know what to do with my time. I screwed around a lot, I wasted a lot of years. I knew I wanted to go on writing . . . But I just never got to it. I look back at it, and retrospection is not, of course, always true, it's always a little manufactured. I suppose I wanted to live, you know. Now that's a terrible cliché, but it also is an excellent truth. I wanted to live, I wanted to see, I wanted to get around. I first came down to the Village then, I didn't know what life was like, I wanted to see paintings.

KRIM: You wrote *Lonely Boy* before you came to the Village.

KAPELNER: Yeah.

KRIM: How long did *All The Naked Heroes* take in the writing, all told?

KAPELNER: Seven years.

KRIM: I see. So a good part of that 15 years went into the *Naked Heroes*?

KAPELNER: Well, I wrote that book and I originally called it *Strangers in the Midnight World,* and a lot of publishers told me to put it away. It was during the McCarthy period. Random House and a few others, there were letters from them asking me to put it away, someone up at Little, Brown, put it away, they wanted to give me money for another novel. I found it very difficult to put away. I got quite a lot of letters, and always specifically, "This is not the time for a book of this kind." Well, then I read the book and I said, I don't understand these people, why shouldn't it be a book for any time, you know, but of course there were people in states of fear. You know what McCarthy did to them. I've always felt that McCarthy was never a villain anyway, it's the people who were in fear of him who were the villains. McCarthy was just some Irish square from Wisconsin, and people just fell by the wayside, fled their attitudes, fled their brains, fled their courage, and made a monster of a man. But the true monsters were those who were the makers of the monster.

KRIM: Yes. But let's not get sidetracked by McCarthy.

KAPELNER: So I read the book. I went up in the country and spent the whole summer reading that book and I said it's a lousy book. I thought I'd write this entire book over again from beginning to end. And that took me quite a long time because I invested a great deal in this book. And I got used to a sense of language which never occurred to me before. Certain sounds of words, rhythms, feelings for words. It could be one of the debits of *All the Naked Heroes,* the romance with words. So then I finished it, McCarthy was gone, and I had no trouble getting it published.

KRIM: How have the critics received your two novels?

KAPELNER: Oh, exceptionally. Strangely enough, the

people out West saw more in the work than the people of the East, and that could be because of the sense of jadedness in the East, which is plausible, because the people of the East are more afflicted by the mass media than the people of the West. There's a little more of an openness about them, the ability to receive. The tendency of the people of the East is that jaded feeling, "Aw now, come on man, what the hell is this all about," you know, they are the beneficiaries of such shit that keeps coming, that shit becomes a habit with them.

KRIM: How did the books sell?

KAPELNER: Not well.

KRIM: Both went into paper?

KAPELNER: Both went into paperback. They were published in Holland, England, and Germany. One was a book club selection. *All the Naked Heroes*. Book Find Club. Didn't sell too well. The publisher did have a strong belief that *All the Naked Heroes* would sell very very well. Unfortunately, he was wrong. As far as *Lonely Boy Blues* was concerned, the editor was Maxwell Perkins. Perkins never believed the book would sell, but he believed that the man who wrote the book would be honored.

KRIM: You mean critically honored?

KAPELNER: Critically honored. He thought that was very important.

KRIM: So he was vindicated.

KAPELNER: He was right. I have always felt that more than three-quarters of Max Perkins' attitudes and feelings and beliefs were always right anyway.

KRIM: In your opinion, is this "blind" instinct what made him a great editor?

KAPELNER: Yes. Because he had no planned design in him at all. He could read any kind of literature and he had a very beautifully instinctive touch, very deep. I don't understand some of the people I met later on, people of the *Partisan Review* crowd and the *Commentary* people, who looked upon him as a square. Well, all I can say is I wish they would be as square as he.

KRIM: Alan, about this question of money, and sales. We live in a money culture. You're a rebel in the money culture as a writer. Is there not a kind of poetic or prosetic justice to the fact that your books have had modest sales?

KAPELNER: Would you clear that up a bit?

KRIM: Is it appropriate that the books have had small sales because of their point of view? What makes a book sell a lot of copies anyway?

KAPELNER: I don't know. I think every book is a gamble. Very few publishers will pick a book in terms of prestige. The days of Horace Liveright, as the oldtimers say, that's gone. If they believe it'll sell, they do take a gamble. In many cases it's a dishonorable gamble because they're gambling with something they don't believe in to begin with. Now as far as my work is concerned . . . let me put it this way. It was absolutely shocking to me when the publisher of *All the Naked Heroes* said to me he thought we were going to make a lot of money on that book.

KRIM: That's what I wanted to ask you. When you write a book, you certainly don't write it to sell a lot of copies?

KAPELNER: I hope I would sell a lot of copies. My God, I'd like to make a million dollars on a book! It's on my terms, I'm not prostituting myself. The point is, I'm writing it for people, people buy books. According to the contract I get a certain percentage. The more people who buy books the more people who read what I have to say to them. I'm not a closet writer; I have a big craving in me. The craving is to say what I want to say, how I want to say it, and hope a hell of a lot of people will read it.

KRIM: Alan, you once used the expression that in order to do justice to someone like Céline you really had to "struggle to be objective." I thought it was a good phrase. Try to struggle to be objective now at this question that I'd like to ask

you. Some writers, and we've run into them, we discussed
Dahlberg just the other day over coffee, become bitter with
the years because they don't feel they've gotten the recognition they deserved. It's likely that you feel that some of your
contemporaries have gotten more acclaim or have sold more
books or perhaps even more important, the so-called serious
critics have devoted more pages to their work than to your
own. Perhaps. How do you balance all these things within
yourself?

KAPELNER: Why, I suppose it would be based on my own
makeup that I can't allow the luxury of despair.

KRIM: You mean this as a man or as a writer?

KAPELNER: As a writer and a man. I also can't allow anyone's "victory" being my defeat, and I've always felt this way.
My whole feeling, you know, every writer, every guy, every
woman who wants to write or paint or dance, I don't care
what they want to do, they're in their own boat and they're
going to go to their own shores. I know when I get to be 50,
60, 70, I'm not going to vegetate like a lot of oldtimers that
cry in some sort of a wild asylum they've built around themselves, and get Jehovah-addicted, you know, "Why have the
gods forsaken me?" I was never able to do that. I was a ball-
player. There were better ballplayers than I. I could never feel
any envy or jealousy if someone hit a double and I got up and
struck out. In a high-school basketball game, if I shot 15
points and someone on my team had 30 points, you know, I
could never possibly envy him 'cause I was glad the team
won.

KRIM: So you're saying that thankfully you lack some of
these competitive streaks?

KAPELNER: No, that isn't it. You know Martha Graham
said a very marvelous thing. She said, whether she actually
believes it or not, and I'm always a little suspicious about
people who write certain things, she said that she's not in
competition with anyone, she's only in competition with herself, to better herself. And then when she betters herself she

sees her other limitations and she tries to override them. Well, I was very struck by that when I read it about 10 years ago. To the point of cutting it out of the newspaper or magazine, wherever I read it, and sticking it above my desk.

KRIM: I assume that this is your way of answering my question. What do you foresee for yourself in the future?

KAPELNER: Well, I'm not going to go to my grave with a shelf of books, that's a cinch.

KRIM: It's too fucking hard to write one good one?

KAPELNER: Of course. I think if you make it on one book, that's enough. You know. I mean, you've had it.

KRIM: You really think that?

KAPELNER: Yeah, if you make a great message. And I'm not talking about CP messages, or Norman Thomas messages, or that sort of stuff, but I mean your own personal message. And if you've made it strong, and you've made it violent and sweet, just what this whole society, this whole world is like, that's a pretty good thing to have done.

KRIM: All right, you've done it twice, or at least you've—

KAPELNER: I don't think for a moment that I've really written what I have in me.

KRIM: Then there probably will be a few more books, there have to be?

KAPELNER: Yeah. See, I'm never going to be senile, 'cause I've made up my mind never to be senile. So I'm gonna write a—I don't know how many books I'll write but I'm not going to reach a state where I'll be unable to write a book. Because I've seen too many old men who have made it strong and well at one time. And then they get to be about 60, 70 and they have fallen into their own private soft cells. And they're tired, and they're no longer hungry. I think my nature will never allow me to be filled.

KRIM: Do you have any notions as to what your next project is going to be?

KAPELNER: I'd like to write about madness. What I'd like to write is what I think is going to happen in the 70s. The

people who are in their 20s now—because they're in complete
retreat, they're into the defensive or rather the aggressive
mechanism of thinking they're in rebellion. But they're truly
in retreat, and then in 10 years, in the 70s, they're going to be
in their 30s, and they're gonna be old men with nothing. And
I think you're going to see a lot of madness.

KRIM: I'm glad you have a strong theme for another book.
How long had you brooded about the massmurder theme of
the new book, *The Air-Conditioned Hell?*

KAPELNER: Well, it actually happened on 10th Street and
Bleeker one summer night several years ago. And it struck me,
the entire thing, of someone—they never did find the killer
—but someone, upon reading my book will probably pound
on my door, detectives, and say that I've done the killing.

KRIM: Yes, you do feel guilty.

KAPELNER: It's a very intimate book. Maybe I did do the
killing, I can't recall. And you know someone said, in dreams
we are the greatest of all murderers. Then I did some research
on it and I found out there were so many mass-murders. Then
there were the individual murders. All this murdering, all this
maiming of people. If not a murder, a traumatic maiming.
And I saw this whole goddamned society in sort of an alive
mausoleum. You know, everyone waiting for death, waiting to
be maimed, crippled, hurt, and there was this terrible meanness going around. And meanness coming from the most *logical* of all reasons, the need for excitement, to escape boredom,
monotony, the humdrumness of their time. And that related
to Negroes, Puerto Ricans, and Jews, Italians, Wasps, and
everyone else. It didn't make a particle of difference. And
mind you, I thought of this a hell of a lot, there was nothing
improvised about the thinking of this, 'cause I had all the
facts before me. And out of it came the idea for the novel. Of
a man committing this murder, a mass-murder. Now, I am a
slow writer, but it didn't take me long to write this book.

KRIM: I think about two and a half years?

KAPELNER: Yeah. I felt like Jesse Owens writing this book.

It was just fantastic, you know. And I first wrote it in first person, I read it and realized I'm not a first person writer. I haven't that knack in the first person. Then I wrote it in third person and it satisfied me.* And that's what this book is all about: a man in revolt against his time, and wanting a better time. And he murders for the better time. See, you had once said in an article that someone's writing was as tough as a murderer. Well, that's what I wanted someone to be, as tough as a murderer, but *commit the act*, so he's beyond being as tough as a murderer 'cause he's now a tough murderer. This story comes from a composite, an avalanche of many similar themes that have happened since World War II ended. There've been so many of these things. Knifers, every damned thing that's been going on. It could be the murder of one, the murder of four or five. Mine was eight.

KRIM: How does a book grow in you? What is the actual process?

KAPELNER: Just sit down and write. Hemingway once said, I believe it was in a letter to Max Perkins, that it took him a long time to find the "habit of writing." I developed the habit of writing. Getting up early in the morning, taking a necessary walk because I knew I'd be sitting all day, and getting back at nine in the morning and having some coffee and just sitting down and writing and sweating it out. My whole writing is always sweating it out.

KRIM: I want to get to a problem that's bigger than both of us. Why is it that when we get down to the typewriter I too sweat it out?

KAPELNER: Because then you have an affair with destiny. Now that sounds terrible, doesn't it? But you do have an affair with destiny.

KRIM: You mean the stakes are greater once you put it on a piece of paper?

KAPELNER: Maybe they shouldn't be, but they are. Like

---

*As this collection goes to press, Kapelner is rewriting his book yet a third time.

you take a prize fighter, you know. You meet him on a street and you spar with him, and he has all the combination punches, and everything, and he bobs and weaves and he smiles, but then you get him in a ring and you wonder, what happened to you, Joe? You were marvelous in the street. But he had no opposition. Once you sit down and write, you have an opposition. Your reader is your opposition. And you have an obligation to yourself, which you don't have when you sit around and talk. Because if I sit around and talk with you, like Seymour we're sitting around, and then you don't agree with me. Oh, all right, man, you don't agree with me, that's perfectly all right. But when I write, Christ, I want you to agree with me. And if you don't, if you don't agree with me—
KRIM: You hate my guts.
KAPELNER: It's not that, I don't hate your guts, but I could blush, you know. I'm not beyond blushing, and that's probably one of my greatest weapons.

1967

part 3

intro

My rebellion against the dead stylistic authority of the New
Yorker was a necessity, as it later was for Tom Wolfe and
eight-tenths of the strident new writers who are twirling our
heads around; I had worked for the magazine as both a lark-
ing reporter and "ideaman" in my early 20s before I was fired
for the double sin of chewing gum in Katherine White's face
and forgetting to zip my pants after a quick No. 1 (read: an
arrogant Joosh boy and not toilet-trained to boot); but it was
only when I was editing a magazine myself, Nugget, from
1961–65 during my earnest make-it-or-perish pilgrimage back
into the bowels of the uptown world, that I felt the impetus
to put down on paper my thoughts about what had been the
most influential magazine of my time. I lost at least one
friend there (Lillian Ross), as a result, and this pained me
and still does. But it seemed to me urgent to attempt this
deflation of what had become in my scheme of values a reactionary publication. More important, to line up this piece
with my notions of total engagement, I was cutting off a possible market by my attack and in turn hoping that my article
by some unlikely curve of fate would open the eyes of the
advertising agencies that feed the New Yorker on the basis of
what it has been, not what it is. In other words, I wanted to

169

hit them esthetically, morally and financially; if writing in this country is to be the significant act it can be, it must radiate out into every sector of a given situation and carry with it the sting and consequences of real action. Significant writers today are not trying to change the world abstractly but con-cretely, naming names, quoting money prices, deals, what so-and-so had for lunch and what his cardiogram says, com-mitting themselves totally to a specific piece in every conceiv-able sense so that a result can issue from the union of art and journalism. There can no longer be any acceptable separation of the economic success of a magazine or publishing house from its taste and moral stance; and no serious writer can blot out his responsibility to actually try and sabotage the econ-omy of a communications setup that he finds noxious rather than healthy. Literary criticism must then become life-action and pose a threat that goes past the livingroom and into the kitchen or bedroom, wherever the vital motor is located. If the attacking writer is ridiculed and dismissed, that is his risk; but writing about cultural institutions which is not concerned with going all the way—literally attempting to change or uproot them, from their very use of language to the quality of the private lives of their stockholders—will never make a fly's dent on the actual reality. I see a coming total journalism in this area which will embarrass you out of every secret you've ever hidden, and if your role is public and cultural, be pre-pared for the worst because a generation much beater than I was will stop at nothing in the exposure of what they see as immoral shit. I consider this inevitable and necessary to the extension of literature as genuine action.

who's afraid of the
new yorker now?

1

There used to be a time, let me tell the younger generation, when the *New Yorker* had sting, when its latest short story was discussed all over town, when any selfrespecting intellectual or chic-ster had to take a stand in relation to it. Out of curiosity and deadly habit I picked up the October 28 issue to see what kind of a review the new Albee play got, and John McCarten's sad, inadequate, slightly snotty two columns only confirmed what an increasing number of friends of mine—and myself—have thought:

Unless there is a revolution on 43rd Street, and it isn't likely, the *New Yorker* as we have known it has had it as a cultural force.

No matter how many irrelevant if statusy pieces the *New Yorker* publishes in the near future by W. H. Auden, Edmund Wilson, Anthony Eden or Mary McCarthy, the magazine has become middleaged, safe and increasingly divorced from the action. The Albee review, by old retainer McCarten, brought this home with a forcefulness that to me illuminates in one lightning-flare all the stale attitudes and

171

plump-bellied complacency that has overtaken this once great magazine. The review, if you've read it (and even if you haven't you can imagine it), is pleasant reading because McCarten—following in the footsteps of the finest *New Yorker* staff writers—uses a combination of the spoken and written language with that deceptive ease which comes from an admiration and imitation of *informal style*. That, I think, will be the *New Yorker's* greatest contribution to sophistication and the country's style at large when, in the dim future, the score is added up and the final judgment made.

McCarten is only the last of a long line of expert Ears, men who wrote the language with absolute attention to all of its nuances as they heard it spoken and who delighted in the precious art of fitting words together. Before McCarten came Joe Mitchell, Wolcott Gibbs, John McNulty, St. Clair McKelway, E. B. White, Geoffrey Hellman, names upon names who fifty years from today, with slight exceptions, might all be taken for the same person—or the same person in different moods. Taste plus a literal shudder at being pretentious lay at the bottom of the creation of *New Yorker* style; and beneath this was, of course, the dominant figure of Harold Ross with his maniacal punctiliousness, but even more important, with his native American journalist's fear of being European or thickly, densely highbrow and hence a fraud. One cannot capsulize with justice the many fine points that went into the making of *New Yorker* style—and anyone who had the experience of working there during the magazine's frontrunning days can tell of the incredible painstaking care and obsessiveness that neuroticized the very air—but even using broad strokes to rough in the picture you can justly reduce the *New Yorker* world to one acute element: style.

So stylish was the *New Yorker's* image of itself that (as can be seen in the numberless "Profiles" written by anonymous human machines who almost reduced art to science) the concern with appropriateness became overrefined to the point where style itself was devalued as brassy display and the article that "writes itself" was substituted as the highpoint of journalistic suavity. Never had a magazine in this country devoted such theatrical care to the subtleties of communication, carefulness, tact, finally draining the spirit of its staff down to the microscopic beauty of a properly placed comma and ultimately paralyzing them in static detail and selfconscious poise, the original ideal of perfection having become in the late 50s and now 60s a perversion instead of a furthering of the journalist's duty to render reality.

But McCarten's review of "Who's Afraid of Virginia Woolf?" is pivotal in a much more crucial sense than yet touched upon because it unwittingly reveals the fear of the new that has threatened the *New Yorker* as an institution and its fine craftsmen as men and women—as egos who had Position and are now foundering in the wave of "barbarism" that has overwhelmed their values. Even during the heyday of intellectual snobbery as canonized by the *Partisan* and *Kenyon* reviews during the 40s, the *New Yorker* felt eminently protected, sure of itself, because the underlying axis of the magazine was always journalistic, concrete, and it excelled with the tangible as did no competitor. Harold Ross or his heir William Shawn might not understand or enjoy James Joyce or even Picasso, being expert newsmen first and artistic dilettantes second, but their roots in the American experience were unquestioned, ruggedly sustained by the journalist's reliance on facts and the exciting job of putting out a toughminded but lightly handled organism every week. This security can no longer exist at the *New Yorker*; inroads were made by the selective inclusion of the eminent highbrows into its pages (Dwight Macdonald, Wilson, Delmore Schwartz, Roethke, Rosenberg, Marianne Moore, etc.), and while once they just decorated the cake devised by Chef Ross, who was always suspicious of them, at this point they brought with them an ill wind of disturbing thought. With the eclecticism of the assured and wealthy, the *New Yorker* thought it could head into the future with literary selfesteem protected by this dressing of accepted intellectuals, who threatened only with words, but it was unprepared for the burst of new values crouched barely behind these older, more hypocritically courteous men—hypocritical only in that while they were in as deadly earnest as the young baby-throwing Albees, Ginsbergs and John Cages they spoke in the university-groomed, buttoned-down manner of their period and therefore could pass as white.

It is the new wave, in every sense, that has cast the *New Yorker* adrift from every familiar mooring and turned it, out of defensiveness, into a castrated and even reactionary publication. As we read it now, there is more crass life and inventiveness in the advertising than in the body copy; from the middle of the magazine to the end you will come upon pages with 5½ inches' width of advertising to three of writing, and the painful thing to anyone in the business is the fact that the writing wastes even the petty amount of space it can still command because of the echo of the old colloquial style, using its now trivial diction and informalities to fill up precious space instead of revolutionizing the style to fit the reality. Magazines live in the world, and no one who understands the bitter economics of magazine publishing would fault a publication for having the beautiful cushion of heavy advertising to rest on; the *New Yorker* earned its present wealth the hard way, and one's professional respect goes out to it on the business level because without revenues you either perish or distort yourself; but the fairyland of four-color advertising and its layout, makeup, zing, thrill, even slickness, from the middle to the back of the *New Yorker* shames the lack of superior life in the editorial copy and makes the irony of this demise of brilliance that much more pitiable. Just recall the stories of Ross not allowing the advertising people even to walk on the editorial floor; and now *they* have the power, not only because they bring in the gelt, but because they are negotiating the basic energy and flashy fantasies that brighten our eyes when we pick up the magazine. Soon they will truly control the

New Yorker, blunt its last edge; and the usurpation will be
just, because these men are as determined as Ross's breed and
are not kidding themselves in their huckster role, while the
diehard editorial neoclassicists, the punctuation castratos who
have gone to bed with commas for a quarter of a century, are
living in a world that no longer exists.

I said above that what I take to be the descent of the *New
Yorker* into an advertising showcase is pitiable, and you could
only feel that way if you once worked there—as did William
Gaddis, Truman Capote, Chandler Brossard, myself, a whole
busload of interesting writers now pushing 40—or if you
were susceptible to the tremendous superegolike authority
that the magazine exerted on the liveliest young literary types
and tastebuds in the 40s. But the emotion opposite to pity is
contempt, and it is in this vein that I would like to conclude.
Contempt, viciousness, snottiness, the reduction of your foe
to absurdity, enormous distance between you and the thing
talked about, dirty fun—all these things come out of fear, and
it was fear that John McCarten demonstrated in his review of
the new Albee play. Fear is not a pleasant emotion to witness,
but it is even worse when it is disguised with pseudo-
wisecracks which leave your reader bewildered as to why you
don't attempt to get into the muscle of what you're discussing. The Albee play (which I haven't yet seen), and what Mr.
Albee represents, seems to me an almost too-perfect symbol of
everything that is wrong with the *New Yorker*, and I would
like to trace it through.

This was Edward Albee's first play uptown, the city had
been buzzing all summer long with news of the impending
event—news, mind you, that once the *New Yorker* when it
believed in its title would have eaten up and happily passed
along to its readers—and everyone hip to this town's tempera-
ture knew that this was more than just another play. It was a
dramatic story from a variety of angles: the marginal man
pitted against the Big Street, the fact that Albee had never
faced the "test" of a full evening-length play, the question of

whether the tone of the times was really ripe for a savagely
fragile avantgardist to hold his own in the hardnose world of
unions and boxoffice, the fact that here was no European
import but one of our very own (so slender, so few) who was
going out to bait the killers of the dream. Much was riding on
this debut, quite apart from the line-by-line merits of "Who's
Afraid of Virginia Woolf?" and John McCarten withdrew
from the entire excitement of the occasion, treated it with the
coolness of catatonia, put it down (which in itself is immater-
ial) in terms that don't apply, and brought off the most pathetic crack of the week in weaseling out of mature criticism
with the words "a vulgar mishmash." What Irishman is kidding what Jew, and haven't we all come a long way from the
vulgar potato famines, eh John?

It is not McCarten as an individual alone who is intended
to bear the brunt of this obituary; it is McCarten as the representative—the very able representative, by the way—of an
entire editorial way of life that has passed its peak and is
descending as ungracefully as every real power does when the
true gism gives out. This is not to say that the *New Yorker*
will not coast with the already established winners for a decade
or more and fur the minds of its readers with the warm feel of
occasional mink; sporadic excellent pieces, their value on the
literary exchange having been appraised long in advance, will
no doubt tastefully appear and momentarily restore faith to
the worried parishioners; but the virility, adventurousness, connection with the living tissue of your audience can only be
restored by rebirth. This is not about to happen in the near
future and could only occur after the present *New Yorker* trust
fades away and 20 years hence stirs the fires of someone who
buys the title and is then animated, directed, by the legend of
a memorable past joined with a love of the living present.

That love—today a savoring of horror because we have had
to live with it, a true delectation of the dislocated age we
inhabit, an elastic and surreal response to cruelty and ugliness
instead of the desperate and unreal attempt to duck its exis-

tence—is absent in the very motor of the presentday *New Yorker*. Its creators are overaged, overinsulated; the truly gorgeous notion of style which they gave to America has invisibly changed into a new style which they are afraid of and don't understand. The magazine is merely cruising now, because it has no place to go except to stay afloat and collect the reward for endurance. But every now and then you'll run across one of its pop-gun artists, like John McCarten, firing away as in the good old days, and then all of a sudden you'll feel embarrassed for the man because he is such a goddamned fool and is so proud of it. . . .

Good night, sweet sheet.

2

James Baldwin's remarkably direct, shocking, uncensored confrontation of white American ignorance in the Nov. 17th *New Yorker* has been singled out as evidence that my obituary on this magazine, for being grossly removed from the reality we all know, was premature. But the freshness of Baldwin's article graphically illustrates how desperately in need the *New Yorker* is of genuine communication, if it is to justify itself, and how unreal its normal posture looks in relation to only one (the Negro issue) of the radical metamorphoses that are transpiring before our contemporary American eyes. Baldwin is one of the very few Negro writers ever to publish in the *New Yorker*, perhaps the only one, and while his appearance there represents a loosening of the perfumed barrier, it also reaffirms the *New Yorker*'s sense of security in identifying itself with a name and an issue that have already been accepted by ashamed white liberals rather than daring to initiate any troubling thoughts of its own.

From a magazine point of view, it is realistic to keep in mind that Baldwin is publishing his views in *Esquire, Playboy, The New York Times Magazine, Harper's, Nugget*, etc., as well as the *New Yorker*. He has suddenly become one of the most pertinent voices of the day because only he, so far, can truly humanize and illuminate the ugly guilt felt by his noncolored countrymen and therefore no magazine editor—whether of the *New Yorker* or *Seventeen*—is insensitive to his tremendous value as a bridge betwen alien camps. (With increased awareness of his unique position Baldwin has become ever more forceful in his role, to the point where in his *New Yorker* article—conscious of his genteel new audience—he echoes his thunder long after felling every necessary tree, and can't resist threatening his characteristically vulnerable, femalized-psychiatrized readership with murder for their timid deceits in relation to his own manly suffering: it was perhaps irresistible in the surroundings, and had them groveling for a week until the next cocktail party, but even Baldwin's mature and fulfilled voice can't entirely sustain the overdramatized burden of avenging prophet which is now permitting his prose to embrace every discursive thought as though it were flame.)

It is not the *New Yorker* who should be naively congratulated on running an outspoken piece by the leading Negro literary spokesman in the U.S. today, valid and blistering as "Letter from a Region in My Mind" was. Both Baldwin and the magazine can be seen as frankly exploiting each other, he for a platform and top-billing right in the hushed center of the Ivy League White Protestant psyche, they for a variety of smart reasons: "courage," prestige, news-value, the hard fact that any article on the Negro is today an automatic circulation-booster, plus genuine open-mouthed admiration of Baldwin and what he stands for in contrast to their own inhibition and lack of editorial conviction. It is hardly possible that William Shawn and the upper echelon who run the presentday *New Yorker* are truly blind and deaf to the new realities that have overtaken most lives—they must get drunk or high with their Negro help on occasion even if they don't ball with them—but so long has the magazine's esthetic been based on a class-oriented sense of repression that one can visualize the sense of shock and love with which Baldwin's warning of vengeance was received. My God, they must of thought when the MS. was handed around, what new life in even this threat of death! And yet it is bitterly ironic that the acceptance of such new actuality can only be made real to certain self-guarded sensibilities when the knifepoint is testing the throat. In the issue of the Negro, and of his eloquent star champion Mr. Baldwin, the *New Yorker* was no doubt succulently willing to yield its white-on-white pages because it sensed a mightier force that could buoy it up and inseminate its jellied blood with meaning; but rather than this being any creative credit to the magazine, it is—in the cold light of editorial values—more probable to read it as a confession of the absence of a positive viewpoint of its own and the desire to spread its legs and offer its body (Baldwin's piece ran 85 pps., advertising-garnished though most of them were) to a genuine infidel at its papier-maché gates in return for the vicarious life it could extract from even a potential executioner.

Publication of the isolated Baldwin manifesto does not represent consistent *New Yorker* policy in the sense that Dorothy Parker, Shaw, O'Hara, McNulty, Perelman and the other minor masters once did—or even as the unlikely stablemates Salinger, Macdonald, Liebling and young Rev. Updike do today—and it is in the lack of cohesiveness that one can see the waning of a definite spirit, and the attempt to substitute plastic surgery for honest limbs and a tangible soul. It has been said in explanation that the *New Yorker* was young and gay when the world was such, and became calculated and grey when history demanded a realistic change of heart; but the world was ancient and agonized long before the *New Yorker* brightened it with a vivacity that might have owed its external froth to the collegiate 20s, but certainly won its unique life because of the gleam in Harold Ross's dry eye.

Style changes of necessity and any magazine, person, attitude minted in the 20s would have to shed its particular glitter when time rusted it or else be laughed into bankruptcy; no one criticizes the *New Yorker* for not being consistent to the short skirt under which it was so nonchalantly conceived, but for the weekly proof that it has been unable to integrate its youth into its middleage with the same integrity. It may well be, as the wise bores tell us, that values narrow with the years and that it is asking too much to ask the *New Yorker* to bite into life with the same tang that enabled it to grow into its present juiceless imitation of itself. If that is so, then let's pity the dull swindle of age which parades as maturity and write it off as still another hypocrisy dripped onto this insultingly mis-educated generation; but the *New Yorker* is too incestuously facesaving to ever healthily admit that its needle no longer bites the flab of its own time, that in function it has become a cover-to-cover tranquilizer precisely for that "little old lady from Dubuque" who, it used to purr, would be horrified by it.

You cannot say, nor was it ever the intention here, that the *New Yorker* doesn't publish valuable or exciting pieces that appear almost as spasmodically as an old movie star's erection: sure they do—Salinger; Macdonald (most effective probably when restrained by space); Liebling (but no longer food or boxing, the vein having been worked dry and repeated because of the magazine's shortsighted encouragement); Tynan when he wrote for them; used warhorse O'Hara still on occasion (although they run him much too often for maximum mileage, apparently out of fear of offending); Wilson when he's not being pedestrianly dated or hopelessly touting old pals like Morley Callaghan and Dawn Powell; J. F. Powers when not being too ultracool about the Catholic world he carries in his pocket; Lillian Ross when in classic form; the neat and deftly-written capsule book reviews, isolated treats. But what the *New Yorker* and its trancelike reflex buyers shut from consciousness is that you have to pick through a weekly issue like a private eye, to spot the article/ story that contains the life, and junk the rest; it's a page-by-page fliptease for which you pay 35¢ and often as not the one redeeming piece—and how often is there more than one?—isn't there.

The mounting piles of unread synthetic *New Yorkers* in the livingrooms of time-squeezed real New Yorkers declares the anachronism of three-fifths of their editorial matter to a city speedster, and makes one realize that the pace and interests of the magazine—the boring tempest-in-a-tulip fiction, the spinsterishly detailed articles—have been muffled like the rationale of Exurbia itself. "Out here in the hinterland," writes Professor Warren French of Kansas State University to me, "we are still interested in Manhattan itself—its life still excites us—but I am sure no one at the *New Yorker* knows how bored we are with accounts of how tough it is to camp out in a $40,000 chateau in Fairfield County. Such an editorial environment goes well with *Silent Spring*, one of the last really exciting things to appear in the *New Yorker*, but one which has nothing to do with the city at all and is another evidence of the concerns of Exurbia."

Exurbia, suburbia or Thurbier, the decline of the *New Yorker* can really be seen in the loss of that very fashionableness which, after all else was said, this magazine always felt snugly in about and therefore genially indifferent to intellectual criticism. Fashion, though it be mocked by bushy minds on the fringe of events, is a visible image of where the sharpest point of interest is in any given period, and fashion-setters can be defined as those so sensitive to the daily life of their time that they can feel its pulse long before thicker skins know that one even exists. When country-boy Ross was intuitively turned on to the Algonquin crowd (Parker, Kaufman, Marc Connelly, Benchley, F.P.A., Auntie Woolcott, etc.), whose unpremeditated sophistication in the pages of the infant *New Yorker* gave encouragement to less extroverted and more subtle talents, a chain-reaction of unparalleled goodies was set in motion that caught the flavor and sharply defined the metropolitan stance of the time.

As close as a nose-hair to its day, the magazine anticipated and created style because it was a totally jumping headquarters for the cleverest wits on the scene—everyone who was anyone wanted to get into the act—and from approximately the early 30s to the mid 50s so phenomenal was the *New Yorker*'s cultural influence that it imposed its character on nothing less than the American conception of the humorous essay, cartoon, "casual" piece, short story, and ultimately revolutionized magazine journalism in this country with its original reportage. Not one uptown New York book publisher was immune to its salty taste (Simon & Schuster almost made an entire career out of eagerly publishing the magazine between hardcovers every three months), practically every newspaperman throughout the country hoarded dumb misprints to submit and read it with glee, in fact every human communications-medium in the days before the present deluge was literally groomed and conditioned by this tart arbiter of How To Say It Right.

But such genuine power can be said to have ended at least eight years ago—as the uneasy giant of American experience hoisted the window on hungry new life that demanded its own appropriate tongue—just when the *New Yorker* began to scoop in sweet advertising money in that recurring failure of U.S. cultural success: namely, starve with a patched elite audience while putting down your exciting opening notes, then clean up on the masses with a pat formularization of your once-hot magic, and by all means con yourself as you bank the winnings until you're inseparable from the new audience and love your own corn like the farmers who lap it up. Money is power, yes, and the *New Yorker* is now sloshing in green where once it held its threadbare Princeton clothes on high with a hidden safety-pin and laughed; but money-power is common compared to the beam of an original idea which can be mirrored endlessly, or the shape of a new look which can change our vision, or the pace of a new rhythm which can quicken our sense of time and therefore alter the significance of events.

The subtle, enormous influence the *New Yorker* once had in these intangible areas, to the extent of intimately shaping the cream of an American generation now in their 50s, has

painfully shrunken because thousands of a new young generation—bulging, bursting, bopping and rocketing at every
mental seam—find nothing for themselves but incomprehen-
sion or condescending miniaturization in the wrinkle-free *New
Yorker* existence salon. "I first discovered that something was
amiss," continues Professor French in his letter, "when I
found (I was then at the ill-fated University of Florida) that
the handful of alert students we had were not reading the *New
Yorker* any more as my handful of friends had when we
haunted the Ivy League some 20 years ago. The *New Yorker*
meant nothing to them, and I was astonished at this, since
it had meant so very much to me and others in the dim past.
I began to see, however, that the *New Yorker* just really had
nothing for them."

In other words, the interest, fascination and identification
with the liveliest aspects of one's time and place—that which
Ross gave the *New Yorker* with the unappeasable sniffer of a
great newshound—has given way to the imitation of such life,
primarily because of the intolerable petrification of the magazine's conventions, and the "fashion" that it now robes itself in
has inevitably become that of the *ancien régime*. The format
of a magazine can be a candid indication of its soul, even
more than the editorial matter, and the obvious fact known to
practiced eyes in the trade is that the predictable *New Yorker*
look—as literally mechanical as the Automat—dissipates joy
and buries brilliance within its monotonous sameness. One
issue looks, feels and smells like the next, and weekly they add
to the undisturbed pyre on the hippest coffee-tables in town
because the alert, nervous, multiple-eyed contemporary is psychologically unable to confront an experience so static that it
depresses him before he begins. What does it matter if
Harold Rosenberg writes penetratingly about painting when
his copy is set as excitingly as an actuarial report, discouraging
visual imagination at the very moment he is trying to cultivate your mind's eye? The sharpest rollicking pieces by Liebling, Macdonald, West, even almost Salinger, slip by the

meshes of the brain into week-later oblivion because of the convictionless regularity of the format, as smooth and faceless as a robot factory. At one time this makeup and typeface spoke coolness, selfeffacement, modesty, taste, but all it means now—contrasted with the competition from bold, jazzy four-color ads that bring with them the booming materialism of the outside world—is a deliberate absence of identity that has become as artificial as any outmoded virtue that no longer serves its purpose. Rather than proving any superiority to the lush commercial jungle that now overhangs its tidy garden, the *New Yorker*'s uninventive and vapid format is almost a caricature of the standard psychoanalytic insight about rigidity of form being a defense against new experience.

If the *New Yorker* is esthetically reactionary—and the time has long passed when you can snoot the visual as applied to a magazine, or anything else, in this aggressively all-conscious era—it is improbable to expect the magazine's implicit liberalism to be anything more than a moral gesture to another phantom defleshed by history and therefore made kiddie-safe. From what we know Ross was apolitical, a 20s toughie cynicized by Menckenism but possessed of enough confident moxie to editorially transcend politics in the sparkling play of the Manhattan world he loved so much; however, with the ascension to the editorship by Shawn, backed up by the Whites (Katherine and E.B.) and the other policymakers, a gloved New Deal hand showed itself which grips the magazine to this day. But instead of being a vote for progress any more than the *New Yorker*'s assembly-line format or archly repressed fiction, this "liberalism" tiptoeingly pitches an effete advocacy of justice which can get wet over the death of Mrs. Roosevelt and small dogs, but conveniently ignores the irony of humaneness of feeling based on the luxury of power. It would never occur to the *New Yorker*'s desk-liberalism that its fineness of empathy is an empty vanity, practiced to assuage its impotence in the face of a reality that asks for illumination and action rather than melodious consolation. But like the possession-weary seg-

ment of America it has come to represent, this exhausted
innovator reclines on the thornless cushion of a passé humani-
tarianism, without once demonstrating the independence to
peer into the revolt which threatens the validity of liberal ideology in our day: namely, that the majority of contemporary
humanity can no longer afford to be humane in a mannerly
charade of the urgent problems confronting them, and the
sensitive hand extended in brotherhood—as in the "serious"
lead essays in "The Talk of the Town"—is foolish to expect
reciprocity when its manicured good will proceeds from a
refinement of the obvious, rather than from the investigation
of what has not yet been defined and demands to be. The
liberal kindness that emanates from the *New Yorker*'s editorial
voice has all the power of a canary used to its cage, and unsur-
prisingly wants to immure its reader like itself, never caring to
acknowledge the elementary insight of contemporary Chris-
tianity that kindness must be radical today if it is intended as
a responsible point of view and not a hollow social grace.

If there was ever an illustration that for our day the liberal
conscience is fast becoming the compromised conscience, a
better specimen than the *New Yorker* could hardly be found:
preaching an outworn union of fine moral discrimination and
epicureanism, it nevertheless buttresses its ooo-la-la conceits
with nakedly materialistic and undiscriminating lures from
the hardassed manipulators of American commercial taste. As
the world shoves its genuine leering face into the pages of the
magazine, not in the editorial niceties but in the encroach-
ingly covetous advertisements, the *New Yorker*'s conspiracy
against reality suddenly takes on the willed perversity of a
porcelain thumb stubbornly thrust in the bloodshot eye of the
truth. And as the outer world grows increasingly more barbarous in its honest appetites—sexual, political, psychological,
sensational—this once-peer is helplessly thrown into static sil-
houette against the greater energies that dominate it. It is
now becoming the passive well-coifed little queen of rough-
trade cultural forces that have surpassed it in vigor, wit, perti-

nence, rhythm, design, excitement, surprise, illumination and selfbelief.

To preserve the fiction held by its now largely convention-al-minded, easily buffaloed public (and the loser-be-fucked ad agencies) that it is a unique, classy, razzmatazz leader, the *New Yorker* must become increasingly eclectic under the rationalizing flag of its buttery liberalism, scurrying to pluck the safely best from here and there and feed it into the cold jaws of its machine format. But unlike magazines which began with such an opportunistic policy and owe their being and style to precisely their callous lack of belief, the *New Yorker* assumed every jewel of its rare life from its spirit. When it rationalizes that, as it is already cautiously doing out of cynical necessity because it fluffed the challenge of imagi-natively redefining its purpose and character in a new America that demands publications which penetrate it with the sting-ing voice of the accelerated present—stretching its now rubber conscience to include tokens of radical chic and impres-siveness on top but not at the bottom where it counts—it will finally become indistinguishable from any other superslick magazine. As a matter of fact, and this sentence to anyone my age who was once in love is hard to write, it already has.

1962

part 4

intro

I met Kerouac only twice, both for brief periods of not more than 15 minutes, and communication between us was abrupt and unreal. What I wrote about the man and writer was the result of feeling, experience and legwork, not friendship. The hippies-Yippies have replaced the Beats today, but they are the logical and expanded second wave; when their history is written it will all point back unerringly to the homemade anarchistic breakthrough of the Beat Generation—the dropouts, communes, drugs, beards, hair, handcrafts, meditation, etc. I owe my own turnon as a writer who had been coldshouldered by my quasi-academic peers of the Cerebral Generation to the revivifying power of the Beats and I can testify in court if need be to the actuality of the Beat messianic excitement. Behind it, in my judgment, was the principal catalytic figure of Kerouac; today Ginsberg and Burroughs get a much bigger and better press and are highly respected by the university intellectuals whereas Kerouac is regarded very fishily as a simpleminded athletic type run amok. It might even be that his final value will have been primarily inspirational: but if this is so, it was extensive beyond current awareness and I am enormously glad that I sweated

189

my way through this overlong and slightly obsessive piece, even incurring Kerouac's oblique anger (via letter) at the less flattering questions I raised about the future of his work. Both of us were in a touchy situation because my article served as the introduction to Desolation Angels (1965) when his reputation in New York was charred and uncertain after mere vogue-followers had deserted for yet a new substitute penis in the search for thrills. Jan Cremer, post-Beat, pre-Provo, cock-eyed kid and terrifyingly cool manipulator of his own destiny, stands astride the two very separate possibilities of pop celebrity and uniquely independent writer-painter. He would like to be a fantasy figure, "a world idol" as he puts it looking you right in the eye without a smile, a rough combination of Bobby Kennedy and Yevtushenko and Cassius Clay (as he told me in 66—see how quickly his images have become ghosts!); his idea of selfdivinity can drive you crazy; and yet I admire both his unusual poise and his courage but have no certainty about which direction he will take. My hunch is that he will be determined by circumstances and therefore become an avantgarde showbusiness symptom of his time rather than the disturbing prophet I truly feel in him. It is almost an arrow pointing the way our times have changed that my own involvements, and those of our shattered American world, have developed in the last decade from Jack Kerouac (who returned to womblike Lowell, Mass., and shucked off every relationship with his own Beat Generation) to Eldridge Cleaver and Abbie Hoffman. Jan Cremer fascinates me because he made a unique individual play out of what would later become hippie materials, cashing in on the style of the young culture outlaws who are now a new world-class, but Cleaver and Hoffman have each in their own way joined the Youth Revolution to socialist-anarchist motors that have taken them into the crumbling center of America. They are leaders—a powerful word on the New Left these days—and young men and women stand behind their words with action. Beats, Provos, Black Panthers, Yippies: what strange names for literature but then what else is literature right now but the eruption of the outraged spirit in language? Dig it while I give and take with these men who project to me more than themselves, who summon up a new quality of experience that grips me and causes me to work out on the most basic level of my own life.

the kerouac legacy

All of us with nerve have played God on occasion, but when was the last time you created a generation? Two weeks ago maybe? Or instead did you just rush to your psychiatrist and plead with him to cool you down because you were scared of thinking such fantastic-sick-delusory-taboo-grandiose thoughts? The latter seems more reasonable if less glamorous; I've chickened out the same way.

But Jack Kerouac singlehandedly created the Beat Generation. Although Allen Ginsberg, Gregory Corso and William Burroughs brought their separate and cumulative "madness" to the yeasty phenomenon of the BG (and you will find them in *Desolation Angels* under the names of Irwin Garden, Raphael Urso and Bull Hubbard), it was Kerouac who was the Unifying Principle by virtue of a unique combination of elements. A little boy tucked into the frame of a resourceful and independent man, a scholarly Christian-mystic-Buddhist who dug Charlie Parker and Miles Davis and icecream, a sentimental, apolitical American smalltowner who nevertheless meditated on the universe itself like Thoreau before him, Jack Kerouac threw a loop over an area of experience that had previously been disunited and gave it meaning and continuity. The significant thing about Kerouac's creation of the Beat Generation, what made it valid and spontaneous enough to

193

leave a lasting wrinkle on history and memorialize his name,
was that there was nothing calculated or phony about the
triumph of his style. He and his friends in the mid to late 50s,
before and while the Beat flame was at its hottest, were
merely living harder and more extensively than any of their
articulate American counterparts. One of the minor characters in *Angels*, an Asian Studies teacher out on the Coast, says
at an outdoor party that the core of Buddhism is simply
"knowing as many different people as you can," and certainly
this distinguished Kerouac and his boys with a bang.

They zoomed around this and other countries (San Francisco, Mexico City, Tangier, Paris, London, back to New
York, out to Denver, yeah!) with a speed, spirit and fierce
enthusiasm "to dig everything" that ridiculed the self-
protective ploys engaged in by the majority of young
American writers at the time. This is not to say that Kerouac,
Ginsberg, Corso and Burroughs didn't have individual equals
and perhaps even superiors among their homegrown literary
brothers; men like Salinger, Robert Lowell, Mailer, Joseph
Heller, James Jones, Styron, Baldwin, etc., were beholden to no
one in their ambition and thrust of individual points of view,
but that is exactly what each remained—individual. The Beats,
on the other hand, and Jack Kerouac in particular, evolved a
community among themselves that included and respected
individual rocketry but nevertheless tried to orchestrate it
with the needs of a group; the group or the gang, like society
in miniature, was at least as important as its most glittering
stars—in fact you might say it was a constellation of stars who
swung in the same orbit and gave mutual light—and this
differentiated the Beat invasion of our literature from the
work of unrelated individuals conducting solo flights that had
little in common.

It can be argued that the practice of art is a crucial individual effort reserved for adults and that the Beats brought a
streetgang cop-fear and incestuousness into their magazines,
poetry and prose that barred the door against reality and

turned craft into an orgy of selfjustification. As time recedes from the high point of the Beat Generation spree, roughly 1957-1961, such a perspectivelike approach seems fairly sane and reasonable; from our present distance much of the Beat racket and messianic activity can look like a psychotics' picnic spiked with bombersized dexies. Now that the BG has broken up—and it has become dispersed less than 10 years after its truly spontaneous eruption, with its members for the most part going their separate existential ways—a lot of the dizzy excitement of the earlier period (recorded in *Desolation Angels* and in most of Kerouac's novels since *On the Road*) can be seen as exaggerated, hysterical, foolish and held together with a postadolescent red ribbon that will cause some of its early apostles to giggle with embarrassment as the rugged road of age and arthritis overtakes them.

But there was much more to the Beats, and to Kerouac himself, than a list of excesses, "worship of primitivism" (a sniffy phrase introduced by the critic Norman Podhoretz), crazy lurches from North Beach to the Village, a go-go-go jaz-zedup movie that when viewed with moral selfrighteousness can seem like a cute little benzedream of anarchy come true. This more or less clichéd picture, especially when contrasted with the "Dare I eat a peach?" selfconsciousness practiced in both the universities and the influential big-little magazines like the *Partisan* and *Kenyon* reviews, was however a real part of a Beat insurrection; they were in revolt against a prevail-ing cerebral-formalist temper that had shut them out of liter-ary existence, as it had hundreds of other young writers in the America of the late 40s and 50s, and the ton of experience and imagery that had been suppressed by the critical police-men of post-Eliot U.S. letters came to the surface like a toilet explosion. The first joy of the Beat writers when they made their assault was to prance on the tits of the forbidden, shout the "antirational"—what a dreary amount of rational Thou Shalt Nots had been forced down their brains like castor oil—exult in the antimetrical, rejoice in the incantatory, act out every bastard shape and form that testified to an Imagination which had been imprisoned by graduate-school wardens who laid down the laws for A Significant Mid-Twentieth-Century American Literature.

One should therefore first regard the insane playfulness, deliberate infantilism, nutty haikus, naked stripteases, free-form chants and literary war dances of the Beats as a tremendous lift of conscience, a much-needed *release* from an authoritarian inhibiting-and-punishing intellectual climate that had succeeded in intimidating honest American writing. But the writer's need to blurt his soul is ultimately the most determined of all and will only tolerate interference to a moderate point; when the critic-teachers presume to become lawgivers they ultimately lose their power by trying to take away the manhood (or womanhood) of others. By reason of personality, a large and open mind, a deceptively obsessive literary background coupled with the romantic American good looks of a movie swinger, Jack Kerouac became the image and catalyst of this Freedom Movement and set in motion a genuinely new style that pierced to the motorcycle seat of his contemporaries' feelings because it expressed mutual experience that had been hushed up or considered improper for literature. The birth of a style is always a fascinating occasion because it represents a radical shift in outlook and values; even if time proves that Kerouac's style is too slight to withstand the successive grandslams of fashion that lie in wait, and if he should go down in the record books as primarily a pep pill rather than an accomplished master of his own experience (and we will examine these alternatives as we dig deeper into his work), it is shortsighted of anyone concerned with our time in America to minimize what Kerouac churned into light and put on flying wheels.

This last image is not inappropriate to his America and ours, inasmuch as he mythicized coast-to-coast restlessness in a zooming car in On the Road (1957) at the same time that he took our customary prose by its tail and whipped it as close to pure action as our jazzmen and painters were doing with their artforms. But Kerouac did even more than this: now in 1965, almost a decade after *Road*, we can see that he was probably the first important American novelist (along with Salinger) to create a true pop art as well. The roots of any innovator nourish themselves at deep, primary sources, and if we give a concentrated look at Kerouac's, the nature of his formative experience and the scope of his concern might surprise a number of prejudiced minds and awaken them to tardy recognition.

John (Jack) Kerouac, as every reader-participant of his work knows, was born in Lowell, Massachusetts, in 1922, a very much American kid but with a difference: he was of French-Canadian descent and the family (his father was a printer, interestingly enough) embraced the particularly parochial brand of Catholicism which observers have noted about that northern outpost of the Church. As far as Wasp America went, Kerouac was almost as much of an Outsider as the radical-Jewish-homosexual Allen Ginsberg, the urchin-reform-school Italian Gregory Corso and the junkie-homosexual-disgrace-of-a-good-family William Burroughs that he was later to team up with.

From his earliest years, apparently—and laced all through Kerouac's work—one sees an extreme tenderness toward animals, children, growing things, a kind of contemporary St. Francisism which occasionally becomes annoyingly gushy to dryer tastes; the sympathetic reader credits Kerouac with having genuine "saintly" forbearance as a human but also winces because of the religious-calendar prettiness in a work like *Visions of Gerard* (1963), the sincere and perhaps overly idealized elegy to a frail older brother who died during the writer's childhood. If Kerouac's feeling occasionally floods into a River of Tears it is nevertheless always present, buckets of it, and one is finally astonished by the enormous responsiveness of the man to seemingly everything that has ever happened to him—literally from birth to a minute ago.

As an Outsider, then, French Canadian, Catholic ("I am a Canuck, I could not speak English till I was 5 or 6, at 16 I spoke with a halting accent and was a big blue baby in school though varsity basketball later and if not for that no one would have noticed I could cope in any way with the world and would have been put in the madhouse for some kind of inadequacy ..."), but with the features and build of an all-American prototype growing up in a solid New England manufacturing town, much of Kerouac's early life seems to have gone into fantasy and daydreams which he acted out. ("At the age of 11 I wrote whole little novels in nickel notebooks, also magazines in imitation of *Liberty Magazine* and kept extensive horse racing newspapers going.") He invented complicated games for himself, using the Outsider's solitude to create a world—many worlds, actually—modeled on the "real" one but extending it far beyond the dull-normal capacities of the other Lowell boys his own age. Games, daydreams, dreams themselves—his *Book of Dreams* (1961) is unique in our generation's written expression—fantasies and imaginative speculations are rife throughout all of Kerouac's grownup works; and the references all hearken back to his Lowell boyhood, to the characteristically American small-city details (Lowell had a population of 100,000 or less during Kerouac's childhood), and to what we can unblushingly call the American Idea, which the young Jack cultivated as only a yearning and physically vigorous dreamer can.

That is, as a Stranger, a first-generation American who couldn't speak the tongue until he was in knee pants, the history and raw beauty of the U.S. legend was more crucially important to his imagination than it was to the comparatively well-adjusted runnynoses who took their cokes and movies for granted and fatly basked in the taken-for-granted American customs and consumer goods that young Kerouac made into interior theatricals. It is impossible to forget that behind the 43-year-old Kerouac of today lies a wild total involvement in this country's folkways, history, small talk, visual delights,

music and literature—especially the latter; Twain, Emily Dickinson, Melville, Sherwood Anderson, Whitman, Emerson,
Hemingway, Saroyan, Thomas Wolfe, they were all gobbled
up or at least tasted by him before his teens were over (along
with a biography of Jack London that made him want to be
an "adventurer"); he identified with his newfound literary
fathers and grandfathers and apparently read omnivorously.
As you'll see, this kind of immersion in the literature of his
kinsmen—plunged into with the grateful passion that only
the children of immigrants understand—was a necessity
before he broke loose stylistically; he had to have sure knowledge and control of his medium after a long apprenticeship in
order to chuck so much extraneous tradition in the basket
when he finally found his own voice and risked its total
rhythm and sound.

Around Kerouac's 17th year, we find him attending the
somewhat posh Horace Mann School in upper Manhattan—the family had now moved to the Greater New York
area with the onset of his father's fatal illness—and racking
up a brilliant 92 point average. (His brightness by any standard confounds the careless "anti-intellectual" charges leveled
at him by earnest Ethical Culture types.) Then in 1940 he
entered Columbia University on a scholarship. Kerouac, so far
as I know, never actually played varsity football for Columbia
although he was on the squad until he broke his leg, and had
been a flashy Gary Grayson-type halfback while at Horace
Mann. He also never finished college, for World War II
exploded after he had been there approximately two years;
but during this period he did meet two important buddies
and influences, William Burroughs and Allen Ginsberg, and
it is interesting to keep in mind that the titles of both works
which brought these men to public attention, *Naked Lunch*
and *Howl* respectively, were coined by Kerouac the verbal sor-
cerer. Burroughs was a spare, elegant, fiercely authentic junkie
and occasional dilettante dabbler in crime, such as a holdup
of a Turkish bath just for an André Gidean laugh, who

earned his role of guru by having lived coolly and defiantly on
the margin of society after being born into its social center—St. Louis' prominent Burroughs Adding Machine family
and Harvard 36. His intelligence was acute, penetrating,
impersonal and sweepingly bizarre. Young Ginsberg was a
"visionary" oddball from Paterson, New Jersey—"I never
thought he'd live to grow up," said hometowner William
Carlos Williams about him—the son of a minor poet and a
suffering crazy mother whom he has written beautifully about
in *Kaddish* (1962), a radical, a Blakeian, a dreamy smiling
Jewish Fauvist, and one can picture the three of them bounc-
ing ideas off each other during apocalyptic Morningside
Heights nights just after America got sucked into the war.

Some day the entire history of these sensational JAZZ-
JUNK-POT-POETRY-IDEAS-ORGASM-GOD! prepara-
tions for the Beat mutiny will be written—Alfred G. Aronowitz, formerly the "Hamlet of the cityroom" at the *New
York Post,* was the first journalist to sense their importance
and has voluminous notes and tape recordings toward a
book that so far has been discouraged because it is "dated"
—but for our particular purpose here, namely Jack Kerouac, it is enough to see how his French Canadian-Catho-
lic-Yankee arc was widened to compassionately include non-
participating acceptance of the homosexuality of his literary
pals, association with interesting criminals and prostitutes,
drugs, Manhattan freakishness of every kind, including those
crazy forays with Ginsberg, Herbert Huncke (ex-con, drugman
and recent writer), Burroughs and Neal Cassady (Dean Mori-
arty of *On the Road*) into the hustling life of Times Square.
An artist of originality, such as Kerouac, is compounded of
many layers, his capacity for experience is always widening, his
instinct for friends and lovers is based on what he can learn as
well as brute personal need; one feels that Kerouac was expanding in all directions at this time, reading Blake, Rimbaud,
Dostoevsky, Joyce, Baudelaire, Céline and the Buddhists now
in addition to his groovy American word-slingers, beginning to

write poetry (perhaps with Ginsberg's enthusiastic encouragement), painting, becoming in other words the manysided
phenomenon he would have to become in order to escape easy
definition and inspire the deep affection of such a variety of
heterogeneous people as he eventually did.

When WW II finally did come, Kerouac signed on as a merchant seaman and sailed to arctic Greenland on the ill-fated
S. S. Dorchester, now famous for the four chaplains who gave
up their lives during a U-boat sinking near Iceland, but he
had been called to Navy boot camp just before that fatal 1943
sailing. After a comparatively short duty in the Navy, Kerouac
was discharged as "schizoid personality," a primitive mental
description not very different from the way a number of his
fellow writers were bracketed by a service unable to handle
their double and triple vision. Now he was to be on his own
(except for his boyishly obsessive devotion to his mother, as
his patient readers know only too well) for the rest of the
race. After the Navy, the remainder of the war was spent as a
merchant seaman sailing the North Atlantic again; then, in
rough order, came a year under the G.I. Bill at Manhattan's
New School for Social Research, the completion of his first
novel, hoboing and hitchhiking across the United States and
Mexico, and the growing attachment for San Francisco as the
first port of call after he came down from his perch on top of
the Washington State mountains as a fire-watcher.

I can remember the word being passed around in New
York in the late 40s that "another Thomas Wolfe, a roaring
boy named Kerouac, ever hear of him?" was loose on the
scenes (and I can also remember the shaft of jealousy that
shot through me upon hearing this). But the significant thing
was that in addition to hard, I-won't-be-stopped writing
during these crucial years—and this extra gland was to make
Kerouac stand out from all the other first novelists clogging
the city—he had an uncanny gift for winging right along
toward new experience; he was the first vocal member of a
postwar breed, the Beat Transcontinental American, for in

New York he numbered among his friends (and happily shook up) such writers as Burroughs, Ginsberg, Corso, John Clellon Holmes (who has a coolly memorable portrait of him in Go) as well as jazz musicians, painters, hippies, while on the Coast he had equally strong currents going with Neal Cassady—"the discovery of a style of my own based on spontaneous get-with-it came after reading the marvelous free narrative letters of Neal Cassady"—and the poets Philip Whalen, Gary Snyder, Peter Orlovsky (Simon Darlovsky in this book and Ginsberg's loyal buddy), Philip Lamantia, Robert Duncan, John Montgomery and others.

Absorbing the life for his work by scatting around the country, Kerouac was also feeding scores of people by his presence, enthusiastically daring the poets to wail, the painters to paint, little magazines to get started (Big Table, 1960-1961, was named by him for its brief but significant career) and in the simplest sense being the human pivot for an improvised subsociety of artists, writers and young poetic-religious idealists alienated from our sapping materialistic culture. It doesn't seem exaggerated to say that Kerouac by his superior capacity for involvement with "his generation" unified surprising numbers of underground Americans who would probably have remained lonely shadows but for his special brand of charisma. And Transcontinental though Kerouac was, the West Coast, and the Frisco area in particular, were to prove culturally more ready for him than the East.

California looks toward the Orient; its young intellectuals and truth-seekers are far more open to untraditional and experimental concepts than their counterparts in the New York and New England cultural fortresses, and it was to be no accident that the Beat chariot fueled up in S.F. and then rolled from West to East in the late 50s rather than the other way around. But more specifically for our knowledge of Kerouac, it was on the Coast, especially from Frisco north to the high Washington State mountains, that climate and geography allowed his Dharma Bums (1958) to combine a natural out-

doorsy way of life with the Buddhist precepts and speculations that play a very consistent part in all of Kerouac's writing and especially in *Desolation Angels*. In this propitious
environment Kerouac found a number of kindred neo-
Buddhist, antimaterialist, gently anarchistic young Americans
whom he would never have come upon in New York, Boston
or Philadelphia; they discussed and brooded upon philosophy
and religion with him (informally, but seriously) and
brought—all of them together, with Kerouac the popular-
izer—a new literary-religious possibility into the *content* of the
American novel that anticipated more technical studies of
Zen and presaged a shift in the intellectual world from a
closed science-oriented outlook to a more existential
approach. This is not to imply that Kerouac is an original
thinker in any technical philosophical sense, although every
artist who makes an impact uses his brain as well as his feelings; Kerouac's originality lay in his instinct for where the
vital action lay and in his enormously nimble, speed-
championship ability to report the state of the contemporary
Beat soul (not unlike Hemingway in *The Sun Also Rises*
some 35 years earlier).

Before Kerouac appropriated San Francisco and the West
Coast, the buzz that had been heard in New York publishing
circles about this word-high natureboy came to a climax in
1950 with the publication of his first novel, *The Town and the
City*. From the title you can tell that he was still under the
influence of Thomas Wolfe—*The Web and the Rock, Of
Time and the River*, etc.—and although his ear for recording
the speech of his contemporaries is already intimidating in its
fullness of recall and high fidelity of detail and cadence, the
book remains a preliminary trial run for the work to come. In
it are the nutty humor, the Times Square hallucinated montage scenes, fresh and affectionate sketches of Beats-to-be, intimate descriptions of marijuana highs and bedbuggy East Side
pads, but at the age of 28 Kerouac was still writing in the bag
of the traditional realistic American novel and had not yet

sprung the balls that were to move him into the light. Kerouac himself has referred to *Town* as a "novel novel," something at least in part madeup and synthetic, i.e., *fictional*. He
has also told us that the book took three years to write and
rewrite.

But by 1951, a short year after its publication, we know
that he was already beginning to swing out with his own
method-philosophy of composition. It took another seven
years—with the printing of *On the Road*, and even then readers were shielded from Kerouac's stylistic innovations by the
orthodox Viking Press editing job done on the book—for that
sound and style to reach the public; but Allen Ginsberg has
told us in the introduction to *Howl* (1956) that Kerouac
"spit forth intelligence into 11 books written in half the
number of years (1951-1956)"—*On the Road* (1957), *The
Subterraneans* (1958), *The Dharma Bums* (1958), *Maggie
Cassidy* (1959), *Dr. Sax* (1959), *Mexico City Blues* (1959),
Visions of Cody (1960), *Book of Dreams* (1961), *Visions of
Gerard* (1963), *San Francisco Blues* (unpublished) and *Wake
Up* (unpublished). The dates in parenthesis refer to the year
the books were issued. At the age of 29 Kerouac suddenly
made his breakthrough in a phenomenal burst of energy and
found the way to tell his particular story with its freeing sen-
tence-spurts that were to make him the one and only "crazy
Catholic mystic" hotrodder of American prose.

This style, as in that of any truly significant writer, was
hardly a surface mannerism but rather the ultimate expression
of a radical conviction that had to incarnate itself in the language he used, the rhythm with which he used it and the
unbuttoned punctuation that freed the headlong drive of his
superior energy. He had invented what Ginsberg called, a
trifle fancily, "a spontaneous bop prosody," which meant
that Kerouac had evolved through experience and selfrevela-
tion a firm technique which could now be backed up ideologically.

Its essentials were this: Kerouac would "sketch from

memory" a "definite image-object" more or less as a painter would work on a still-life; this "sketching" necessitated an "undisturbed flow from the mind of idea-words," comparable to a jazz soloist blowing freely; there would be "no periods separating sentence-structures already arbitrarily riddled by false colons and timid commas"; in place of the conventional period would be "vigorous space dashes separating rhetorical breathing," again just as a jazzman draws breath between phrases; there would be no "selectivity" of expression, but instead the free association of the mind into "limitless seas" of thought; the writer has to "satisfy himself first," after which the "reader can't fail to receive a telepathic shock" by virtue of the same psychological "laws" operating in his own mind; there could be "no pause" in composition, "no revisions" (except for errors of fact) since nothing is ultimately incomprehensible or "muddy" that "runs in time"; the motto of this kind of prose was to be "speak now or forever hold your peace"—putting the writer on a true existential spot; and finally, the writing was to be done "without consciousness," in a Yeatsian semitrance if possible, allowing the unconscious to "admit" in uninhibited and therefore "necessarily modern language" what overly conscious art would normally censor.

Kerouac had leapt to these insights about Action Writing almost 15 years ago—before he sat down to gun his way through *Road*, which by his own statement was written in an incredible three weeks. (*The Subterraneans*, which contains some of his most intense and indeed beautiful word-sperm, was written in three days and nights with the aid of bennies and/or dex.) Whether or not the readers of *Desolation Angels*—or contemporary American writers in general— embrace the ideas in Kerouac's Instant Literature manual, their relevance for this dungareed Roman candle is unquestionably valid. The kind of experience that sent him, and of which he personally was a torrid part, had a glistering pace-discontinuity-hecticness-promiscuity-lunge-evanescence   that begged for a receptacle geared to catch it on the fly. At the

time of Kerouac's greatest productivity in the early 50s, the
humpedly meditated and intellectually cautious manner of
the "great" university English departments and the big literary quarterlies was the dominant, intimidating mode so far as
"serious" prose went; I know from my own experience that
many young writers without Kerouac's determination to go
all the way were castrated by their fear of defying standards
then thought to be unimpeachable. So tied up were these
standards with status, position in the intellectual community,
even "sanity" in its most extensive sense, that writers who
thumbed their nose or being at them had to risk everything
from the categorization of simple duncehood to being called a
lunatic. But Kerouac, "a born virtuoso and lover of language," as Henry Miller accurately pointed out, was literarily
confident enough to realize—with the loyalty of a genuine
pioneer to his actual inner life—that he would have to turn
his back on the Eliot-Trilling-Older Generation dicta and risk
contempt in order to keep the faith with reality as *he* knew it.
Obviously this takes artistic dedication, courage, enormous
capacity for work, indifference to the criticism which always
hurts, an almost fanatical sense of necessity—all the guts that
have always made the real art of one generation strikingly different from the preceding one, however "goofy" or unfamiliar
it looks and feels to those habituated to the past.

What many of Kerouac's almost paranoically suspicious
critics refuse to take into account is the fundamental seriousness, but not *grimness,* of the man; his studious research into
writer-seers as varied as Emily Dickinson, Rimbaud and Joyce,
the very heroic cream of the Names who rate humility
and shining eyes from the brownnosing university play-it-
safeniks; and his attempt to use what he has learned for the
communication of fresh American experience that had no precise voice until he gave it one. This is not to say that he has
entirely succeeded. It is too early, given Kerouac's ambition,
for us to make that judgment; but we can lay out the body of
his work, 14 published books, and at least make sense of what

he has already achieved and also point out where he has perhaps overreached himself and gestured more with intention
than fulfillment. As with any creative prosewriter of major
proportion—and I believe without doubt that Kerouac
belongs on this scale for his and my generation—he is a social
historian as well as a technical inventor, and his ultimate
value to the future may very well lie in this area. No one in
American prose before Kerouac, not even Hemingway, has
written so authentically about an entirely new pocket of sensibility and attitude within the broad overcoat of society; especially one obsessed by art, sensations, selfinvestigation and
ideas. Kerouac's characters (and he himself) are frantic young
midcenturyites whose tastes and dreams were made out of the
very novels, paintings, poems, movies and jazz created by an
earlier Hemingway-Picasso-Hart Crane-Orson Welles-Lester
Young network of pioneering hipsters. Nor are these warming
modern names and what they stand for to Kerouac's gang
treated with distant awe or any square worship of that sort;
they are simply part of the climate in which the novelist and
his characters live.

We ought to remember that the generation which came of
age in the late 40s and mid 50s was the product of what had
gone immediately before in the dramatization of the American imagination, just like Kerouac himself, and his-and-their
occasional romanticization of the stars who lighted the way
was not essentially different from what you can find in any
graduate school—only emotionally truer and less concerned
with appearances. So credit the King of the Beats with having
the eyes and ears to do justice to an unacknowledged new
American Hall of Fame that was the inevitable result of our
country's increasing awareness of the message of modernity,
but remained unrepresented in fiction until Kerouac hiply
used it for his subjectmatter. Yet art is more than literal social
history, so that if Kerouac is a novelist-historian in the sense
of James T. Farrell, F. Scott Fitzgerald or the early
Hemingway, he like them must show the soul of his matter in

the form; the artist-writer's lovely duty is to materialize what he is writing about in a shape indivisible from its content ("a poem should not mean but be").

It therefore would have been naive and ridiculous for Kerouac to write about his jittery, neurotic, drug-taking, auto-racing, poetry-chanting, bop-digging, zen-squatting crew in a manner like John Updike or even John O'Hara; he had to duplicate in his prose that curious combination of agitation and rapture that streamed like a pennant from the lives of his boys and girls; and it is my belief that precisely here he stepped out in front by coining a prose inseparable from the existence it records, riffing out a total experience containing fact, color, rhythm, scene, sound—roll 'em!—and all bound up in one organic package that baffles easy imitation. In this sense art has always been more than its reduction to a platform—and it is interesting (in a nonjudgmental sense) that Allen Ginsberg and John Clellon Holmes have always been more articulate Beat ideologists than Kerouac, who has always squirmed out of any programmatic statements about his "mission" because it was ultimately to be found in the work rather than a Town Hall debate. Except for that machinegun typewriter in his lap—or head!—he was seemingly deaf and dumb or reckless ("I want God to show me His face") and bizarre as a public spokesman; simply because this was not his job, and any effort to reduce the totality of experience communicated in his books would have seemed to him, like Faulkner, a falsification and a soapbox stunt rather than a recreation—which is where the true power of Kerouac and narrative art itself comes clean. As Gilbert Sorrentino has pointed out, Kerouac accurately intuited our time's boredom with the "psychological novel" and invented an Indianapolis Speedway narrative style that comes right out of Defoe—Defoe with a supercharged motor, if you will.)

If Kerouac's books are then to be the final test, and if the writing itself must support the entire weight of his bid—as I believe it must—has he (1) made his work equal its theory?

and (2) will the writing finally merit the high claims its author obviously has for it? To begin with, we should consider the cumulative architecture of all his books since *On the Road*, because in a published statement made in 1962 Kerouac said: "My work comprises one vast book like Proust's except that my remembrances are written on the run instead of afterwards in a sickbed. . . . The whole thing forms one enormous comedy, seen through the eyes of poor Ti Jean (me), otherwise known as Jack Duluoz, the world of raging action and folly and also of gentle sweetness seen through the keyhole of his eye."

Let's try to break this down. Kerouac regards his work as highly autobiographical—which it obviously is, with only the most transparent disguises of people's names making it "fictional"—and a decade after the beginning of his windmill production he has found an analogy for it in *Remembrance of Things Past*. Proust's massive spiderweb, however, gets its form from a fantastically complicated recapturing of the past, whereas Kerouac's novels are all present-tense sprints which are barely hooked together by the presence of the "I" (Kerouac) and the hundreds of acquaintances who appear, disappear and reappear. In plain English, the books have only the loosest structure when taken as a whole, which doesn't at all invalidate what they say individually but makes the reference to Proust only partially true. In addition, the structure that Proust created to contain his experience was a tortuous and exquisitely articulated monolith, with each segment carefully and deviously fitted into the next, while the books of Kerouac's "Duluoz Legend" (his overall title for the series) are not necessarily dependent on those that have gone before except chronologically. Esthetically and philosophically, then, the form of Proust's giant book is much more deeply tricky, with the structure following from his Bergsonian ideas about Time and embodying them; Kerouac, whose innovations are challenging in their own right and need no apology, has clearly not conceived a structure as original as Proust's. As a progressing work, his "Legend" is Proustian only in the omniscience of the "I," and the "I's" fidelity to what has been experienced, but it does not add to its meaning with each new book—that meaning is clearly evident with each single novel and only grows spatially with additions instead of unfolding, as does Proust's. Finally, the reference to Proust's work seems very much an afterthought with Kerouac rather than a plan that had been strategically worked out from the start.

If structurally the "Duluoz Legend" is much less cohesive and prearranged than the reference to Proust implies, what about the prose itself? I believe that it is in the actual writing that Kerouac has made his most exciting contribution; no one else writing in America at this time has achieved a rhythm as close to jazz, action, the actual speed of the mind and the reality of a nationwide scene that has been lived by thousands of us between the ages of 17 and 45. Kerouac, no matter how "eccentric" some might think him as a writer, is really the Big Daddy of jukebox-universal hip life in our accelerated U.S.A. His sentences or lines—and they are more important in his work than paragraphs, chapters or even separate books, since all the latter are just extensions in time and space of the original catlike immediacy of response—are pure mental reflexes to each moment that dots our daily experience. Because of Kerouac's nonstop interior participation in the present, these mental impulses flash and chirp with a brightly felt directness that allows no moss whatsoever to settle between the perception and the act of communication. Almost 10 years before the "vulgar" immediacy of Pop Art showed us the astounding environment we actually live in—targeted our sight on a close-up of mad Americana that had been excluded from the older generation's comparatively heavy Abstract Expressionism—Kerouac was happily Popping our prose into a flexible flyer of flawless observation, exactness of detail, brand-names, icecream colors, the movie-comedy confusion of a Sunday afternoon jam session, the spooky delight of reading *Dr. Jekyll and Mr. Hyde* in the woods of Big Sur, all sorts of incongruously charming and touching aspects of reality that were too slender and evanescent to have gotten into our heavyweight literature before.

The unadorned strength of the prose lay in the fact that no detail was too odd or tiny or inhuman to escape Kerouac's remarkably quick and unbored eye; and because of his compulsive-spontaneous method of composition he was able to trap actuality as it happened—the literal preciousness of the moment—where other writers would have become weary at the mere thought of how to handle it all. Such strength coupled with humorous delicacy, and made gut-curdlingly real by the "cosmic" sadness especially in evidence in *Desolation Angels*, cannot be disregarded by anyone seriously concerned with how our writing is going to envelop new experience: "If it has been lived or thought it will one day become literature," said Emile Zola. Kerouac's influence as a writer is already far more widespread than is yet acknowledged or even fully appreciated, so extensive has its reach been; Ginsberg, Frank O'Hara, LeRoi Jones, folksinger-poet Bob Dylan, Hubert Selby, John Rechy, even Mailer, John Clellon Holmes, Lawrence Ferlinghetti and myself are only some of his opposite numbers who have learned how to get closer to their own rendering of experience specifically because of Kerouac's freedom of language, "punctuation" (the etiquette of traditional English as opposed to American) and, in the fullest sense, his literary imagination.

Yet this same prose reveals itself as well to be at times little-boyish, threadbarely naked (so that you want to wrap a blanket around both it and its creator), cute-surrealistic-collegiate, often reading more like breathless short telegraphic takes than "writing" as we are accustomed to the meaning of the word. This is the risk—that the spontaneity is only paper-deep and can be blown away by a stiff new cultural wind. Since there is no "character" or "plot" development in the oldfashioned sense, only an accretion of details—like

this—with the voice of the narrator increasingly taking on the
tones of speech rather than literature—so that it might have
been taped instead of written—just as Jack taped four chapters of *Visions of Cody*—the words have a funny lightness—
like feathers or kids' paper airplanes—they trip along like
pony hoofs—no deep impression left on the page—with a
kind of comicstrip simplification—everything impatiently
kissed on the surface—but is experience only that which we
can see right off?

To be realistic, Kerouac's writings can seem like nonwriting
compared to our steelier literary products; he has dared all on
a challengingly frank, committed, unweaseling rhythmic fling
that can get dangerously close to verbal onanism rather than
our conception of fundamental novel-writing. The books
themselves often seem like sustained underwater feats rather
than "works" in the customary, thought-out, wrought sense.
You get the impression that they landed between covers only
by accident and that if you removed the endpapers that hold
them together they would fly away like clouds; so light and
meringuelike is their texture, so fluid and unincised their
words, so *casual* their conception of art that they seem
doomed for extinction the moment after they are set down.

I find it inevitable, even for admirers, to seriously entertain
the possibility that Kerouac's work will not outlive the man
and his period; already he has told us all his secrets and apparently bored—by the uninhibited exposure of his soul—readers
who have no special sympathy for his rucksack fucksack
romanticism. And yet this is the risk he has taken; the general
reader to whom he has romantically exhibited his genuine
being is as merciless as the rolling years, as uncharitable as
winter, as restless and fickle as the stomach of a millionaire.
One cannot help but think, poor Jack, poor Ti Jean, to have
flung his innermost flower into the crass hopper of public
taste and the need for cannibalistic kicks! My personal belief
is this: whatever is monotonous, indulgent or false in Kerouac's prose will be skinned alive by sharpeyed cynics who

wait with itching blades for prey as helplessly unprotected as this author is apparently condemned (and has chosen) to be. Kerouac has been flayed before and will be again; it is his god-damned fate. But I also believe that the best of his work will endure because it is too honestly made with the thread of actual life to cheapen with age. It would not surprise me in the least to have his brave and unbelligerently up-yours style become the most authentic prose record of our screwy neo-adolescent era, appreciated more as time makes its seeming eccentricities acceptable rather than now when it is still indigestible to the prejudiced middleclass mind.

In subtle and unexpected ways, haunted by the juvenile ghosts of his childhood as he might be and therefore unnerving even his fondest intellectual admirers, I think Kerouac is one of the more *intelligent* men of his time. But if the immediate past has been personally difficult for him—and you will see just how painful it has been, both in this book and in *Big Sur* (1962)—there is little to say that the future will be easier. He is a most vulnerable guy; his literary personality and content invite even more barbs, which wound an already heavily black-and-blued spirit; but the resilient and gentle nub of his being—whose motto is Acceptance, Peace, Forgiveness, indeed Luv—is stronger than one would have suspected, given his sensitivity. And for this resource of his wilderness-stubborn Canuck nature all who feel indebted to the man and his work are grateful.

The danger now confronting Kerouac, and it looms large, is one of repetition. He can add another dozen hardcover-bound spurts to his "Duluoz Legend" and they will be as individually valid as their predecessors, but unless he deepens, enlarges or changes his pace they will only add medals to an accomplishment already achieved—they will not advance his talent vertically or scale the new meanings that a man of his capacity should take on. In fact one hopes, with a kind of fierce pride in Kerouac that is shared by all of us who were purged by his esthetic Declaration of Independence, that time

itself will use up and exhaust his "Duluoz Legend" and that
he will then go on to other literary odysseys which he alone
can initiate.

Desolation Angels is concerned with Beat Generation
events of 1956 and 1957, just before the publication of *On
the Road*. You will immediately recognize the scene and its
place in the Duluoz-Kerouac autobiography. The first half of
the book was completed in Mexico City in October of 1956
and "typed up" in 1957; the second half, entitled *Passing
Through*, wasn't written until 1961 although chronologically
it follows on the heels of the first. Throughout both sections
the overwhelming leitmotiv is one of "sorrowful peace," of
"passing through" the void of this world as gently and kindly
as one can, to await a "golden eternity" on the other side of
mortality. This humility and tenderness toward a suffering
existence has always been in Kerouac, although sometimes
defensively shielded, but when the Jack of real life and the
hero of his books has been choked by experience beyond the
point of endurance, the repressed priest and "Buddha" (as
Allen Ginsberg valentined him) in his ancient bones comes
to the fore. All through *Angels*, before and after its scenes of
celebration, mayhem, desperation, sheer fizz and bubble,
there is the need for retreat and contemplation; and when
this occurs, comes the tragic note of resignation—manly,
worldly-wise, based on the just knowledge of other historic
pilgrimages either intuited by Kerouac or read by him or
both—which in recent books has become characteristic of this
Old Young Martyred Cocksman.

Let no one be deceived. "I am the man, I suffered, I was
there," wrote Mr. Whitman, and only an educated fool—as
Mahalia Jackson says—or a chronic sneerer would withhold
the same claim for Kerouac. His mysticism and religious
yearning are (whether you or I like it or not) finally ineradica-
ble from his personality. In this book he gives both qualities
full sweep, the mood is elegiacal, occasionally flirting with the

maudlin and Romantically Damned, but revolving always around the essential isolation and travail that imperfect beings like ourselves must cope with daily. If critics were to give grades for Humanity, Kerouac would snare pure A's each time out; his outcries and sobbing chants into the human night are unphony, to me at least unarguable. They personalize his use of the novel-form to an extreme degree, in which it becomes the vehicle for his need and takes on the intimacy of a private letter made public; but Kerouac's pain (and joy) becomes his reader's because it is cleaner in feeling than the comparatively hedged and echoed emotions we bring to it with our what's-the-percentage? "adult" philosophy.

Like Winston Churchill—admittedly a weird comparison, but even more weirdly pertinent—Kerouac has both made and written the history in which he played the leading role. The uniqueness of his position in our often synthetic and contrived New York publishing house "literature" of the 60s speaks for itself and is in no immediate danger of duplication. If is goes unhonored or is belittled by literary journalists who are not likely to make a contribution to reality themselves, the pimples of pettiness are not hard to spot; Kerouac, singled out by the genie of contemporary fate to do and be something that was given to absolutely no one else of this time and place, can no longer be toppled by any single individual. The image he geysered into being was higher, brighter, quicker, funkier and sweeter than that of any American brother his age who tried barreling down the central highway of experience in this country during the last decade.

But the route has now been covered. Jack has shown us the neon rainbow in the oil slick; made us hear the bop trumpets blowing in West Coast spade heaven; gotten us high on Buddha and Christ; pumped his life into ours and dressed our minds in the multicolored image of his own. He has, in my opinion, conclusively done his work in this phase of his very special career. And I hope for the sake of the love we all hold for him that he will use those spooky powers given to all

Lowell, Mass., Rimbaudian halfbacks and transform his expression into yet another aspect of himself. For I think he is fast approaching an unequal balance—giving more than he is taking in. Two-way communication is fading because during the last 10 years he taught us what he knows, put his thought-pictures into our brains, and now we can either anticipate him or read him too transparently. I sincerely believe the time has come for Kerouac to submerge like Sonny Rollins—who quit the music scene, took a trip to Atlantis, came back newer than before—and pull a consummate switch as an artist; since he is a cat with at least nine lives, one of which has become an intimate buddy to literally thousands of people of our mutual generation and which we will carry with us to oblivion or old age, I am almost certain he can turn on a new and greater sound if he hears the need in our ears and sees us parched for a new vison. He is too much a part of all of us not to look and listen to our mid 60s plight; to hear him speak—and it's a voice that has *penetrated* a larger number of us than any other of this exact time and place, trust my reportorial accuracy regardless of what you may think of my taste—just turn the page and tune in.

1965

i jan cremer

Jan Cremer at the age of 25 can rank unashamedly as the brazen illegitimate son of both the crazy 60s and of such Big Daddies of imaginative autobiography as Louis-Ferdinand Céline, Henry Miller, Jean Genet and Maxim Gorki. What makes his book all the more mysterious in its triumph is that Cremer was primarily known in scruffy underground circles abroad as a professional narcissist, publicity-hound, tourist-hustling Action Painter—an American expression coined by the New York critic Harold Rosenberg and applied most beautifully to Jackson Pollock which Cremer imported into Holland—a trans-European cocksman and selfannounced "world idol" who in his own unsweet words wrote this document to "seize power, strengthen my image and make MONEY!" He will accomplish each of these goals, thumb his elegant nose at the bourgeoisie of two continents, continue to make gold facsimile copies of his book each time it sells another 100,000 copies—he has already started this Elvis Presleying of literature via the Dutch edition—and with the back of his hand he will show distinguished literary men twice his age the difference between talent and authoritative originality. His book should break the heart of all but major novelists because each of its chapters contains in itself the amount of life that one confronts in a conventional novel. That a man so

217

young, so contemptuous of "seriousness," frankly absorbed in
his own ego to the point of pathology from an American middleclass psychiatric position, should break through every predictable human prejudice by the sheer authenticity of his
being is a significant event that separates this book from "literature" at the same time that the book inevitably creates its
own niche in literature which has no precise equal for it. It is
unique in its not only "unprecedented" but, until you read
it, more or less unimaginable blend of quietly and sharply
observant narrative—almost reminiscent of the big 19th-
century Russian novels; then equally naturally comes its
blunt and nasty Dutch hipster-slang lingo which admittedly
borrows from an international pool of American Negro-Beat
inside talk but has an undeniable effect in deflating the Ger-
man-type pretentions that infuriate Cremer about Holland;
yet this is still only a beginning about the writing—from here
it explodes into what can only be taken to be fantasies or
wish-fulfillments of murder and mutilation committed by
Cremer on those countrymen of his whom he hates for the
same reason that he manfully curses the country itself, its stul-
tifying cowlikeness which squashes human growth. But the
weird quality of these scenes of sadism and murder is that
they seem to be inspired by crude American toughguy pri-
vate-eye work like Mickey Spillane and Henry Kane yet with a
humanly real, moving, pitiful Dutch setting. The emotions
they set up in the American reader, who sees with dread the
violence of his own country's fantasies acted out with stoic
seriousness in a place he has always thought of as "quaint,"
"charming," are upsetting and almost erotic in the pleasure
Cremer forces us to experience in sadism. It is impossible to
describe in detail each new piece of ground Cremer's writing
covers, and it should be made clear that he works all of these
veins at more or less the same time—there is no switching-on
and off in any manipulatory sense, you are immediately
caught up in the *story* of his life and he is a most powerful
and deceptively original storyteller on just that "universal"

level. But his story is not just an unusually engrossing narrative even though it is loaded with hipster-masculine derringdo
and probably—certainly!—heightened, invented, brutally
imagined events; the story is primarily a confession of his
being, a la the great modern confessors mentioned as his
fathers in the first sentence although it is very doubtful if he
has read them, but confession in Cremer's hands is also a
weapon. He will tell you frankly for example about his fascination with every conceivable form of moving the bowels, he
will speak simply about turds and their shapes and the kinds
of bathrooms he likes to enjoy this basic necessity in, and you
know with each sentence that he is putting you on the spot;
what he says is true, not shameful at all, but the majority of
us feel uneasy—at least in this country—about thinking or
talking too explicitly on the subject and he makes us feel
small and grateful for his freedom (not license) in not just
being himself but *having a self to be.* Thus he awakens without any polemical addresses in the least the self we haven't
dared use under the pressures of either conformity, insecurity
or ignorance, so that we can respond in a fuller way to experience than we usually do. He is by no means an uplifter or a
"nice" man, put that thought away quickly; he is aggressively
(often refreshingly) conceited throughout the book, paying
off old scores one might think, but doing this with a com-
posed and slightly frightening sense of innate superiority
which makes the reader sometimes feel like the lesser man.
This arouses resentment because it puts down one's own
ego-possibilities but it is usually soon rectified by the reader's
increasing familiarity with the boldness of Cremer's actions
toward everyone: running naked with a knife in his teeth in
the Amsterdam streets to frighten a parasitic hanger-on who
thought he, Cremer, was a professional killer, deserting from
the Foreign Legion with the probability of a court-martial (he
got away with it). The sex of course—and the book is
drenched with sex, probably somewhat craftily to catch the
modern market and certainly in keeping with Cremer's own

admittedly, scornfully lowbrow American paperback
tastes—again screams envy in the ordinary male reader
because Cremer seems to have slept, made it, with several
hundred choice girls. But once again a curious and highly tes-
tifying—to Cremer—experience occurs: exaggerated or not,
and the probability is that the majority of these experiences
took place except that we see them through his own usually
blazing painter's eye which would be different from the way
another witness would see them, they are really exciting,
honestly "pornographic" in the good groiny way that adults
should describe sex to other adults; but the gaminess is lifted
up and will be for even embarrassed readers by the enormous
selfdeclarative enthusiasm Cremer has for women as people of
exotic beauty as well as agents for his penis. He dresses them
for sex, poses them as just a happy pot-smoking (imagina-
tion-freeing) lover would do, it is all convincing, but he is
richer than most lovers because he is a genuine artist in the
most elementary sense of wanting to paint them and make
the ecstatic moment permanent—he is not a utilitarian middleclass man, intellectual or not, who wants to satisfy the
flesh, period. The very best fucks and love-bouts in Cremer's
book are human, nasty sometimes, you feel the nails of the
woman in his/your back but also his boredom 10 minutes
later and it reminds you of life, not fiction. He also irritates
you because he is young and impatient and apparently spoiled
by his good fortune with pussy galore, but then again he walks
away from setups where those of us perhaps not quite as charismatic would hold on. Cremer as he comes to us through the
pages of this unedited letter to the world accepts very little
that is cheap and no matter how heroic many literary figures
are they often accept cheap lays—which this at times snotty,
prideful Dutchman won't do. Once again his *spirit* toward
sex, women—he naively boasts about the number of his girlfriends in a humorless and foolish U.S. collegeboy way, slightly
aggressively as if we won't believe him which is human
enough but disappointingly immature—is what is groovy and

genuinely itch-making, firstrate horny, regardless of whether
Cremer is laying it on thicker than he laid it in. But a
reader would be a vicarious sucker in several ways to confine
his view of this book to sex or to think that Cremer has confined his life to it; the more one thinks about it the home-
movie sex is there for pride's sake, to show the "American
world" which he admires that he's as virile as Heming-
way-Mike Hammer-Richard Diamond-godknowstherestoftheir-
names except probably an Americanophile like Jan Cremer.
Also, to again acknowledge his shrewdness, the sex is present
because Cremer knows it will "sell" and this boy is a garment-
center operator when it comes to selling, which we'll discuss
when we get to the tremendous cynical artificiality or amoral
gamesmanship of his offstage career. But finally the greatest
thing about Cremer's sex scenes is the unconscious honesty
that also permeates his entire book and rises to the inspiration
of what used to be called genius before the word became
debased: like an idiot he will tell you how a chick who loved
him put on her black nylons with the traditional hardon-mak-
ing garter belt and the spike heels, what Jack Kerouac once
called the Forty-second Street jerkoff image, and the detailed
zest with which Cremer acts out the whole scene is poignantly
real because you can see him living out some mad, to him
beautiful inspiration from the dingiest American girlie magazines and having his all-American fuck, so to speak, right in
the heart of the Dutchland he despises—a strange and moving
poetic gesture made memorable by his creative and unashamed
eroticism and his lonely unspeaking love for this country
which at that time he had never seen. He is a naturalist, at least
the sentence-by-sentence technique is very competently realistic on the surface even when encasing the fantastic flights, but
if a poet is one who in the end *sees* further than a prosewriter
then Cremer's uncanny vision makes him transcend his
medium. Vision for the details in full view that no one else
sees, for example a description of how he and the whole crew
smuggled cigarettes, pot, heroin, razor blades and scores of

other items into a foreign country from comically absurd
secreting-places on a Dutch merchant ship including the
toilet, rudder, etc., a perfect, modest, immediately visible
funny picture. But finally vision is just that born *awareness* of
seeing that has always cast meaning into the blanknesses of
life and is an objective human virtue quite apart from the
see-er's personality. Genuine seers—using the word unpreten-
tiously just as "to see" in the preceding sentence and now
extending it in the logical culmination that must have been
involved in its mystical usage—must always be perceived by
others who have been on the receiving end of their vision; but
it is futile to look for them in the world because one must
deny their existence up to the moment when denial is impossible. A seer—and in however impure or immature or too-
worldly a form he appears the concept fits Jan Cremer on
both the elementary level and on the higher one—has only
one important function, which is to see more and further
than the majority. Not because of any unperceivable, witch-
like, fourthrate "devil's power" but because he or she can literally see more reality than their fellows and then with varying ability compress this vision into statements that are startling to us because we haven't followed their route and are
presented with only the sum. Admittedly seers can err out of
common weakness, Cremer errs; perhaps the powerdrive that
he projects offstage away from his writing—the pop
celebrity-idol aura—reveals what could become a major abuse,
or prostitution, of a disturbingly rare human quality which
should ideally be protected rather than selfexploited. You
have to talk about the man this way because he uses the work
to redeem himself; no sniveling redemption, hardly, it's a
total giving apart from what he may have omitted (which is
his secret alone)—a creative giving with a green fist, so to
speak, not a neurotic heart-squeezing with forgiveness written
over it. But it is naive and misleading not to see that Cremer
the man wants to use the success of this first large public
impact to advance his notoriety and therefore cushion him

against adversity in a dangerous world. One forgets how much
of a hustler, conman, trickster he encouraged himself to be,
trying to establish a Name as a painter-personality in an indifferent Holland, goaded by a history of lumps and kicks delivered by the world since he was an infant during the German
occupation. This tremendous concern with money that one
reads about in the paperstorm of Dutch publicity releases that
followed the original publication and success of *Ik Jan
Cremer* in March, 1964—a chauffeured Rolls Royce in
London, a silver Mercedes for conspicuous home consump-
tion, all this showy razzmatazz—can it be attributed to the
early poverty alone or, as one fears, is this again protection
against the majority that can't perceive the lonely uniqueness
of having vision in a suspicious world where everything must
be callously proved? The public wheeler-dealer Cremer, the
young man *not* writing or painting, must feel confident that
his superior power to see will affect and ultimately influence
those people and situations with which he gets involved; but
the habit of showmanship from precocious years as a Dutch
dada-stuntman (*"Amsterdam's Eighteen-Year-Old Action
Painter Will Perform Before Your Very Eyes!"*) reduces the
potential purity of the power, puts an alloy in it, which makes
all that one hears about the legend of this hipster Peer Gynt
different from the person who emerges from the book. The
goodlooking young hotshot of real life may accomplish public
wonders like the new quadruple-threat boys and girls who
pace his generation (Streisand, Yevtushenko, the Beatles,
Kubrick, Bobby Dylan); but because of his selfconsciousness
as an actor in the world of headlines, in contrast to the unselfconscious freedom his visionary eye can navigate on the page
or on a canvas, these seemingly needed ego-triumphs or
I-Happenings are more like a Dunninger in a nightclub
making the squares pay good money for all the miserable
tanktown years rather than magic for its own sake. To psy-
choanalyze Cremer is ultimately a bore, because the most significant part of his impressiveness comes from something as

immutably a part of nature as a sixth finger or a third eye, but
he evokes it by such deliberately challenging statements about
his work as the often-repeated "I wrote this book for one
reason: to make money!" He almost seems belligerent about
getting you to believe it, but it could well be a puton disguising a young originator's fear that he will be taken as seriously
as he takes himself. If this comes to pass, what a burden as
well as a final relief; he would have to labor in intense privacy
when all the tempting action today is in mutual work-as-play,
and the solitary work of art, unless it becomes an act of discovery, is usually a dreary narcissistic grind flattered by tradition and encouraged by businesslike psychotherapists for their
aimless patients. All this at the expense of that poor, abused,
misunderstood, exploited but finally indifferent human mira-
cle which the gleam of new consciousness in art always is.
Cremer owns the gleam loosely—it must be unbearable to
possess it in full, at least the awareness of your unceasing responsibility to articulate it, how can you live without working
night and day like a measured madman knowing it will die
with you and is much more important than its keeper?—
perhaps because Cremer is afraid to tighten his hand on it
and take it all the way. Which is certainly not the way of the
world except indirectly, when the work ultimately returns like
a gift to humanity after the creator—or curator—has killed
himself in its care and feeding and curses his last ugly days.
Why then shouldn't Jan Cremer desire to swing when he can
seemingly score high, wide and handsome in several directions, "star in his own movies, establish a new concept for a
daily newspaper, produce and sing on his own rock 'n' roll
records," all the limitless massmedia possibilities which are
now open to the new avantgarde celebrity of our time unlike
his "alienated" brother of the past? When the Beats, particularly Allen Ginsberg and Gregory Corso, invaded the formal
outlets of literature in the late 50s and staged the equivalent
of a newsreel-covered riot at Brentano's in Paris until their
underground publications were put on sale they were foolishly

mocked by the university-bred "in" group. But what they unerringly showed is that a desperado generation raised amidst the massmurder of the Second World War, the deceits of the peace and the disintegration of meaningful middleclass ethics has little patience in prostrating itself to some toothless trinity called Dedication, Poverty and Art. Mostly streetkids like Jan Cremer whose combined classroom and church was the movie dream-palace, they grew up wanting in some form to be Stars, that greatest image for the vindication of the personal ego that America gave to the world; and even though they had the unusual sensitivity that was to eventually make them artists they immediately smelled out the hard reality in Hollywood-style fame, money and power. Unlike an older generation of serious highbrow painters-writers-poets who were proudly superior to what they thought was the unprincipled vulgarity of pop culture, these tough and ambitious lowermiddleclass "barbarians" saw no reason why you couldn't use Hollywood techniques in the invasion of the pure arts and why the rebel dramatizer of new truth couldn't become a national—or even international—celebrity like a movie star. It is right in the middle of this radical transformation of the position of the artist in our society, the opening of unprecedented doors to mass-celebrity, possible political power, an immediate influence through magnified communications greater than ever before, that Jan Cremer has appeared. The temptations are enormous to "cash in," as they say, and therefore cash out as a major revolutionary voice; it is probable that Cremer will further commercialize or theatricalize his uniqueness in this new superlush era confronting us but he will never totally become like anyone else before or after.

1965

black panther meets
lox-and-bagelman

Cleaver's soul may once have been on ice, but that ingredient
as well as head, heart, fists, guns, icepick and basic black prick
is now aimed right at you, baby; this (*Soul on Ice*) is an
angry, more accurately, tormented book—and Cleaver is getting all of his rocks off to such a gashing extent that he tears
holes in your white emotions that can never again be plugged
up with the quick-drying cement that chemistry makes available to every American with the spoiled luxury of a hardware
store two blocks away. Cleaver wants to demolish that copout
bandaid chemistry even though he is too realistic (not all the
time, this is an ambivalent book with chords that come out
like Chinese music even though Hero Eldridge wants to
Americanize them so that there is no mistake about his intentions) to primitivize everything; but he is primitive or elementary in the grand sense; he is against faggotry—he kicks
Jimmy Baldwin around as if J.B. were his gunsel, in the true
homosexual sense of Dashiell Hammett's use of that word in
The Maltese Falcon—Malted Milk America, Beatle music,
Uptight Ofays Who Don't Know How To Shake Their Asses,
The White Power Structure (naturally), The Corruptive

Penal System, American Colonialism, White Ultrafeminines
and Black Supermasculine Menials (his disturbing polarizing
words for the U.S. division of labor in which his own nation
within a nation has been ruined and deballed until now as he
tells it) and hands out 100 other demerits to his and my
"democracy" the right to which he seems to have EARNED.

I say seems to have earned because there is dramatization
in Eldridge; he's not a writer for nothing—even though he
uses the language with a sobriety which is I believe a true
reflection of his soul, of the bigness of his feeling, of the cold
bigness of his feeling, and it creates a new kind of black sym-
phonic range in our prose which is a form of art as well as
tough statement. Eldridge Cleaver says to me and probably to
himself that he is telling the truth. But truth to a writer is
arrived at through art, language, technique, and you would be
naive not to see that Cleaver like any writer is working under
the limitations and strengths of his talent for expression as
well as what he "really thinks and feels." Do you read me,
reader? I'm certain you do (I guess) but I've reached the
point in life—unlike Cleaver—where my uncertainties are
more powerful than my certainties and I have to tell you this
if you want an honest count on this book from one man
(me) wrestling literature with another (Cleaver) with no
impressions barred.

Cleaver's certainty has been saved up, a treasure of hate,
my friends, until it comes out of him with axe and pick
which—to be candid about this America which he hates more
than he loves but like every black American on the deepest
level would like to love more than he hates—hacks you up;
there is no bullshit creaming over this land such as the present writer has indulged in when he's been the deepest in that
paradoxical bag, the American Jew, yes the Two Shapes,
America and Jew, and the long headride any such member
of the human race like the American J. has to go on to figure
out his identity in the so-called scheme of things. Cleaver will
have nothing to do with such complicated speculations. He is

the member, the representative, the articulate voice (along with LeRoi, Ishmael Reed, Calvin Hernton among the new black brilliant banditos using nouns, prepositions and hammers) of a people who have just discovered themselves and also discovered with contemptuous pride the weakness of You and Me. And that's the essential point: even though Cleaver (like Ralph Ellison in a different context) has done his "homework"—a black man in America has had to be twice as good as a nonblack to win his niche and show the profound style of his touch (great style, I agree), Cleaver keeps telling us in these pages—taught himself with a sense of depth and importance things that less serious people will never take the pains to teach themselves, even though Cleaver has burned his midnight oil and wrought a fine mind for himself, it is the fat and corruption and Freud-justified "neuroses" that we nonblacks have rolled around in as moral slobs which brings the blood to his imagination.

Why not wipe out such lameys as ourselves? is a thought that LeRoi, Reed, Hernton and now Cleaver have brought to the front within my immediate knowledge; and why not, given the existential ironies under which they have had to live their multiple-joked, authentic Black Humor lives? By that I simply mean the amazing putdown enforced by Western society on merely the obvious flag of their pigment—why not kill in your heart, rape out on the streets (as Brother Eldridge did), wear the wildest bop earrings or beret or shades or spangles you can dream up as the super-freak in a world of white ghosts, why not whip it out and motherfuck the entire *Stranger* (Camus', that is) universe that a weird, incredible, unbelievable, insane, you name it, fate has popped you into? I (too) am merely trying to dramatize the state of mind or, deeper, being out of which Cleaver expresses himself; and why his book goes beyond Cleaver because his specific personality has been shaped by the Idea of Black all over the world and now into the universe itself; but then I also have to say that as the Other Person and nonblack

whom Cleaver must ultimately sit down to the table with, as a
result of reading him, and UNLIKE him, see this Idea as
finally a human one and not Black at all; and while I or someone like me will one day be killed because of this birth of a
great new perspective in our ancient, often rotten world, a
half or even a quarter century from now it will be a normal
part of the constant stream of basic change that expands
man's consciousness, alters history, broadens the appreciation
and knowledge of one's human brothers, sweetens the sting of
everyone's mortality when color has long been erased or only
used to highlight the basic oneness of all of us—thoughts too
abstract and probably overoptimistic to touch Cleaver right
now, understandably but sadly so.

Cleaver as a writer, and I must always return to this base in
reacting to him, doesn't always have the knowing fingertips,
the literary sophistication, the ease among the stars, the foot-
work that a high cliff asks for when you walk it, that his
deep-pump overflow toward all of experience demands; I find
his touch heavy when it should be easy, his irony explicit
when I prefer a hint, his rage cold when I prefer my murder
warm (which obviously is his point, that from his coalblack
cannon-mouth he can not afford any warmth toward me), his
Big or would-be Big Cock a threat which I acknowledge but
also a drag because I'm not a cunt but a man like himself.
Yet, what I'm building up to saying, is that the Other Man
writing this knows, feels, understands, is willing to take Cleaver's smear of me and mine to the point where it makes me a
bigger and better representative of the nongod God that lives
above our separate individualities as something to aim at; he,
Cleaver, explodes and tears to shreds like a cat with a roll of
toiletpaper many of the romanticized American myths that so
many of the middleclass—decent, let no one talk you out of
it!—people I know and half-am used to love out of ignorance
of what the bottom-dogs of our society were going through
and I love him for it; yes, I, responding, wording my report to
you of the Cleaver experience feel he is a potentially great

American because he is giving the society which made all of us a new DIMENSION not only of conscience (which is too abstract, as abstract as Eldridge can get when he juggles strategies for World Revolution and Black Realpolitik out of his too-professional dialectical pride) but of concrete reality which it behooves all of us to incorporate in our vision and then our institutions so that we can get closer to what we always wanted to become as individuals living together in a social order which is finally our own creation and responsibility. Cleaver may believe that he is writing for himself and for the Black Brother and Sister—I can hear him saying this at a meeting of the Panther elite when the white Peace & Freedom theoreticians have left the room—but let me tell him and tell you that he is writing for us and that we need him the way we need money and love and a smile from someone we respect.

But Eldridge, who has spent almost half of his adult life in prison, where this book was mostly written, dreamed, sweated, speaks of necessity out of a much different mortal pinch than this writer with those steel bars crossing his prose like punctuation; it's stupid for a white man (and I've recently been needled by a black man who digs me but thinks my minority lot is soft into finding another color category for myself, as a Jew, so I'll say not white but Olive Man) who has never been hit with American society's tangible repressive humiliation, prison, to try and wipe those bars away in a curve of the mind on paper—like here; when this reporter went up to Sing Sing for the now dead *New York Herald Tribune* to do an Easter Sunday story he was knocked on his mental-emotional ass, his paltry reserve, by the 80% majority of spades who dominated the prison and set its tempo, embodied the very idea of prison in America today, and whatever public responsibility he had as a selfabsorbed loner was appalled by what the country he still believes in has done to its own kind. Cleaver, of course, has no such illusions; if America is to live for him as something more than a clown's hell (as a longtime ofay watcher he

still gets bitter amusement out of our antics even while wanting to take a machinegun to the entire system) it will have
to be made into a different society, by ourselves, than the one
which has NOT been hell for me and would be Revolutionary Bullshit to say so. But not for Cleaver to say so, which is
an important distinction when we try to remake our society
on the basis of differences of experience rather than lumping
it all callously and unfairly together on the illusion of a
common togetherness which—and this book is the proof—
does not exist. To Cleaver the U.S. is "this shitty land" and
from the comparative dungeon where Eldridge has looked out
at our national life it is coils and coils of excrement, no
matter how deodorized by the sanitary absurdities that clean
up the surface but allow the base (Harrington's *Other America*) to rot in obscurity; yet, as Cleaver knows, what America
has done to its black citizens is only really monstrous in the
light of our democratic pretensions. Men and women of color
have always frightened the hell out of the entire West, not
only this nation, and their total incorporation into every
Western society is only just now beginning—to my knowledge it is not only a specific blot on this country, guilty as we
are, but on every grouping of men, women and children in
this part of the world. But Eldridge, rightfully, is not interested in generalizations of this sort. As an American himself,
the recipient of the entire baggage of myth about freedom
and opportunity and pluralism which seems to make sense to
people whose complexions don't stamp them as outsiders and
losers in this still Anglo-oriented society of ours, he levels his
hatred primarily against our own mutual homeland (father-
land, parentland) because it has betrayed him and thousands
of other nonwhite Americans with its democratic slogans and
pretensions. This is what he can not tolerate: that either
black or white oldsters (include the present writer, 46 as this
is written) should be suckers enough to buy the phony American Dream, hollow, gassy, based on the selfdeluding Head
Cells without Body, not backed up, a fantasy. Eldridge, like a

young, black leftist D. H. Lawrence, wants to strip away the phantom of "capitalistic democracy" and embody in its place a vital socialism which immediately does away with "imperialism" and "colonialism" (I put these words in quotes because they are now catchphrases of the New Black Left which to me omit the more complicated details of our interior economy as well as our current trading habits with other nations; out of the vaulting ambition of his radical prison thinking it seems to me that Cleaver is merely substituting a new set of romantic concepts for dated ones). When he says that "Negro bondage" at home is based on American imperialism abroad I appreciate the way the key fits into the lock of his theory, but I am not convinced because of the very neatness of the idea; I don't feel the American Negro is now in bondage, for one thing, especially not here in the East Village in March of 1969, and I am distrustful of the metallic edges of such concepts which strike me as necessary for Cleaver's "total picture" thinking but are much too mechanistic to make me believe they are valid.

Let me explain all of this in more detail: Eldridge Cleaver, like Richard Wright and Theodore Dreiser in a solid U.S. tradition before him, has taken the writer qua writer's abnormal sensitivity to injustice (Hemingway: "Madam, it's the sense of injustice that makes a writer") and, uncontent with that, has developed his political awareness and insight to make capital out of that original emotion. He no longer wants to comment on an unjust society and his own existential plight, he wants—needs—to change it. The emotions of suffering that come out of his book can apparently not be borne by him unless he can convert their fierce hurt into the mental energy that will undo them and bring about a new set of conditions in their place. In this sense he is typifying what is going on among all the new, fresh black writers in this country; merely to write autobiographically about their experience is not enough, in fact if you extend this thought far enough the answer that comes back is that, to them, art is not enough

unless it becomes a revolutionary weapon that will affect
society in just about the same way that a bomb will.

To concentrate on Cleaver alone, and not those who share
this general attitude, his revolutionary needs take the form of
an often brilliant grasp of the interrelationships between the
individual and the social forces that conspire to crush him,
and we are impressed (highly impressed) by the intelligence
he brings to his own compulsion to understand what has happened to him. No only is there intelligence, which one can
find in dozens of political-cultural analysts who storm the
pages of every left publication today from *Ramparts* to *Dis-
sent*, there is in Cleaver an intensity, an emotional depth,
a PERSONAL necessity to break through the bars that
imprison him, literally and metaphorically, which lifts his
search to the level of art. But what kind of an art is it? Certainly not a selfsufficient one; it is tied by his life to the revolutionary Black Movement in this country, its very purpose is
implicated in the success of that vanguard of which he is a
leader and the overthrow of existing conditions which degrade
him—if I read him correctly—in almost a personal sense. His
art, then, is not related to itself so much as it is predicated on
intolerable conditions; Cleaver must therefore be involved in
direct action (politics or even armed rebellion) to supplement
what he writes, and what he writes must in turn add to what
happens out on the street. His writing then is a double mixture that comes out of personal need and functional effectiveness on the Black and New Left barricades, which means
that in order to "speak to the people" he often has to educate
them by his revolutionary analysis of a specific situation
rather than permit himself to speak in a language that they
don't at first understand, or which doesn't have any immediate effectiveness.

What I am trying to say is that Cleaver is in the position
toward the people who depend on him of leader, spokesman,
revolutionary, charismatic man and every other important
life-role you can think of as well as "writer"; and while this is

exciting, and gives the prose itself some of the urgency of action, it means that even before he had to flee the country to escape being returned to prison he didn't have the simple time to concentrate on deepening the writing itself inside of its own world. If that is too general, I'll be explicit: the most crucial pieces in *Soul on Ice* are outspoken personal opinions or analyses, comments from the depth of his own being on the miserable world around him, and these are cast in the form of statements that could almost be spoken to an audience as well as written. Their strength derives from their total commitment and their contempt for the weakness and timidity of conventional comments on the same subjects: the police and the "armed forces," black lust for white pussy, the dignity of black women, the political psychology of rape, the war in Vietnam, etc. But they are solo efforts in the sense that other individuals, as complex as Cleaver, do not enter his pages. He is commenting on THEM but they are not interrelating with him, as in the pages of a novel, up until now the literary form that has been most lifelike.

If you believe, as I do, that the immediate future of prose in our country is a richer nonfiction than any we have seen before, then you may follow my thought that Cleaver's omission of human beings other than himself in his pages is the result of the semipropagandistic position that he has put himself into which freezes out the resisting human element and abstracts it so that his mind can move more quickly in running a revolutionary campaign through print. I can't say that he is primarily a pamphleteer because he is too honest, stubborn, thorough, tenacious to walk away from his interior experience in order to make an external impression. But the complete width of a real-life experience, not only its heights and abysses, demands the complex roundedness of other beings unless a writer wants primarily to be a "spokesman," which usually ends up being a glorified form of editorial writing. If he does not—and I think that Cleaver is a creative writer in every potentially conceivable sense—then the revolutionary action to which he is committed has to take place within the pages of his work rather than take the form of comments on a life outside itself, which will soon change in the course of just a small amount of time and leave the impassioned words high and dry. If the writer in Cleaver is willing to sacrifice his writing to external events, then that is a choice that must be respected even while one knows it is delimiting and can not be undone as time moves away from the event in question and creates new ones; if, on the other hand, he creates events himself, incorporates within his work the full dimension of reality that he now reacts to OUT THERE, his radical vision will be acted out in his own work instead of used as a spur for the political activities of others. I miss, in other words, revolutionary portraits of Huey Newton and Bobby Seale and his own wife in relation to Cleaver; and by portraits I mean the full extent of truth, analysis, complexity and integrity that he gives me in relation to the broad world but not the intimate one in which he lives. I miss his using the full resources of the novel on the world of "truth," which would include his brilliant insights, but not on nameless or distant beings whom he treats with the indifference of objects. I would like that passion for truth extended to the individuals with whom he must live his life; otherwise I get sweeping statements about recent history rather than the more difficult living experience itself.

As things stand, Cleaver reveals himself to be a penetrating advocate, a literary lawyer, a skillful debater, and as he constantly breaks through the stone wall of inarticulateness we cheer him on because we know what he has gone through to find his tongue. We admire him because of the obstacles he has overcome and we respond to the unsparing momentum that has led him through that wall because of a human grit superior to most. All of that is admirable, but our focus is then centered on Cleaver the man, and the man's ideas, rather than on the immediate interacting world of which Cleaver is only a part. What we get is autobiography plus

scalding statement, but to my mind this is only part of the
Cleaver reality; the other part is his actual experience with
real, named men and women, his specific failures, triumphs,
infidelities, all of which would document his ideas and test
them out. To be a true revolutionary writer, in my view, is to
challenge reality through the dangerous risks you take in your
work, the real people you confront in it, the lengths that you
go to tell the truth about others as well as yourself, the example of reality-in-action that you summon into being by your
art. This is much different than just speaking boldly and even
brilliantly; it is the WHOLE STORY that I want and that I
miss in Cleaver. No one can shrug off the new picture of a
revolutionary reality, especially the so-called Establishment,
but they can pat you on the head for words alone. It is, however, the picture that outlasts the speechmaking, the actuality
of scene and dialogue that survives the monologue, the
PROOF that dominates the eloquence.

What we now have is a "heroic" individual, a teacher, a
man who has attained nobility in his way, even a human
being with the gifts of political and moral leadership, but not
in my eyes the total writer (at this point) who really scores
against reality in a lasting sense by making every inch of his
vision manifest in the work rather than dependent on external
situations impossible to control. Show me life as it is lived by
you and yours, Eldridge, show me the people who are significant to you, tell me how you react, with revolutionary shame-
lessness and amusement, to bourgeois codes of art, GIVE ME
A NEW ACTION PAINTING OF REALITY as well as its
ideological outline and my mind's eye will be forever changed.
Ideas I can argue with—opinions can be batted down by my
contrary nature—brilliant analysis can be regarded by me as
merely intellectual exhibitionism—but the total experience of
a new attitude to life ACTED OUT on the page makes me a
member of the cast and changes me where polemics never can.

To be realistic, Cleaver might feel—there is something of
the prison hipster in him which laughs at innocence—that his

role is to fuck the enemy with everything at his command (brains, scorn, lyricism) but never to give away secrets from home. He lived marginally with the Panthers and guns and for all I know necessary killings or at least crimes which he refers to cryptically in this book, and with so many strikes and scars against him it might be a daydream for me to ask him to show the whole truth. But it is a fact that words which are only directed outward become little different than speeches which can impress, increase the stature of the man in life itself—not at all to be downgraded on the scene in which we live and it is not my intention to do so—but all of this is different from being revolutionary with your material, taking that fleeting world, all of it, the "pigs," Huey, Bobby, Kathleen, your parole officer, and somehow integrating your real life with your intellectual-radical one so that the full weight of a statement about reality is there in all of its kinky dimensionality.

All of this may be speaking into the wind on my part, obviously; readers may even find it presumptuous, which I can't help because it is necessary for me to speak this way, and more important Cleaver may never have a chance to ever again brood over literary problems in a way that matches the full reach of his stern and independent mind. He is on the run, as you know, wanted for "breaking parole" and being hunted. Eldridge has said he will never go back to jail. He was rumored to be in Mexico City in February of 1969 and in Africa in April; where he actually is I don't know, but it is clear that survival is right now his main concern and that personal truth has probably become a luxury. In literature it is the other way around.

1969

should i assume
america is
already dead?

I don't know Abbie Hoffman but I know the people around him· Jerry Rubin (small, beaded, selfpossessed and distant when I made one of the futile nominating speeches for his Vice Presidency at the 1968 N.Y. Peace & Freedom Party Convention on the basis of his intelligence as shown in the underground press), John Wilcock, Ed Sanders, Tuli Kupferberg and Paul Krassner. They are all writers, radicals, activists, and all have very quick and creative minds. But when I say they are writers I should qualify that and say WORDMEN, because the selfimposed isolation of writing as opposed to performing in public, Doing Their Thing before an audience they can actually see responding to them, has come to seem like what Abbie would call "masochistic theater."

Why jerk yourself off when you can ball? I can hear John or perhaps Ed say, why artifically lock yourself up in a room when the action is out on the unpredictable and chance-ridden streets? Why sanctify the written word when it grows stale by the time you put it down (let alone get it printed)

compared to the immediacy of the spoken one? I have to
except Wilcock from this generalization, of course, because
he is all journalist, possibly a great one, certainly the most
independent and consistent underground newspaperman of
my own generation in spite of occasional crank infatuations.
But even John's use of words is impatient, immediate, functional, I know he is suspicious of "writing" and wants a style
as close to speech as he can get it, and since I am involved in
the human gamble of trying to have an impact on events
through the use of written language at the intensity of art I
find John's work utilitarian rather than ultimate. It is excellent to its purpose but not branded in your memory (or at
least mine): my obsession is for a para-journalism that combines soul and straight fact in such a way that the reader is
challenged, persuaded, invaded and literally powered into
positioning himself in relation to the new future that the act
of writing has just created.

In other words, in this time of increasingly direct action, I
am still trying desperately to hang on to my faith in the written word, make it highly contemporary, see where it differs
from the spoken word (the latter perceived through the ear
and by gesture while the written word uses that great organ,
the eye, as well as the invisible ear) and I am shaken by
Abbie's fascinating handbook of Yippie survival tactics, *Revolution for the Hell of It*, when he says flatly that "words are
horseshit." "Action," he tells me, "is the only reality; not only
reality, but morality as well." How, I ask myself, do Tuli
Kupferberg and Ed Sanders relate to this concept when they
began as poets with a deep involvement in language (Sanders
in particular, as opposed to Tuli's dry and supersly wit, has
already added to our language with his "grope" imagery and
all the squack-squarf-poonscomp animal wildness that went
into *Fuck You*/A Magazine of the Arts) and now seem more
than willing to subordinate it to the musical action of their
rock group, The Fugs? Yes, I know, Sanders talks and freaks
his verbal vision on stage and both of them write lyrics—"Kill

for Peace," etc., now apparently offered as pop poetry in *The Fugs' Songbook*—which communicate a definite revolutionary point of view that supplements the work they were doing when they wrote words on paper for the eye; but the necessary theatricality of their being rebel ENTERTAINERS doesn't allow them to explore this language for its own sake. A song has builtin limitations and the lyric is only part of the experience; how do they rationalize their dream as poets by putting these words into only half-action? The answer is probably that they need a participating audience at almost any price, the problem of all outcast modern writing, but the cost is high and disturbing when writers themselves think of print as prison and Al Jolson replaces Dylan Thomas as an example of genuine communication.

I will get back to Abbie in a moment, since his brand of nonverbal activism (and yet to add to the paradox he has gone and written a book with words to give credence to his ideology!) seems to me central to what's happening out on those streets of the imagination, but in the privacy of my own mind I am sorely troubled by the downgrading of the written word on the part of writers-turned-activists. I think it represents a turning-away from everything that literature is supposed to have embodied and the implications of the "uselessness" of the written word cut deeply into my own existence, to be frank about it. My conscious life, and I'm now a month shy of being 47, has been bound up with that printed word from the beginning; and since I came of spiritual age in the late 30s, when the American novel was the most vital creative outpouring in this culture, I identified every hope of my own being with prose and now I'm stuck with it in a revolutionary time (in every sense) where TV, film, new theater and the climax of all these dynamic visual forms, "body confrontation"—the very physical presence of the living man—seem to be of much more reality to the radical leadership of the new generation than the abstractions of written language. But I have a deeply vested interest riding here, not only for myself but every writer my own age, and out of that total investment I have tried to match the needs of action by putting my own body and being in the way of the reader by means of gut commitment right before his eyes; I have tried to be physical in my work at least, if not out on those mythic streets, and if I continue to write prose (and what choice do I have after 25 years if only to maintain my identity, make a living, collect some of the ego-dues I think are legitimately owed me because of risks far beyond the call of expediency?) I want to increase my involvement with each word so that the person on the other end KNOWS he is undergoing an experience and hardly an abstraction at all.

I say all of this to show that not only Abbie but the present writer and hundreds like him are enormously sensitive to the irrelevance, right now, of what we used to call "literary writing" as opposed to survival expression; and I mean that last phrase in every sense, running from one's craft to one's life—they are all the same. The communication of our day that is going to truly reach others has to come out of the abyss where men and women are struggling for their sense of purpose, and the existential reality of the instruments they use like the written word, or it will be communication from another age. But Abbie and his team are so tuned in to sensations, trips, the notion that "fantasy is the only truth," that I wonder if a writer like myself is assumed to be a heavy fool for taking the pains to try and tell the truth about himself in a literal way as a means of establishing contact; and then getting something going, in the sense that the artistic authenticity of his statement (or lack of it) is the measure of what will happen to it as an act in society that has to be reacted to.

But of what value is my goddamn theory and my practice, I have to ask myself, when a generation of PRINCIPLED nonreaders like Abbie (if I can trust what he tells me) couldn't care less? Of course the answer must be that I will continue to do this private brand of communications work if only for myself, to keep my own record straight no matter if I have no

other readers but my own pair of eyes when I pick up a pencil
to edit what I have written. But even my limited confidence
has been damaged, frankly, by the thought that I might be
pounding my typewriter, my being, in a void when the people
I want to reach out to (and I would like to get a word-
relationship going with everyone but as a man being borne
forward on a collision course with death I would also very
much like to hold the young out of such middleaged weakness
as wanting to "count" and being "important") are more
involved in motherfucking, defying, getting terrorist kicks,
getting their heads smacked, jamming the radio rather than
receiving, the entire noisy apocalypse described by Abbie this
way: "When you're involved you don't get paranoid. In a riot
I know exactly what to do."

Abbie's generation, or let's say the generational view that
he brings to a sharp zinging point (since at 31 he's considered
"old" I've been told), is geared to visible action in a way that
my literary generation never was; I came of age after the
Communist zenith in this country had already passed and
given us writing that was inferior, using the most generous
standards, to the work produced by the more complex Trot-
skyite-socialist group that clustered around *Partisan Review*
and was not afraid of being ambivalent, ambiguous, plunging
into the entire mess of themselves and the world without easy
answers. I nevertheless broke with the cerebral style of the
PR-Commentary crowd a decade ago because I couldn't move
in every important sense under its insulated intellectual net-
ting and got turned on to my own particular motorcycle of
word-action via the well-caricatured Beat Generation. As I
turn around and look back from the rush of the present activism—the making of new history that has me backed against
the wall of myself, especially the values raised by Abbie's
book—I see the Beats as the primitive or at least unsophisti-
cated center of radical energy for so much that has come to
threatening full flower now; the personal anarchism toward
"the Establishment" (let's sink that word!), the white nigger

conspicuousness as a result of long hair and short bread, pan-
handling, dope, concern with the East, communes, new dress,
so much that has now become a casual reality for what Abbie
calls the St. Marx (Pl.) dropouts.

But through all of this transition in America from Beats to
Yippies one man's concern (this one's) was not so much with
outward change but the liberation within that could allow
him to say his say with more freedom, openness, fullness and
depth—with no taboos or hangups as to subjectmatter, using
confession when necessary, new and more vivid imagery, even
a more "religious" personal-journey tone without being
accused (as I often was in pre-Beat days) of sloppy subjectivity. What I am saying is that the explosion that has been set
off now, and I feel that its momentum is going to travel
through the 70s without letup, was in its beginnings part of
my Beat second life and perhaps that's why I'm so conscious
of it and so equally conscious of my own double view toward
it: the fact that I'm not a wholehearted member (as in a
broad sense are John and Tuli, neither kids, with perhaps
Paul Goodman as a foster father and Allen G., Tim Leary,
Bill Burroughs, etc., as parent figures) and the obvious reality
that I'm worried about my own future as writer-man in relation to this sweeping emphasis on life-action instead of
word-action. Or, to take Abbie very seriously in this context,
the new need to be an "artist" (as he legitimately calls himself) out in public, to be an artist in the flesh, to make The
Word flesh without hiding indoors behind a machine but
"wearing a flower in your fist"—like Abbie.

The fresh chutzpah and flair of his stance impresses me so
much that I feel I have to justify my own indoor years and say
to myself and to him that I, too, have wanted to put my life
on the line almost as a way of redeeming the idea of LITER-
ATURE from aimlessness and shrinkage into the secondrate,
just as I have always backed off from the temptation of writing "fiction" and possibly making a nice score because the
form seemed to me too easy, riskless, evading my equivalent

of the street-reality, no "body confrontation," no blood, challenge, embarrassment, pain, exposure—in other words, none of the danger that is the very name of experience today. I might have been wrong in that decision and it may very well have come (as young writers have told me) from a restricted idea of what a novel, or a postnovel, can be; but at least by my own standards of significance I have never succumbed to a less real "fiction" when I could dramatize the area of fact I had lived through and that might have a direct effect on other beings who enter into a trust with me when they read my words. I say this not to boast, for I have nothing to boast about in the mood that is upon me now, but to show that writers can risk their skins in their own way as much as brave young guys like Abbie and Rubin who lie down in front of National Guard tanks, enter the House UnAmerican Activities Committee dressed like Revolutionary War soldiers or clothed in the American flag; or like the pig-bearers who broke up a pro-Humphrey meeting in 68 by bearing that animal's head upon a plate in simple nakedness and knocking the liberal wind out of such a selfrighteous type as Shelley Winters, who was shocked all the way to the bank, as they say. I don't see such actions as "crude and childish"—as I've heard them put down in the so-called mature literary-intellectual community—but rather as a unique combination of political imagination and courage. Living Revolutionary Theater, that's the name of Abbie's game, and it's a thousand times less melancholy, grim, overserious, introspective, hungup on warts and decimal points of being, the whole bad bag of Self, than my own (and my generation's) microscopic inspection of experience has been.

It's a relief for someone like myself to swing and cheer with Abbie's clear and uncomplicated prose—he has no need to impress because he thinks words are no important things and uses them to tell succinctly where he's at, which is everywhere ("I am the Revolution") at once—and it gives my heart a great lift by making reality both a simpler and more potentially rewarding place than I have known it. Dear Ankey, Beverly, Peter, Willie, Weldon, Rhoda, all my dead tormented suicide friends, couldn't you have waited to read Abbie and gotten the tonic injection that I have gotten, were you all in error to have found your lives hell when you could just as well have found them great—"One learns reality is only a subjective experience," says Abbie confidently, "it exists in my head"—and now you've paid for a downbeat view WHEN IT COULD JUST AS WELL HAVE BEEN THE OTHER?

Yes, possibly, hopefully, but that well-known voice within, a nagging voice which I don't want to hear, even, says, "But is Abbie's view reality as you have known it, is this existential gaiety about 'fucking the system,' owning the streets, balling on roofs, seeing visions of Bob Dylan in treetops, the so-called politics of ecstasy, is this the real thing for you?" The answer that comes back, that I don't particularly want (who wants difficulty above pleasure?) is no, not for me, much as I'd like to think in this technicolor cartoonstrip style it doesn't do justice to the thousand stubby details of being alive which have always been a fascination to me even when they were painful. Abbie wipes them out too blithely (but what a fine, defiant wipeout against life's invalidism!) with his new moral and tactical shortcuts which make short shrift of layers of experience that preoccupy less glamorous people: for example, he convincingly tells me why the Old Left is "shitting in its pants" (because they don't understand the simultaneous bombardment of contradictory experiences), but he doesn't tell me how to live successfully with another human being, whether I should replace my glasses with contact lenses, whether I should have an operation for hemorrhoids or try to get by with Preparation H. He gives me the world on a psychedelic platter but he almost entirely leaves out the SUBSTANCE of one's personal life that continues to dog one all of one's days. It is that substance, that reality, that march through the glue of actuality that I'm stuck with, as are millions of people, and when I look to buoyant Abbie for help he is sitting on a windowledge megaphoning down instructions on how to manipulate the media. Abbie, I don't want to manipulate the media, I want to get by with a little help from my friends!

And yet as I see Abbie's attitude toward our anachronistic society and its absurdities gaining power and belief, penetrating the massmedia because of his and his friends' ingenuity and fearlessness, penetrating the phony armor of our reactionary official personages (Mayor Daley, Captain Fink, James Wechsler, deposed LBJ, people in positions of public authority who used to frighten me because they were alien and backed up by the clanging power of the state), I realize that right as I might be about where Abbie lets me down I have been timid and selfconscious about confronting institutions that NEED an Abbie to yank their pants down and I embrace him for his guiltless political homosexuality. Further, can it be that my own and my N.Y. Jewish literary buddies' bias toward American experience—wanting to be a member of this nation in a central sense rather than the outsiders we felt like as adolescents, identifying ourselves with the warming mythos of the country through Whitman and Melville and Hart Crane and Wolfe rather than resisting like menschs until it could prove itself to us as something more than promises, romantically digging its variety and even the flavor of its evils as part of the magnitude of the great picture—has become dated, of nothing but sentimental (non) value, a shell disguising what is really going on? I have to accept this as a possible charge against my vision, my point of view, the very identity that I have conceived for myself, and when I feel the full moral crime of my possibly unreal madness toward this country in Abbie's throwaway remark, "Assume America is already dead," I wonder if I have been putting myself on all these years and must now pay for it. Abbie is right—different views of reality or not, I am the proof in the headsearching he puts me through—when he says of the Yips and himself: "We are dynamiting brain-cells. We are putting people through changes. The aim is not to earn the respect, admiration and love of everybody—it's to get people to do, participate, whether positively or negatively."

Abbie has gotten me to participate—jesus, yes—he has knocked me off my balance, made me question my own relevance, dig once again for my own sense of what is real; and yet he has done all of this through the pissed-upon written word which I must take more fanatically than he because to me it MUST contain the fluid of life, intelligence, purpose, while to Abbie it's only a backhanded means to action. I and those like me have none of those escape-hatches (riots, public bacchanals, etc.) except that printed word which he rightfully demeans from his point of view. But don't forget that he also tells me that people over 40 don't know how to live with antitheses such as his booting out the word while exploiting it, that juggling these illogics is the "secret" of the revolutionary-pop scene, so it is less important to me to seize on his own inconsistencies (as I sense them) than to profit by his vision and measure what I and those like me have tried to do against its surprising luminousness. It seems to me, in the light of the imaginative flare that Abbie has shot up, that I and my most diehard literary friends have failed to see through many of the compromised arrangements that have taken place at the top of American life; that the longing in ourselves to make it into the main arteries of the national body has corrupted us in varying degrees into accepting bourgeois achievement, heavy and dull, that Abbie no longer takes seriously. He uproariously laughs at institutions which we also have attacked—the easy targets of the *Times*, *Time-Life*, NBC, CBS, Pentagon police, Congress, all of it—but the revealing thing is the difference in EMPHASIS, the informal grace and detachment in his style as compared to the heat and emotional fervor from our side. What one sees in the mirror of Abbie's absurdist approach is that we have apparently been much too straight in taking on these cultural monsters; we took them at their own values, so to speak, credited them with a middleclass straightforwardness of motive, the making of money, which Abbie almost vomits up because it seems to him a defamation of existence in front. They are his stone, unashamed enemy—apparently his LIVING principles are the abolition of all private property, money, and the setting up of totally free institutions and stores where you and I use them at will—and this belly-anarchism of his beautifully simplifies his behavior, there is no wavering at the source if again I can trust him from his words.

Added to this, Abbie seems to feel none of the selfaccusatory guilt that those of us brought up in the delicate strands of middleclass personal relationships (family especially) still feel even today toward those who may have persecuted us; there is in his book, to me, a COOLNESS, even a ruthlessness, which I envy but can not emulate and still keep kosher, and through Abbie I suddenly really see Mark Rudd, the SDS, the Up Against The Wall Motherfuckers, their human exemplars like Che, Ho Chi Minh, Mao, Castro, etc., but all converted into an American style (and language!) which in this tough form has never really been on our scene before. And as far as "Amurrica" goes—which is the way the young slashers mock it but, cornball Yid that I am, I truly can't— keep in mind that Abbie was almost a post-Bomb all-American Boy, not awkward, introverted, "tormented," which was almost the sacred passport of admission into our literary world. Speaking from his cool pride Abbie tells me that he was always a competitor, a medal-winner in almost everything he took on (from hustling pool to stealing cars to modern dance), and it is the joining of this selfconfident, extroverted, almost hip businessman's URGE TO WIN with his revolutionary disbelief in everything that I and thousands like me once assumed was normality that makes me watch him sharply—to the point where I'm already exploiting him as a probe into my own cancers.

But in case you think that I underrate myself unfairly, am too generous at my own expense, which I know I'm not, let

me say that Abbie also makes me understand conclusively
that words are not "horseshit"; because each item that he has
taught me has come through his own WRITTEN language,
it carries everything about him (I can read writing, I believe,
the way a fortuneteller can read palms), his facile psych
major IQ, the lack of texture in his prose which means the
lack of deep sensuality in the man, his genuinely mod combination of humor and insane determination, the extraordinary
combining processes of his head where the cues he has picked
up from Artaud, McLuhan, Dylan, Che, Hollywood, TV,
Lenny B., the Beatles, Mailer, Ginsberg, Heller (all his influences are very "right" but it is fair odds that he will one day
be dated by them even as right now he is ahead of the pack)
become metaphors for him to bounce points off you. What a
user you are, Abbie, as I hope you'd be the first to admit! But
the very significant thing, which should never be forgotten, is
that Abbie Hoffman has brought the thinking of a cocky nonliterary cat ("Jerry Rubin is a writer, but I know I can whip
him publicly because I'll use any means necessary") to those
sneaky little words and just by doing that has made a really
fresh contribution to an art that he sneers at. More than that,
much more than that to me, he has by going in a new direction, organizing a new cross section of thoughts that create a
genuine blueprint for his own synthesis of dada-acid-flower
revolution, setting down his unclichéd, unselfconscious, clear
and perky prose, given someone else an important experience
which confirms to that person, finally, the nature of his own
contribution as opposed to Abbie's.

I finally come out of Abbie's high, quick, funny, smart,
slightly thin world confident that I must take myself as seriously as I ever have ("People who take themselves too seriously are power-crazy, if they win it will be haircuts for all,"
Abbie tells me and I agree and still know I must do what I
have to do) in order to communicate to readers as a person
who is squeezed into doing the boldest part of his living in
words. I write out of necessity, just the way Abbie acts, but

my oldfashioned grind is still a means of commitment in this day of instant (and marvelous) Abbies and the way I know I can do it, throwing my body wrapped in the very horseshit words that make man man before any tanks that can be invented, reassures me that the doubts which often sweep my being about the purpose of my trip and the limitations of my ability are less important than I thought when I started this piece. Abbie's book for deep emotional reasons brought out every specter I have feared about writing, age, being out of it, being out of action, seeing John and Tuli and Ed and Rubin take the Word into the public arena and putting me uptight with envy and selfdoubt until I screwed the paper into the machine once again for the ten thousandth time out of having NO PLACE ELSE TO GO with my head; then Abbie really straightened me out, at lcast for now, and I know he must be an East Side medicine man in the sense that Creeley once said of Kerouac that he had "healing hands."

1969

part 5

intro

Nugget *was my home for three and a half years from September of 1961 to March of 1965. With pinched money, a hard-boiled red-nipple picture policy that contested what I was trying to do with the editorial matter, in fact a hipster-Establishment schizophrenia that regarded* Playboy *as competition on the one hand (as seen by my publisher Michael St. John) and* The Village Voice *on the other (as seen by me) we nevertheless put an exciting magazine on the newsstands that fought the hairier twat books to a draw and was the peppy prose equal of* Esquire, Show, *the later* Cavalier, *you name it. We published Baldwin, Mailer, James Jones, Calder Willingham, Gregory Corso, Wolf Mankowitz, John Clellon Holmes, Dan Wakefield, Colin Wilson, Marvin Kitman, Ralph J. Gleason, Terry Southern, Jack Gelber, Leslie Garrett, Dizzy Gillespie, Nat Hentoff, Nelson Algren, Bill Manville, John Wilcock, Charles Simmons, Len Zinberg, John A. Williams, Chester Himes, Richard J. Walton, Michael Harrington, Pietro Di Donato, Chandler Brossard, John Rechy, Franz Kline, James T. Farrell, David McReynolds, Ross Wetzteon, Kenneth Rexroth, Eliot Fremont-Smith, Gael Greene, Brian O'Doherty, Sid Bernard, Davis Grubb, Albert Goldman, William Saroyan, Jack Woodford, Otto Friedrich,*

255

Thomas Gallagher, Paddy Chayefsky, Gene Lees, Rey Anthony, Lionel Olay, Richard M. Elman, Joyce Greller, Joyce Elbert, Ralph Ginzburg, etc., plus at least two unknown writers every issue. What was remarkable about the operation to me is that by family background, temperament and taste St. John was a conservative man who had taken over the magazine from his dead father after only one issue and wanted to turn a profit; but he was also as independent as the eagle on the backside of a quarter. His editor for many years had been George Wiswell, a cautious man of excellent taste who had published Grace Paley, Jack Kerouac, William Gaddis and many other writers of quality; among so-called girlie magazines Nugget *always had restraint and distinction and St. John himself was responsible for the fine reputation that the magazine had in the trade. But when I came with my post-Beat enthusiasm and comparatively embattled and rattling tastes, he backed me some 90% of the distance although money and a "safe" reputation among advertisers hung in the balance and the brute fact is that we lost our shirt. My point is that he was a publisher who having once decided on an editor stuck with him until the flood was jaw-high; St. John, I'm sure, did not entirely sympathize with the sample editorials reprinted here and he had to defend me and the magazine's new tone to his money-religious distributor who thought I was a Communist and probably psychopathic as well. High over 45th St., for almost four years, we tried our impossible experiment and lost. But I had taken my sensibility into the world of dollars and deals and horseshit and met a man who was willing to gamble his capital on my ideas. It was an act of faith to me, coming as I had from the submarine of myself as I have told of it in* Views of a Near-Sighted Cannoneer, *and it led step by step (as you might build up a skinny kid) to my present synthesis of art and action, imagination shot right into the groin of events, and the use of the massmedia as the vehicle. By the way I also wrote titles, subtitles, all the unsigned material in the maga-*

*zine as well as the three editorials that follow; they are not
Seymour Krim writing for Seymour Krim but rather seymour
krim writing for Nugget just as he lay awake at night praying
for it until it went down and he returned to praying for himself. Boris Lurie pounded me into writing my first piece of art
criticism, made me rewrite it with that Russian secret-police
tenaciousness of his, and I have included it here because while
I had my head full struggling with Nugget another world was
pulling at me with the same urgency to be recognized and
acclaimed for its value. What a seethe we live in on this continent, in this town (N.Y.), in my hard-driving and never-
quitting era—skyscraper balls, that's what you need!*

the unimportant
writer

Never have we seen such insane competition in our business as exists today. Magazines and newspapers have always been zestful about cutting each other's throats and circulation, but this traditional sport has been hypoed by the interference of the highpowered Agent and the godlike Agency.

As the financial rewards have gone up for a word-product that hits it, shrewd business minds have taken to selling literary talent as coldly as a pimp sells flesh—to the highest bidder. The writer may write out of a desire to reform the human race, but his representative automatically cheapens the writer's bloodsoaked message by the very method of hawking it.

The irony, which has already driven some writers crazy and will doubtlessly crack up more of them, is that the Agent and the Agency glory in the very smell of dollar-success that the serious writer spends his lifetime condemning as an end in itself. Writers are people, yes, and they like their share of the bread, yes, but from our observation their highest purpose is to communicate an urgent vision to another. This is their literal reason for being and they take themselves more ear-

259

nestly than any other breed we know. Now think, if you will, how disgusting to the writer's ultimate purpose is the method by which glib salesman-types clutch the message in a well-manicured fist and wave it under the noses of hungry editors.

It may be a profound communication for brotherhood and sanity, for love and saintliness if you will in this loveless and saintless time, which our writer has redeemed from the pit of his mortality. But it immediately becomes a piece of goods to be marketed, even though the very conception of a "market" in human life may have motivated the writer's entire blast and strike for justice.

It makes no difference any more: you can write about the most pitiful horrors known to troubled mankind and grow rich on the saleability of suffering, for there is no longer any sense of appropriateness or proportion in this decade of Writing As Big Business. All is sausage for the economic grinder, all noble statement is reduced and mocked by the merchandising climate which strips the work down to packageable size. This is the world we live in, make no mistake about it. But what compounds the pity of it all is that the writer doesn't know where to turn. If he complains to his Agent about the crassness of literature being turned into a piece of manufacture like soap, the realistic one merely says: "Be reasonable, sweetie. I didn't invent the market. I'm only using it for your best advantage."

True, as far as it goes; but it doesn't go far enough. What happens, and could very well have killed a Hemingway with his animal-sharp nose for fraud, is that the writer becomes a tool of the economy instead of its spiritual leader and conscience. The writer, no matter how extraordinary his work, is providing a mere technological function to be exploited by the Agent, Editor and Publisher.

In New York, the editorial center of the country, the writer is much less important to the complicated heavy industry of literature in the 6os than the three "practical" figures mentioned above. He can be operated on, bought, sold and dismissed because he is not as significant (can always be replaced!) as the men and women who use him for their own purposes. Oh yes, glowing words can be scattered his way and the poor shnook's ego can expand like a case of mumps for a season, but poor fool he is indeed if he takes it seriously. Words are deadly cheap to the people who puff your writer up, because they are playing for higher stakes and in a game where the writer is a mere idiot child whimpering about verities that every "adult" knows is nurseryschool jazz compared to the mammoth merchandising network.

The sketch we have given you of the true value of literature in our world comes out of our experience as editors and publishers. We, too, like every magazine, have bargained the flesh of writers as coldly as if we were dealing with numbers and then expiated to our analysts for our souls' sake—but it doesn't cut ice. We *know* what the reality is and the direction in which it is being expanded. We can pretend to no piety, except for the fact that within an ugly situation we try to leaven it by telling as much of the truth as we can. That, it seems to us, is the only possibility of help and slight redemption.

1962

lenny

We come, with mixed feelings, to the Case of Lenny Bruce. You probably have an opinion—who doesn't?—but sit still long enough to hear ours. First, so that no matter how finky you finally think our stand is, let it be triple-clear that we don't think Lenny should go to jail for *any* reason except to play a benefit. As you know, he is facing possible prison terms for both "obscenity" (in Chicago—where else?) and the possession of narcotics (on the Coast). The obscenity rap is questionable in every sense, bringing into play as it does unsettled ideas of taste, propriety, freedom of expression, just how far an artist or performer is entitled to go. To us the only limit is the imagination. But for the majority of people these questions are up in the air all over the country and to make Lenny the martyr for all the dirty mouths around is vindictive and unjust, even if at times he seems to desire a niche in history as a Copacabana Jesus.

As far as the narcotics charge goes, everyone knowledgeable in this area knows that our laws stink. A small army of psychiatrists, lawyers, general MDs and reporters will tell you how indisputably barbaric it is to call addiction a crime in 1963. A user has all the free choice of a terrified passenger in a careening New York taxi; it's out of his control and to be punished for that is just about as stupid as society can get. As in

the question of so-called obscenity, enlightened public opinion can only stand by Lenny (whether he is a user or not isn't
the real point) and agitate even harder for some progressive
legislation in this crummy backalley of American life.

But the phenomenon of Lenny, as you know, goes much
deeper than his contest with the law. His admirers—and they
include two of our most outspoken jazz critics, Ralph J. Gleason and Nat Hentoff, as well as some of the most perceptive
newspapermen and social critics strung across the country—see Lenny as a fearless black knight who is lancing the
pustules of our age. They use the word "genius" in speaking
of him and there is no selfconsciousness when they do so.
This is especially true of nightclub and entertainment writers,
men who cover this beat and can truly appreciate how radically Lenny has changed the entire criterion of afterdark
entertainment in the last six years—changed it from forced
frivolity, gags, oneliners, to the most ferocious kind of humor
that claws into the blisters of sex, race, religion, hypocrisy, etc.
In their eyes Lenny could no longer be thought of as the conventional comic dear to burlesque, radio, TV, nor even as an
extension of the acidly clever Mort Sahl. He became (we are
told) a kingsize social prophet trying to awaken a sick,
numbed populace from its moral coma.

O.K. We dug the sloth out of our ears and listened closely
to every word in Lenny's five taped-on-the-spot albums. We
caught him at the Vanguard in Manhattan and got our
friends to send us long reports on his appearances in courts
and clubs all over the country. Revolutionary individuals are
the lifeblood of the arts, and ultimately of society, and
Nugget is acutely sensitive to their presence because—
frankly—we want to learn from them and incorporate their
message into our pages.

And Lenny comes out about 50-50, no more and no less, on
our scorecard.

Here's why. Although an original satirist and a brilliant
mimic—a man who grew up on movies the way other people

read books and can zip through a dozen convincing roles in an 8-minute bit—we found a monotonous sameness to his material. The world, yours and ours, isn't made up *only* of junkies, Hollywood, other comics, minority groups, sexual aberrations, four-letter words and so on. As good paidup hipsters, we nevertheless found ourselves getting restless by the tight horizons that enclose Lenny's world and getting angry when he tried to act as if this was *everyone's* view from the bridge. It just ain't and it's surprisingly provincial of Lenny to think it is. It's as if someone with nightclub pallor tried to pretend that sunshine was either square or didn't exist—a cunning distortion of reality.

We admired Lenny's deft roasting of obnoxious types (once again his expert and loving mimicry is invaluable) but found his neo-Christian moralisms naive and pretentious, redeemed only by his obvious sincerity. But can actual ignorance be excused by conviction? When Lenny came out with the cheaply sentimental line that "Jimmy Hoffa is more of a Christian than Christ because he hires ex-convicts" we thought he was kidding—this shallow halftruth is profundity? But he wasn't kidding. Lenny the Jazz Circuit Hegel truly believes this thought and is flattered in his pontifical minor blasphemies by better-educated critics who swallow the sheerest adolescent crap from him with "Go, man!" enthusiasm.

But all of this is only the most superficial part of our gripe. The most objectionable aspect of Lenny to us is something much more serious. We refer you to the standard refrain that he's been muttering lately, which gets quoted in the papers this way: "It's just like Kafka." What Lenny means in his avantgardey, statusy ("Kafka? Certainly I dig Kafka, baby, you think I'm Bob Hope or something?"), inaccurately chic way is that the society he has willfully baited now pesters him with legal subpoenas, denies him entrance to England, in short makes his life a small hell of redtape and harassment.

And it's just in this area that our sympathy grows tough.

Mature artists and rebels throughout the well-known ages

have assumed, early on, that they were in opposition to their
times and that they would be suffering from picture postcards
in the brain to expect kindness from the social order they ridiculed. From Swift to Céline, they whined not, neither did
they knock down $2,000 per week for their hatred of phoni-
ness and injustice. But Lenny is that new, mod phenomenon
who can preach God's message to belching Scotch-guzzlers
while he gets rewarded with more yearly loot for his "courage"
than most of us will ever see in a lifetime. There is something
spookily unreal, incongruous, outrageously theatrical about
this kind of new nightclub holiness. It flashily erases all the
sacrifices men and women throughout history have always
made to cling to their unpopular vision. Lenny, the Boy
Martyr, would have his stake and cop headlines in Variety
too: a crucifixion on TV as the climax, maybe, with $200,000
plus residuals to go to his mother and ex-girlfriends (because
don't forget, he has a practical Jewish head as well as a saintly
universal one).

We've suggested some of our reservations about Lenny's
Crusade but surprisingly enough we hope time will prove us
wrong. We hope the cheapness and semiliteracy and preten-
tion and ignorance that we hear in Lenny is our own stiffness
or deafness or (who knows?) envy and that he will emerge in
the eyes of the immediate future as the sacred, shamanlike
figure he is touted as being. Because if this doesn't happen
what a stew of adolescent halftruth and wiseguy selfdeception
he will have handed out to an already confused and reeling
audience: us.

1963

NOTE: *The originality of Bruce's art developed in a much
weirder and unexpected way after this was written and I became
an addict like the rest of us; but I've let this stand because he had
read it and asked me to edit a fast-buck collection of his miscellany
on the basis of dealing straight with him. He faded away, literally,
while we were setting it up.—SK*

mr. madam

The day of laughing at tropical fruits is obviously over: snicker, make cheap cracks, and you stand ready to meet the charge of repressed homosexuality in yourself. Not only has this most taboo of American minority groups (niggers and kikes, step aside!) lived through the worst of its period of ridicule, the homosexual community itself in the last five years has become more aggressive and forthright than ever before in the nation's experience. Whether you consider queerness a "disease," as do the rearguard of orthodox psychoanalysts, or a legitimate if unpopular way of life—as do the new breed of outspoken homosexual militants—there can be little doubt that male and female deviates have come out of the shadows in America.

Nugget is proud, therefore, to have this opportunity to run a condensed but unbowdlerized version of Kenneth Marlowe's extraordinarily *straight* autobiography, *Mr. Madam*. In one sense this book is the factual counterpart to John Rechy's groundbreaking grope novel, *City of Night*, part of which we also had the privilege of publishing. But in another sense it is totally different. Where Rechy wrote about the world of the male hustler, not necessarily homosexual himself but catering to the sexual fantasies of older and richer men, Marlowe takes you smack into the smalltown, grassroots environment of the

American faggot. Here you see him as a kid thinking differently than the straight boys on the block, trying on women's
clothes out of compulsive instinct, being picked up by an
older man and initiated into the fears and pleasures of the
act, slowly seeing people and places with the perceptive eyes
of a young man who knows that destiny has worked out a different fate for him than it has for most of us. The book's
authenticity is unquestionable; and although Kenneth Marlowe was not a professional writer before he resolved to tell
the whole story about his entry into the Gay World (he was a
professional female impersonator and hairdresser) his words
are so much to the point that you'll be pinned to your seat as
we were. Only those "butch types" who are queasy about the
truth because of the anxiety or aggression within themselves
will—in our opinion—set up a screen of impatience.

The Gay World, as Kenneth Marlowe lightly refers to it,
comprises some 5 to 10 million adults in this country and it
should be evident at this late date that evading its there-ness
will not wipe it out. Nor will moralizing, lecturing, pep talks
or punishment. In the majority of our states homosexual practices are still a crime, where if you're caught you can go to jail.
As the law is now constituted, this is equivalent to punishing
a person because he or she has purple eyes or ears without
lobes—punishing them, that is, for what nature or environment has determined they should be rather than for a crimi-
nal act made out of choice. The majority of homosexuals,
Marlowe makes clear, do not have this luxury of choice. And
yet through no fault of their own the large majority of the
American homo community have had to lead the lives of civilized outlaws, blackmailed and jailed by the Vice Squad, harassed by private industry as well as the Federal Government,
treated as scum by U.S. state laws that might have been
designed in the Middle Ages.

Within this often unbearable pressure—perhaps because of
it—men and women built this way have created that Gay
World of lightness, fluff and camp that has given them a sub-

culture which percolates and fizzes across the length and breadth of the country. And, of course, this same throbbing pressure has also herded the most talented of them into professions (hairdressing, theater, modeling, antiques, dance, recently education) that are tolerant of their slant and offer a minimum of persecution. If the butch opponents of homosexuality find fun in the fact that "fairies" are often drawn to the same five or six standard jobs, they should think about the idea that a rewriting of American law would permit the often marvelous creativity of homosexuals to show itself unashamed in many areas that are still out of bounds. There is every reason to believe that the social and legal harassment of these people has narrowed their careers to certain predictable occupations and even exaggerated defiant mannerisms that would have found a more natural expression in a less judging and uptight society.

But let's not drip any false tears and ruin our mascara: although the homosexual has been victimized and often distorted into a caricature by the hostility of all-American types, certain canny benefits have come his (and her) way too. When you are always in danger of exposure, or being turned against by the square world, you are on your guard, baby—and few groups as a whole have the alertness, sensitivity, wit and need to convert rough experience into high stylish pleasure as do homosexuals. This is the reward life has given them for being so-called twilight people. It surely isn't enough, and the artifice sometimes gives way to the ravaged human underneath, but for now it often makes a wild gaiety out of what could be misery and it certainly makes Madam Marlowe a man to appreciate.

1965

no show

ROCCO ARMENTO   STANLEY FISHER
ESTHER GILMAN   SAM GOODMAN
GLORIA GRAVES   ALLAN KAPROW   KUSAMA
BORIS LURIE   J.-J. LEBEL   MICHELLE STUART
RICHARD TYLER

I was kindly asked to write this introduction to the No Show for two oddly pertinent reasons: I am the editor of *The Beats,* an anthology of Beat Generation prose and poetry, and the editorial director of *Nugget* magazine. If you couple the outcries of Beat literature with the direct erotic charge of a magazine like *Nugget,* you have a unique marriage of elements which could not have been dreamed up before this specific, cockeyed period we're living in. Both the writing and the pictures glory in sources of repressed life that couldn't very well find their way into such publications as *The New York Times,* the *New Yorker* or even the *Partisan Review.* At its best, this exposure of flesh and frankness is too disturbing for the intellectually mink-lined operations named above and at its frankest it bitterly offends traditionalists who want expression which is subdued, selective and discreetly clothed.

Without forcing the question, I see an unmistakable connection between a magazine like *Nugget* and the present exhi-

271

bition. Although our ambition and daring have not yet gone
the lengths of artists like Boris Lurie and Sam Goodman,
because we are a mass magaizne and can only subvert hollow
tradition and dullness by easy stages, both the magazine and
this exhibition share a passion for contemporary imagery. We
both are mediums for the release of the most vivid, racy and
caustic sights and scenes which all but overwhelm the sensitive American eye. The painters in this show, from the shrill
siren-warnings of Stanley Fisher to the obsessive phallic
imagery of Yayoi Kusama, are however much more aggressive
and individualistic than what we have so far visually permitted in *Nugget*. Even a sassy mass-publication like ours must
bend an ear to the cash register in order to survive, and this
means that we must be ever alert to entertaining as well as
alarming. But the majority of the works in this exhibition are
entertaining only as an afterthought I believe; their primary
intention is to communicate, or more accurately, *be* a savage
experience that owes little to that diplomatic finesse which all
commercial art must cultivate. These artists are totally
unbuckled to their vision, so to speak, letting escape all the
smelly gases that cause constipation in so many other com-
partments of psychological and even artistic life.

This in itself is reason for genuine respect, I believe, even if
you recoil or are angered by the calculated extremism of some
of the work. Why? Because serious art in a rather cowardly
mass society such as ours must constantly assert to the public
that it is motivated by a different purpose than the decorative
or simply artful work which is gobbled up by massmedia
man without indigestion. America today is no place for selfrespecting beauty which doesn't threaten complacency. We
have too much slickness in every compromised area of our
lives to need art that soothes. Marvelous French masters are
not in tune with us right now. We need art that screams,
roars, vomits, rages, goes mad, murders, rapes, commits
every bloody and obscene act it can to express only a shred
of the human emotions that lie prisoner beneath the sanitary
tiles here in adman's utopia.

Most of us, people as well as painters, live every 24 hours in the midst of constant and previously unimaginable bewilderment these days. We are dazed. One's values, sense of purpose, psychic equilibrium, are zip-gunned from every side by the new barbarism that American culture has rained down upon us. No one who can feel is spared the absurdities, indignities—the sense of drowning in a stew of taxicabs, Coca-Cola machines and tight-jeaned asses—that the "material carnavalia" of our society has pyramided beyond laughter or tears. This is the life we know with our own eyes; but it is so incredible by previous standards that we try to gloss experience with the formal consolations of another period. These artists are too much in love with the monstrosities of contemporary life to fake their vision: the bulk of the work in this show is an appropriately brutal effort to cope with a brutish environment.

Allan Kaprow's piece is an exception to my eye: it is cool, calculated and effective in a controlled and delimited sense. He has classic taste, but the point of view is too cautious to be representative of what you will see. Esther Gilman's broken Christ shows the disenchantment of a private religious experience, perhaps bitter disillusionment is the closer description, and it no doubt succeeds but on a comparatively gentle level of wanhope. Michelle Stuart's sadomasochistic portraits and Yayoi Kusama's orchard of penises seem closer to the precise point of paint and fantasy, all done within terms of the female sensibility—so different from my own that I am an insensitive translator of all three ladies' language and advise you to react to their broken melodies with your own sensory equipment.

But with men like Lurie, Goodman, Fisher and Tyler, the work hits you like a rock hurled through a synagogue window. Smash!— and a 100 emotions follow in its wake, blashphemy, violence, hatred, release, fear, disgust, anger. After having suffered a critical brushoff in their early March Gallery exhibitions—the Vulgar, Involvement and Doom shows—this group of unfashionables have now made it shockingly clear

that they've invented a slambam art of the 6os which is going
to turn a lot of people around. They use every handy esthetic
device (collage with mixed technique, overprints, what Boris
Lurie calls a "simultaneity of attack") that will torpedo the
eye and rape your soul of its clichés. They ARE a band of rap-
ists in a sense, impatient, unsparing, openflied and ready for
action—"hot" pop artists out for copulation rather than cool
ones doing doodles before a mirror.

The garishness of their color, the posteresque externality of
emotion, the flashy, honkytonk "Beat Coney Island" tone and
lack of shading in the materials—all these are deliberate tab-
loidlike devices to give you the real yummy taste of our
squawking American nightmare. "A match skating in a
urinal" was Hart Crane's almost chaste image of disgust 30
years ago; now it has multiplied into these bashed-in TV
sets, girlie pinups next to concentrationcamp mass graves, in
short the unedited film strips of the contemporary id which
usually end up in the mind's wastepaperbasket. To be honest,
I am at moments uncomfortable with the garment-center
schlock and hysteria that squirts out from some of the work
even though I understand its necessity. A good example of
this is the Stanley Fisher piece which hangs above my fire-
place, purchased from his "Help!" show. What is remarkable
about it is that it actually brings Times Squre and its hus-
tling-chick, suicide-pill desperation into my house. I feel
naked before it, it is such a trophy hunted down in the jungle
of public life that it seems to be alive. I resent it because it is
so raw, vulgar, smeared, screechy, hardly separate from the
fevered streets that inspired it. And yet I love it because of its
reality. Not being a painter, it seems to me extraordinary that
the reality which I and thousands of my generation must cope
with every day has been seized and thrown cursing into art.

Let us not kid each other. The life we are forced to live in
New York and America today often seems like a bad pot-
dream, paranoid and cruelly absurd beyond conventional
description. Much of the work in this exhibition seems to me

the closest approximation of this contemporary madhouse,
which is our unchosen lot, that I have seen. Some of it is as
uneven as a rollercoaster and the artists vary from conman to
saint, often in the same package. But what a picky little
matter compared to more urgent needs. The times have
decreed the noise and insanity that rise from the streets and
drop down from the sky, and as the times always do, they
have inspired a group of artists to use this time's own personality against itself. How right and necessary for us all!

1963

part 6

intro

Here are letters I have written to writers, to my old and new hip tabloids (The Village Voice *and* New York Magazine), *an extended letter-type answer to an article in the* Sunday Times *book-section that became itself an article in the* Sunday Times *book-section—all responses, counterpunches, verbal reflexes, informal writing acts which seem to me characteristic of this decade in New York. Our lives are lived on the run and letters fix a moment that will never come again. And just as I take pains with letters—and have written and rewritten scores of them to arrow my exact meaning into someone's being—I take equal care with statements written for the jackets of books or to be used in ads. These are included also. I work on all of these letters and comments as hard as I do on anything I have written because it is all literary communication in the fullest sense. We are naive to think the literature of the future will be confined to books. I have written notes TO writers and blurbs FOR writers as events of writing in themselves: I can't afford to be proud toward any form that permits you to react. Each statement to or about a fellow writer was an effort to put my total weight behind work that I believed in—or as you will see disbelieved in—and also to assert my literary voice in its own right. As you probably know writers are not paid for making the remarks that appear on the back of books or in the newspapers; it is considered flattering to be asked but it is finally a mutually advantageous petty game in which the publisher gets free publicity on merchandise he is pushing and the writer gets exposure for his thoughts and name. Many writers (including myself) go through an intense ambivalence about making these statements which are cynically solicited by the publisher with his knowledge of the writer's hungry ego. I've laughed at myself doing eight rewrites of one sentence for a blurb, a sentence that was never used—yet I go on doing it because I want to be* HEARD. *That's what I'm here for. I believe in a writer who is indifferent to the shabby motivations behind the blurb-game (and every other insincere collaboration between publisher and writer) and* USES *it as an instant carrier for messages that he thinks are significant. I believe in statements, expressions, every form of verbal persuasion and literary commitment within an alien medium (like advertising). Writers who once thought themselves superior to the massmedia in its most corrupt sense are now beginning to realize that it is possible to speak through it without backing down an inch. Pointed writing can withstand every medium designed to smear it and grow wings of inspiration when it fits its truth to subway stations, matchcovers, mensroomwalls, record jackets, bulletin boards, posters, broadsides,* SIDEWALKS—*every prop of immediacy where wordmen as yet unborn will communicate with a minimum of false literary pride from mind to mind as quickly and urgently as they can find (or make!) the channels to do so.*

letter to nat hentoff

Nat:

My original letter to you—the one I asked you to destroy unopened by my staying up all night (on dex) to beat the mailman to your office with my note—said that I thought *Call the Keeper* was THE hip novel of the day, hip in the finest sense. When I finished the book (I sped that first letter off halfway through) I felt that this reaction was premature because I found certain drastic inconsistencies in scene and mood that partially broke the spell for me. But let me speak about why the book, even so, was a fascinating probe, a new landscape. No one that I know of has written so naturally about the really neocontemporary Manhattan scene of political-Black Power-sex-soul-"in"-reality. All the magazine years that you've spent on jazz and radical protest seem to have their proper reward now that you've turned your nonstop hand to fiction. Over the entire book was, for me, a new kind of sophistication that comes from an immersion in the areas that have preoccupied you for the last 10 years—leftwing politics, the New Black image, the ambivalent contemporary New York Jew, most important the sense of moral crisis and enlightened pessimism that haunts all your work.

I was struck at first in *Keeper* by the clarity and "rightness" of your ear, without strain, in creating New Black dialogue; I

doubt if I've seen it done better. In addition to this was your
ability to get inside the Negro psyche, male and female, in a
way that was almost totally convincing to me. Dianne strikes
me as a very real heroine and I was surprised that you, a non-
queer guy, could make me believe in her reality as engross-
ingly as you did. Billy I felt completely at home with; his pot,
easygoing sadness, cool withdrawal, all struck me as true to a
style and attitude going on right now that I've met up with in
certain stylish Negroes who have made an uncertain success in
the pale world. I'm afraid I'm somewhat rooted in the past,
fictionally speaking, in that I still want a believable reality in
characters when they are created to duplicate life. The majority of your Negro characters and their scenes had that reality
for me, which I said over the phone was superjournalistic. By
that I mean—and you concurred in a way—that in newspaper
and magazine journalism it's often hard to show how one ultimately sees a situation because of fears and obligations to the
actual living persons involved. But in the case of your book,
one of the reassuring and impressive things to the reader is
your obvious easy familiarity with what you're talking about.
Anyone who is worried about the tough Negro threat today,
and the violence that surrounds it, can get more information
about the mood of the New Black from *Call the Keeper* than
from a ton of strictly slab-on-slab factual material. In a sense
your novel is the other side of the coin, the material you had
to suppress both in a superficial or strictly to-make-the-sale
sense and probably more deeply in a subconscious or unconscious sense because of your obligations to a sympathetic
defense of the New Black in your polemical writing. But all
this I'm sure you're aware of.

First, then, to an old realist-naturalist oriented reader like
myself, I was convinced by the lifelikeness of the opening of
the book. I felt uneasy with the plot all the way along because
I distrust melodrama and feel an element of contrivance in it,
but I accepted it without too much inner difficulty because I
accepted your using it—the plot—to reveal the workings and

attitudes of your people. The plot was an excuse, I thought, to make revelations. Nevertheless as the book progressed I felt it (plot) was somewhat artificial; as I say, I bought it on sufferance as a device that would enable you to probe. But Kafka (not to be fancy) wrote about nightmare situations also without resorting to standard melodrama and I think as the subtlety of your fictional thinking grows the obvious "plotting" of your work will give way to a storyline that comes directly out of the obsessions of your characters without the convenient "accidents" from without, like the murder of Sanders. I never entirely believed in your Detective Sanders although I can certainly see why he interested you as a Negro bully in contrast to your Negro Good Guys. He was too stereotyped for me—knee in the groin, the Arch Bastard, etc. Frankly, I thought he was not too far removed from a comic-strip conception in his consistent prickishness although your artistry made him go down easier than if he had been written about by someone more clumsy. Nevertheless, to be honest, he had routine echoes for me of a thousand bad-movie novel villains whom we've all been subjected to. His novelty, of course, was that he was a spade; but apart from his important plot value in the development of your story I (and I think most sensitive readers) had to put up with him as a Type instead of reacting to him as a person.

I wasn't going to get into Horowitz at this point, but since both he and Sanders are cops, and they are the two characters that strike me as least real, I'll give you my thoughts. First, I think H. is a new kind of character whom I have never seen delineated before. You told me over the phone that he is the chief malevolent character in the book. That surprised me because even though I sensed that his efficiency, coldness, what Dianne called his "cobra" quality, were totalitarian virtues, he still was too ambiguous for me as a whole to stick him in the Bad Guy pigeonhole. He represents a very complex or fresh vision on your part. The fact that he's a Jew makes him that much more interesting, because he is a Jew without any apparent insecurity, with sexual and he-knows-how-to-handle-himself assurance, in a word all the qualities one usually associates with the *goyim* instead of Jews. Damn interesting, I thought while reading, but I couldn't buy his reality. His conversation sounded like a parody, in style, of the eggheadism that Jimmy Breslin sometimes accuses you of. (That's merely the handiest descriptive phrase that comes to mind, I dig you both as writers but for different reasons.) In itself, the uninflected intellectualism of his talk approached the monstrous and very likely you intended some of that highly selfcontrolled IBMish quality, perhaps all of it; but set in the context of the wonderfully funny, sharp, realistic talk of Shirley, Dianne, John the Avenger, Billy, he becomes ludicrous as an acceptable member of the cast as far as his surface style goes. Ludicrous to me, anyway, after getting to know cops in my brief newspaper work and in particular my having interviewed at length Sandy Garelik, the smartest Jewish cop I've yet run into. I think, to try and nail it, that the conception of Horowitz is fascinating; but the execution and his relationship to the rest of the cast struck me as somewhat out of key. (By the way, Nat, it's damn easy to pick flaws and very much harder to create the targets for the flaw-picking.)

But once Horowitz is put on the sideline, at least for the moment (you said that he will reappear in fiction you intend to do and I will be very interested in getting to know more about him), I can't say enough about the way you really make the other characters *your* material. I mean this. The entire spade quality, the East Village-New Jazz-New Political nerve that you have exposed before in nonfiction comes alive in such an easy, believable way that if I were in the Viking ad department I would sell the book as a kind of "imaginative handbook" of What's Happening. It's illuminating in a way that I haven't met up with before because it's really quite possible that no one knows as much—or, put another way, has the ability to say as much—about a symptomatic scene that is increasingly becoming a very important one in American life. Your instinct as a reporter—and I don't or couldn't mean the term pejoratively because I've been one myself and have the highest respect for the role—has led you into an area, in my opinion, that fascinates many people because their own personal lives run up against the New Black-white cold war all the time. To quote an old phrase of Arthur Koestler's that I often use, you have your finger on "the pulse of contemporaneity," or at least a very jumping part of it. When I use the word reportage, I *include* the ideas. They seem to me as much, perhaps more, of really contemporary where-it's-at-reporting as the bulk matter itself. I get the feeling that you're going to develop this interrelationship of character and idea and, again, I think most strongly that you're on the right and most pertinent track.

Call the Keeper, whatever its flaws as a whole, seems to me genuinely significant because it opens up an area to imaginative rendition that is almost ahead of the beat. Your time-sense, as a music critic, is also a time-sense in a bigger area; an awareness of where the important "sounds" of our day are being blown and what the reverberations are likely to be. What I'm saying roundabout is that you can illuminate the headlines and the subheadlines of this time by fictions that give depth and breadth to what the majority of us read only thinly in the papers and see on TV. This is a gift, in my opinion, that's badly needed and will find, inevitably, a very appreciative audience even if it takes a while to sink in. I think your novel is only the opening shot in this area. It seems to *demand* a series of novels that cut into contemporary (super-contemporary) life and open them up for the intelligent but ignorant reader. The present book has insights, attitudes, feelings about the Negro scene that give me, just as a white cat out on the streets, added ammunition in my contact with edgy or hostile or contemptuous Negroes. It is acutely aware (and I am trying not to overstate in the least because I don't want to dilute any possible value these comments might have

for you) of a "presence" in the downtown scene that will be
equally valuable to other just-plain citizens in their interrelationships in what, for most of us, is a very tricky and
anxiety-making area. In that sense your fiction—a series of
novels—seems to me a truly valuable and unique contribution
if you can sustain your energy. It could well be a social contribution that *anticipates* events in the Negro-Peace-Jazz-New
Political spectrum. Besides that, the characters you create and
their attitudes toward pressing issues of our day again give the
reader insights that will enable him to *cope* with confusing
and frightening experiences for which there is no precedent.
He can actually look to your book for guidance—how much
fiction can I say that of?

What I'm saying, Nat, is that too much contemporary
fiction is irrelevant; that's why journalism seems right now to
have stolen fiction's cherry. If you can help bring into being a
truly relevant fiction, with more dimension than typical journalism permits without a hassle, it will not only match events
but have perceptions that will go ahead of them. Today the
time-sense seems to be shortened. Large generalizations, such
as traditional novelists were inclined toward, have become
clichés. We need novels like *Call the Keeper* because they are
not indulgently literary yet they use the greater freedom that
literature still has and most journalism is only reaching for. I
think this first piece of adult fiction of yours could be the
beginning of a new genre and the door-opener for a new
"news-fiction" form brought into being by the needs of our
time. I can't embrace it as I do a fully and perfectly executed
work of art, but I think it's worth more than most of the
novels I've read recently (when I along with others can get up
the enthusiasm just to open them); and whatever seems to
me unbelievable or unconvincing in *Call the Keeper* is minor
compared to where I think it is valuable, pertinent, fresh,
honest and ahead of the accepted beat.

I will telepathically be in your corner for the next one; and
this from a guy who has been a silent critic on several occa-

sions of your polemical V*oice* soundoffs, your putting down
of Heller's *Catch-22* for Bill Manville's *Breaking Up*, etc. I
think you're finding a new dimension in your writing that's
exciting for me to swing with. And I LOVE to swing—so
thanks for giving me jollies that no one else is.

All good wishes,

Sy

P.S. I've omitted a few details (such as Septimus hitting
Horowitz in the nose and H. not defending himself) that I
should have gone into as evidence of moments that seemed to
me farfetched. Overall, as I've said earlier, they didn't bother
me; but they strained credulity for the moment. However, on
the plus side, these fantastic moments also give a spooky resonance to certain scenes, create wonder in the mind. So it's a
tossup; and the more I think of it, the more intriguing
becomes the surreal joined to the real—I never thought of it
before, but it's exactly the way I feel all too often when I go
out of the house (my shelter, my mind, my order) onto the
unbelievable streets (shelterless, mindless, chaotic and like it
or not instructive and creative).

Friday–Sunday, December 15–18, 1966

letter to jack newfield (unmailed)

Jack:

You were the spokesman of the New Left to me in its most inspiring sense: confident golden ethics unashamed to go right into the wardheeler's parlor, spontaneous honest warmth as a new instrument of politics, the sharp eye to see the betrayals imposed on us by our government but the refusal to use the Establishment's dinky pragmatic compromises by demanding a new total environment where sensitive-complex people like ourselves could live with endless human possibilities. Long before I met you I was a chargedup scholar of your work in the *Voice*; to say that I admired your ability to give new scope and flashing insight to flat political reporting is to put it most mildly. I read you with excitement because you illuminated the haze of the immediate political and social scene with remarkable freshness, perception, ease of expression—above all the ability to make fascinating new connections between the formerly isolated areas of Tammany Hall and Camus, Bobby Dylan and LBJ, every imaginative equation that makes use of our entire 1967 consciousness instead of speaking to only one walled-off compartment.

When Fred McDarrah told me that you were at the Hotel

Warwick press conference for the Beatles in late August of
last year, I badgered him to point you out to me (you'll recall
I was covering it for the *Post* during my brief workout for
them) and I think I embarrassed both of us by my square
pumping of your hand in the middle of that strange shrieking
mob. It was not easy for me to do; I knew you were Dan
Wolf's protegé at the *Voice* and we both know that almost
chemically there is this insoluble scartissue between Dan and
myself which neither of us seems able to heal; but I would
have pretty nearly walked on my knees to show my appreciation to you because even though there is 15 or 17 years' difference between us—and I am as sensitive as any of my
40-and-over tribe to the threat from the young—I felt that
your writing contribution was not a narcissistic one (as mine
has been on occasion), it threatened no one who wanted a
groovy future for himself and others, it popped the scales
from the eyes of my contemporaries and myself who had
become confined to a one-way street of seeing, it took a newly
sophisticated political antenna into the world of events and
demanded that this world meet you on your own level—you
didn't compromise for it and I loved your work for that,
learned from it, in fact tried to unknot my own prose in the
light of your example of fluid intelligence in action on the
page.

That's why, when we got to know each other, I was almost
exultantly myself and unguarded (sometimes overbearingly
so) in speaking everything I knew to you like an older but not
always wiser brother; you saw me drunk and wild, saw me roy-
ally sound off to Jimmy Wechsler on that crazy night up at
Channel 13, saw the end of my rough love affair with J.S.,
were the recipient of my 2 A.M. notes on the crucial journal-
ism-fiction crisis which actually led me into newspaper
work—to put it where it's at, you were my friend. There is
nothing that I could give that I would have held back from
you because the combination of your ability, commitment
and above all the hope for the next decade that you repre-

sented as the most articulate journalist for the New Left
represented in a strange and moving way a hope for myself. In
my own generation (hateful word, but I don't know what else
to use) the hard-fast Marxist politics of the *Partisan Review*
and often *Commentary* Left always struck me as being as
alien as the same doctrinaire, semi-European attitude applied
to literature. My experience was strictly American and in my
most impressionable years there was no brand of swinging,
open-collar radicalism for people like myself; although I knew
and alternately respected/argued-with very shrewd radicals
like Dwight Macdonald, Harold Rosenberg, James T. Farrell,
David Bazelon, Willie Poster, etc., there was at that time no
encompassing view for a young man like me that could contain my overwhelming personal experience and also let it join
with a significant public movement. Yes, Macdonald spoke of
the "root as man" and not just dialectical materialism in his
socialist-anarchist days when he was editing *Politics*, but the
theoretical language in his magazine was nothing native to
me, always something I had to strain to identify with. To
shorten all of this, it was only when the New Left created a
humane, pot-smoking, offbeat, spontaneous, informal, to my
mind very and specifically American breakthrough that it all
made perfect sense to me, made it a continuation of my
involvement in the Beat scene, created a union of the ethical
and literary approach to experience so that both the
personal-public sides of me could dovetail easily, sensibly,
excitingly.

I felt that even though I was past 40, and this was a spiritual leap forward of the young, that I understood what motivated it, was part of it, that in an uncanny way I had survived
all the shit I'd been through so that I could finally sit on the
floor with my brothers and sisters and smoke a stick out in the
open and listen to Little Richard or Tim Hardin on the hifi
and go from there into frank talk about the ghetto, in other
words *pull together* all the disparate parts of my life because
at last a new morality had come along in America that under-

stood me and that I understood. And you, Jack, were the
symbol of all this for me: through your writing, talk, insights,
etc., I felt I was hearing the real promise of your generation
and I knew I felt at home—spiritually at home, the finest
home of all and the hardest to get to.

It was therefore the most natural thing in the world for me
to show you the final draft of my newspaper piece, the one I'd
been wrestling with for six or seven months as you know, over
lunch at the new Cedar about a month and a half ago. I was
showing it to one of my own kind, wasn't I? I was very concerned as to how you would respond to the piece, since you
had already written in Jerry Agel's *Books* that new U.S. journalism had usurped much of the thunder of the "political
novel" (as evidenced by Koestler and Malraux, I think they
were among your examples) and, as you recall, after reading it
I sent you a fairly intense letter saying in my best selfrighteous style that you had only gone part of the distance in your
article—that the best journalism today was usurping the
entire novel (you had said "perform the function of the
novel") and using literature as a potential wedge into reality
itself, into the overturning of it by mirroring life from an
aggressive angle that could influence events themselves.

You "liked" my newspaper piece, you said at the Cedar,
and I was sorry that there was slight reservation in your voice
(because *you* were doing the job I was theorizing about on
the *Voice* while I had really been out of action since the *Trib*
folded on April 24, 1966) but I appreciated your pointers:
that Tom Wolfe was closer to Ted Williams than Joe
DiMaggio if I was going to use a baseball image, the reminder
that Camus had edited *Combat*, that George Orwell covered
the Spanish Civil War for British weekly papers, the fact that
almost all of the New Journalists had begun as sports writers
(including yourself) because in your words "there is a builtin
drama in sports." You also spoke about the new freedom of
newspaper form on the *Voice*—"you can make a story short
or long, as you feel it"—and I happily jotted down your com-

ments because you were my *Wunderkind*, the kid I was not ashamed to learn from and be edited by when it came to sharp details about journalism. I figured it was mutual, but I didn't know exactly how mutual by a long shot—not until today.

To get to the point, you have fleshed out your own perceptive notions of the so-called New Journalism in your review of Dick Schaap's *Turned On* book in today's Sunday *Times Book Review* with ideas and almost phrases embedded in my "Newspaper as Literature"* piece and passed them off as your own. I tell you straight that 45 minutes ago my neck-hairs bristled, something I thought only happened in lousy short stories, when I read the first three paragraphs of your piece. This fleshing may have been thoroughly guiltless and guileless—to give you the benefit of the doubt, because these ideas are certainly in the air—but I also saw this appropriating tendency in *A Prophetic Minority* and once mentioned to you that I was surprised in your chapter "The Beat Generation and the Un-Generation" to see a few phrases of mine from the introduction to Kerouac's *Desolation Angels* show up practically intact. (My description of Ginsberg, for example, as "the radical-Jewish-homosexual" becomes in your book "the Jewish-radical-mystical-homosexual," etc.)

What particularly pisses me, apart from what might be a touchy oldfashioned sense of personal betrayal and even more important a sense of creeping cynicism about what I thought you stood for, is that it will still be two months or more until my piece sees the light of print in the August *Evergreen* and some of its edge will now be blunted. I know you have been thinking in a broadly parallel direction, but the very separateness with which you speak of the Big Three reporters in my article, Breslin, Tom Wolfe and Hamill, in relation to other N.Y. daily reporters is precisely the way in which I discuss them; the fact that they are in their 30s, as

---

* See p. 339

you carefully note, as opposed to the older "clerks of fact" (Pete's phrase) is a pertinent point in my piece; the fact that these reporters are using many fictional techniques and will use more is one of the main points in my article, further backed up by a direct quote from Tom Wolfe which I obtained firsthand, although I agree you roughly sketched out this observation in your 1966 piece for Agel; and the main idea that I brooded on and tried to act out for almost half a year while I was a reporter for the *Herald Tribune*, that the New Journalism (to quote your sentence in today's *Times*) "pits the sensitive reporter—and all his feelings and intelligence—directly against an event," seems to me a direct paraphrase of a sentence in my article which says, ". . . it concerns the *whole man*—the acting out in print, as Hamill intuitively senses on certain stories, of the subjective being as it collides with objective happenings."

You to on to say, shining for the readers of the *Times*: "It is the experience, in all its complexity, that is communicated, not just irrelevant housing projects of facts bereft of essence." My sentence was (admittedly heavier since you get a little mud on your shovel when you do the digging yourself): "It is no longer the mere formal outlines of an experience that we expect from a Breslin, Wolfe or Hamill, but its entire quality, overtones and undertones, in a word the 'saturation reporting' (Wolfe's phrase) that we used to get from novelists but now need daily to understand the untrustworthy world in which our own small destinies are being negotiated."

That's it, Jack—those first three paragraphs of your Schaap review in which you pluck the balls of my own right out, absorb them in your own excellent but cannibalistic way, and leave me holding 10 pounds of gristle to wow the readers of the *Evergreen* with two months from now. I believe those three paragraphs sunk my friendship with you (as you probably knew it would and obviously didn't care) and smeared much beyond you, too—namely, what you stood for, what it summoned up to me in the hope and difficulty of my own life. Just now, reading your fifth paragraph when you've already gotten into Schaap's book, I see this quote as well while you're complimenting Schaap on his writing: "Spare, understated Hemingway prose, whose very lack of emotion generates feeling." Knowing from the *Trib* cityroom what a younger buddy and admirer Schaap was of Breslin's, I'm sent back to my own article, just as you read it more than a month ago, to this sentence: ". . . the art in Breslin's shrewd hands being to underplay details packed with emotional consequence and by flattening them allow their intrinsic value to float clear . . ." Not exactly the same, but close enough, coming on top of everything else—close enough, old buddy.

I wish this were all in my head, Jack, but I don't think—in fact I know—it isn't. We all borrow, journalists especially, working under the guillotine of the moment and grabbing for the apt thought or phrase. But this isn't borrowing—it's rape, damnit. And the Goth comes bearing flowers, words of hope, sanity, ethical eloquence, intelligence, and tells me at the final climax of A *Prophetic Minority:*

"The New Radicals are speaking harsh truths in a new and irreverent voice . . . They are saying that the whole society— from the academy to the anti-poverty program—has become too bureaucratized and must be decentralized and humanized. They are saying the draft is undemocratic. They are saying that revolutions are tearing the colonial clamps off three continents, and that America must stand with the poor and not the powerful. They are saying that automation is making a guaranteed annual income and a redefinition of work imperative. They are saying that ethics and politics have become divided and must be reunited.

"If they are emotional or badly informed about other things, on all these issues the New Radicals are right. *The older dissenters should pause and acknowledge these new voices before the Generation Gap becomes a canyon of mistrust.*" (Italics mine.)

I paused and acknowledged, I even loved a little, and right

in the middle of all those slogans and glib generalizations that now seem like so much birdseed let me just sign off. By the way, I'm glad that my speculations about the artist shaping reality itself through journalism were too too farout for you to profitably make use of—thanks for your prudence. You've left me my own funny bag as my only safety, to climb in it as deep as I can, and that's something I never would have learned without you, babes.

Seymour

May 7, 1967

two letters to
the village voice

Dear Sir:

It is practically impossible to observe our daily American culture and our own dishonorable behavior without feeling emotions that once would have flipped men and women of merely normal conscience. Today such moral turnabouts as the one I'm going to mention are taken so much for granted that it is almost naive to comment on it. Nevertheless, just for cocktail-hour laughs, consider the recent ad in *The New York Times* boosting Edwin Newman as the hotshot drama reviewer ("Watch him tonight and you'll see why") for NBC's Eleventh Hour News.

If you recall, Mr. Newman conducted a solid, skillful interview with Mary McCarthy in Paris about a year and a half ago which turned into one of the most successful and replayed of NBC's celebrity closeups. Mary McCarthy was in top form—as brilliant and fluent a conversationalist as anyone alive today, even more impressive (in my view) with the spoken word than the written—and at an impassioned moment in the interview she told Newman that her test of the health of any particular society was the state of its theater.

Newman said nothing in answer to this, the camera playing across his deadpan face while Miss McCarthy leaned toward

297

him with that spontaneous, moving eagerness she gets. As the
silence thickened, she then asked Newman if he agreed and
Mr. Newman said sadly that he was afraid he did not—that
he far preferred movies to stage plays and found attending the
live theater a chore if not a genuine bore.

This honesty of Edwin Newman's, aired and in at least one
case (mine) applauded before millions of viewers, has now
become transformed into the smooth dishonesty so prevalent
in the vital communications business. The man who truly dis-
likes the theater, and has said so publicly, has become No. 1
theater critic for the huge NBC network and in influential
publications like the *Times* you will increasingly see the
phony dignified ads proclaiming Newman's competence and
authority in a field he once came close to despising. To bend
over backward and try to understand this travesty of even
minimal justice, one can imagine that Newman would probably say that he is basically a newsman and that his current
role as star drama reviewer for Channel 4 is merely an assignment that he didn't choose for himself. Under cover of journalistic "professionalism" he and his employers can shirk off
the basic immorality (or is it the weariest kind of amorality?)
that makes him a pundit in an area stifling and uncongenial
to him·

Edwin Newman in his own eyes and those of the careless
public, starved for authenticity, is obviously a Good Guy—
unpretentious, humane, substantial, experienced, "real." He
comes across that way. And yet in a more crucial sense, as it
affects human integrity, art, theater, and the desperate moral
health of THIS society, he is in his new position adding to
the perfumed shit which is dumped on everyone because of
the expedient ethics of cynical, bigtime electronic journalism.
And don't kid yourself that it is unimportant to the individuals involved. Every newsman who took his oath to serve the
truth in some scuffed cityroom 10 or 15 years ago, and is now
riding on the power of the Tube, knows each time out when

he is playing false with what has been entrusted to him ...
until that day when he blissfully forgets.

Of course nothing will change: if you got Newman on the
phone today he'd tell you that he's much more appreciative of
the theater than he was before, that he spoke out of ignorance
on the Mary McCarthy show, that he hasn't seen a movie for
months (kicked the lousy habit!), and that he has more
humility about stagecraft than he ever dreamed possible
before.

And the phony dignified ads will continue to appear in
their perfect setting, the phony dignified *Times*, and Edwin
Newman's dry convincing words will continue to be propelled
out of those honest chops at 11:20 on Channel 4, and we the
eternal suckers will go on lapping up that something far less
than the truth which is eroding and falsifying us as individuals and as a people.

Go, America, tell it like it ain't! That's our new world-
famous role, isn't it?

Seymour Krim

Feb. 8, 1968

studs daley

Dear Sir:

In the print-storm of coverage someone must have pointed it out but I haven't seen it: Mayor Richard J. Daley steps right out of the pages of James T. Farrell's indicting and now prophetic novel, *Studs Lonigan* (1935). From Chicago's South Side to the parochial school with its "sour-faced nuns" to the ward clubhouse, here is Studs's friend Dick Daley, who wasn't killed by the booze. It all fits with hair-raising probability· Farrell is now 64, Daley 66—a little research might actually find Daley in the trilogy under a disguised name. If he's not there in the flesh his punk spiritual twin is on every page; to understand why Chicago happened let everyone from Humphrey (who prettily quoted Thomas Wolfe in his acceptance speech when it was Farrell's bitter hour) to *The New York Times* editors take another look at this granite reporting of 30 years ago. The Convention was the inevitable postscript of what happened when Studs's boys became grandfathers.

Seymour Krim

Sept. 19, 1968

letter to
new york magazine

Editor:

Howard Junker is apparently so carried away by Philip (No Jewish Freak He) Roth that he can't merely say *Goodbye, Columbus* was an exceptional collection of stories for a young writer in his 20s to produce; he has to knock the competition. When Junker says Roth copped all the awards "in a year without a major novel" (and then lists, among others, William Burroughs' *Naked Lunch* without batting an eye) he is doing his ace lefthander a disservice. Junker uses the word "major" as hollowly as a general, not someone who cares about literature.* Burroughs' book, whatever one's personal taste, is already a weird, era-typifying landmark in contempo-

---

*Junker does care, actually, and responded with a very spontaneous and open acknowledgement of Burroughs' wild supremacy when this grouching note was printed; I reprint it not to embarrass a good man but only to give a continuing picture of my nervous reaction to every literary-journalistic burp going down on the New York scene. I'm writing this background matter from London, where I've escaped from the minute-to-minute exercise of emotion that Manhattan machines out of you, but while I've left one life I haven't yet joined another—so America (if you care) don't worry!

rary American prose; Roth's collection, finely poised and precocious as it was, is a conventional package compared to the former in influence, lasting interest, controversy, etc. I think even Roth, a decade after the fact, would admit this.

Seymour Krim

Manhattan

Feb. 10, 1969

literature makes
plenty happen

George P. Elliott's defense of literature as a gentleman's art ("Poetry Makes Nothing Happen," *The New York Times Book Review*, Jan. 28, 1968) is just about the most deadening invitation to become a writer today that I can imagine. Mr. Elliott, his eye trained on the museum of the past and the most pedestaled busts of the present (Yeats, Auden, Faulkner) seems to have no notion of the crisis that literature is facing in 1968: whether it can compete with newer and for today's public groovier artforms in the mere excitement of being alive. For him to dote on the very questionable fact that, in his paraphrase of W. H. Auden, "literature makes nothing happen"—so questionable that I think it's untrue in spite of Mr. Auden's slick generalization—is almost throwing in the white rag for writing when everything from acidrock to new cinema to the revolutionary street theater is trying harder than at any time in recent memory to bust wide-open our preconceptions about the possibilities of reality.

Why not admit that much current U.S. "creative writing" is fighting a sickly fight against its hungry young competitors because selfelected custodians like Mr. Elliott and Headmaster Auden want to stick it under glass, or in the freezer, in the

305

overcivilized conceit that it is too good for action out in the riot-torn cities. Whoever heard of a great literature written with the express purpose of being kept from smiting its audience, or teaching it humility before it was sent winging? You'd almost think from Mr. Elliott's timid guardianship that writing actually belonged to writers (ha!) and not to the deepest needs of a generation, especially a totally shookup one like the short fuses, you and I included, who smolder on the modern streets. How can Elliott speak so blandly and genially about the final ineffectiveness of serious writing when more besieged people than you can count write primarily in order to survive—surely an effectiveness second to none.

And if the writer writes to survive there must be readers who also depend on communication from this swaying parachute, who desperately hold to the lifeline of sentences. As the noises of unreality, hard sell, coy buy and official computerthink sneer in our ears, perhaps the entire balance of our country and the new values we need to redeem ourselves as a once-decent people hinge on great and vengeful words that are also art. Let Mr. Elliott not deceive himself that literature was ever made, in any time, without the intention of changing something: the writer himself, the outer world around him, even the disorganized materials of existence that had to be shaped in pain to make sense and even a glimmer of justice out of the mortal mess.

Examine the word "change" any way you like and it still represents the alteration of a process. What I am saying is that there are many important kinds of change or "making something happen" that writing can produce even if until now it has not revolutionized society. But who has the authority to say that writing is essentially a superior kind of word-game that may result in, to use Elliott's words, "esthetic admiration" (sounds like "interior decoration") when the people who play it are in each generation—or *were* before Elliott, Auden & Co. cooled them—the most serious spirits of their time? Believe me, literature up through the bloodbath of history had other little purposes beyond "amusing, entertaining," as Mr. Elliott puts it, and the first of these was to protest against the world and the conditions of life so fiercely that a hole was forever burnt into the conscience of mankind. Think about the Bible and go back or forward from that point in time and you can not evade the fear and trembling that literature has not only changed men, it has created them.

Mr. Elliott says that "these effects of [literature] cannot be demonstrated," but he is wrong. The effect of his article could be demonstrated to have driven a young would-be writer, who might otherwise have attended a session of a prose workshop that I umpire for the Poetry Project on the Lower East Side, into the movie or theater workshop instead. Young literary talent today wants action, rough body contact with society, and if Mr. Elliott says it is an illusion to find it in prose you can bet your inflated dollar that should he be taken seriously a new generation will happily leave the field to his pipesmoking literary club—why should they want it?

That is a clue to your effectiveness in a practical sense, Mr. Elliott. It all seems to depend on *how* you take your role as writer as to whether and to what degree and to what end you will cause change. Let me hazard a guess—namely that your own removed view of the power of literature will help remove from its ranks those kids who want a more immediate form of expression. And it will draw closer to literature those "literary" types who agree with your conception of the pragmatic futility of writing. That's "making something happen," isn't it? And then along comes a writer who may attract into writing those activists who agree with me that "creative literature" should be equivalent to an implosion/explosion and can blast a doorway that didn't exist before into the inner and outer future. And others, who may resent today's writing being represented by high-explosive freaks like myself, may well prefer a safer area of activity than their conception of what the new writing style is.

So it seems that both of us can provoke change at an ele-

mentary level—affect the kind of literary climate that will
exist—and this is only a prelude to a broader change in values
depending on which of us prevails. In other words, I think
that whether one believes writing can "make something
happen" or not is entirely up to the writer himself and what
he imposes on his reader. It is the lone individual who turns
on literature's flame and banks it in this direction or that, not
an Elliott-type program that presumes to speak for others—
there can be no program, no certainty, no scientific poll of
effectiveness, because we are dealing with faith, which is spiritual and probably the essence of literature. It must be in
faith only that I believe the will to action can be created in
men through written language, and Elliott does not. And on
the basis of these two attitudes we act as writers and virtually
predict our own effectiveness or lack of it.

In my view Mr. Elliott's inability to believe even in the
desirability of literature influencing events shows the narrow-
ness of imagination that has made serious writing in this
country recently take a back seat to the New Journalism, film,
multimedia theater, truth-comedy (Lord Buckley, Bruce,
Sahl) and pop song-poetry (Dylan, Baez, Leonard Cohen).
These communications to a present-tense public have nothing
to do with "an object of esthetic admiration" as a goal; that is
the talk of tired, oversophisticated men; like all fresh art
today, the intention of these long-suppressed bursts is to stab
their audience into transcendental awareness. They are made
for the moment of their performance, like a metaphor of
modern living. History (assuming there will be one) will
judge whether these performances are to be singled out as
lasting art, but at least their practitioners do not get confused
as to what should come first: existential communication from
I to Thou with the fate of We possibly hanging in the balance.

Maybe it will take this invasion of the performing arts onto
ground that literature always accepted as its own—that it was

the most serious conceivable comment on an age—to wake up elite contemporary writing to the gloomy selfknowledge that it has been hiding out entranced in the classical ruins. Can there be any question that over the last 10 years "fine" literature in our country has abdicated hitting power to the new nonliterary forms that have not been weighed down by the curse of too much wisdom ("Auden . . . is our wisdom poet," says Mr. Elliott with genocidal pride) and are proud to be alive?

To be alive, as I understand it, is to fight for change; a person or an artform can't live significantly without using energy differently than it has been used before. And the time one lives in determines by its needs what is done with this life-force. It is no accident, for example, that a number of writers, myself included, have in the last decade stripped down to bearing personal witness to their experience rather than "fictionalizing" it in order to force public acceptance of the subjective mind in motion· Show me what's in your head, I ask of a writer, and if it is closer to the vital grain than mine I will gladly yield up my reality to yours and selfishly incorporate your head in mine—because I want to be where the most brilliant action is.

But Mr. Elliott gives me no action that I can use; because of his philosophy he "makes nothing happen" to me; he'll leave that to Bob Dylan or the Beatles and then write a piece telling me what thirdrate or adolescent poets they are. What he refuses to understand is that his "mature" comments are beside the point if they aren't replaced with something better than what the new generation of wordmen are already doing—energizing, enlarging, deepening my sense of being, increasing my awe before the possible, making me more aware of what I and the world are not but could be (and if not in this lifetime then in those I can conceive of). This is the real change: because once my imagination is stretched by a convincing new literary experience I can never be totally the same and the artists who have done this to me change the sliding scale of truth that motivates my actions—even to writing this answer.

"To the extent that a piece of writing is art, it makes nothing happen": a beautiful epitaph for that stone under which George P. Elliott would lovingly bury the power of The Word!

1968

blurbs and statements

DONALD BARTHELME ("Come Back, Dr. Caligari"):
To the Editors of *The New York Times Book Review:*
R. V. Cassill's review of *Come Back, Dr. Caligari* (April
12, 1964) gives barely the slightest whiff of how fresh Donald
Barthelme's work is, how much talk it has stirred up, how it
has fictionally goosed the *New Yorker* and jimmied open the
imaginations of other more pedestrian writers. Mr. Cassill is a
distinguished novelist in his own right (and the author of at
least one unforgettable short story, the deadly "Fracture")
but he certainly was not the prompt critical outrider that a
talent as unexpected and outrageously contemporary as Barthelme's deserves. Mr. Cassill has just made it that much
harder for this unique writer to find his true audience, which
is an ironical role for a teacher and advocate of an artform
that is being overwhelmed on all sides these days by the flashier massmedia.

Seymour Krim
New York City
1964

ERJE AYDEN ("The Crazy Green of Second Avenue"):
Ayden is a goodlooking world-weary young Turk living in

311

East Hampton who has learned our language only in the last
five years. In his pure first novel, *The Crazy Green of Second
Avenue,* he uses these new words with the unmasked clarity
and directness of a Gertrude Stein or a Sherwood Anderson;
line by line it is as truthful and unfaked a prose as any we
have had in the last five years. The artlessness of the writing
makes the experience of reading Ayden as refreshing and startling as drinking from a natural brook in the center of Rockefeller Plaza. With total unselfconsciousness this writer cracks
the shell of customary reality and takes us back and forward
in time, space and imagination at the whim of his brain; yet
so natural, uncontrived and real is each new picture that we
entrust ourselves to his dreamlike cinematic technique with
surprising ease and appreciation. His story is an Arabian
Nights tale of the bitched contemporary scene told in the
first person and redeemed only by the fanatical joy of sex; we
have all lived it, perhaps not as imaginatively or honestly, but
enough so to make identification with the protagonist
immediate and uncomplicated. Ayden's scenes of physical
copulation are frank, basic and barbarous to the point of challenging the puny concept of sex held by every selfcongratulating Village swinger. Pervading these pages is an offhand
aristocratic integrity expressed in such a simple way that
common speech gains values of silver and gold in place of the
copper pennies we are used to. In my opinion the experience
communicated in this small book, by virtue of intensity, bare
truth and a form as fresh as a wild flower, combines to make a
unique assertion of art for our time and place. I recommend it
to you as something both hip and precious.

                                                                    1965

GILBERT SORRENTINO ("The Sky Changes"):
    Mr. Sorrentino's integrity is tough and special. He nei-
ther spares himself nor others. That he can write like a—not a
Bengal, but a Brooklyn—lancer, covered with bitter inconspicuous glory, only enables us to see with ashamed clarity

what severe and intractable standards he upholds. Sorrentino is not only a firstrate writer, he is a wild literary conscience of his generation who must be reckoned with by every American avantgarde writer and reader in action right now. The full extent of his influence as a ringed-fingered custodian of the truth has yet to be felt.

1966

LESLIE GARRETT ("The Beasts"):

It is a great pleasure for anyone familiar with his spooky short fiction to see Leslie Garrett rise from the New York literary underground carrying his grotesque world intact. Readers encountering him for the first time are to be envied; for the cruel shudders he induces in this first novel are only the beginning of a raven-winged flight of the imagination that makes one think a hipster's Poe has come among us. Garrett is prolific; pointedly embarrassing because of his sadomasochistic understanding; a genuine storyteller; and a beautifully corrupting fantasist whose works will soon be widely read, filmed and become essential black fables for our hang-your-head-and-cry era. Beware—this man can show us the rotten side of life as we are normally afraid to confront it but unconsciously love it.

1966

W. H. MANVILLE ("The Palace of Money"):

Bill Manville is an easy rider, a deft sweatless natural writer who nevertheless has not reached the heat of his creativity with his two formal "novels" as he did with the semijournalistic *Saloon Society*, his first book; written out of his midnight patrols for (himself first and then) *The Village Voice*, that original collection stamped a time, a place and a below-14th St. style as vividly as Runyon did Broadway or Weidman the garment center. Manville's one characteristic contribution in this second novel is the free, informal, perfectly convincing sexplay, so low-key that it can't be resisted but so frank that it can emotionally get to every lover. Other than that, his money-mystiqued, I'm-Scott-you're-Zelda fantasy is tinsel, finally, when he should now be tempering his own brand of swanky, hardly visible muscle. Is Dashing Bill going to fizzle out in the grand old American one-book tradition after his champagne christening? These last books of his, whatever he may think their refinements, are not speaking to the people the way he has already proved he can and what else is writing for in this or any time?

1966

HUBERT SELBY, JR. ("Last Exit to Brooklyn"):

Hubert Selby has extended the range and possibilities of contemporary American literature with a single book. It is in a class by itself and its author now has the great responsibility of taking his relentless vision even further. This first statement is too committed to be only a beginning and too original in its impact to be a conclusion. He can only go forward creating a world that would shame even God if he existed.

1966

HUNTER THOMPSON ("Hell's Angels"):

The vivid strength of Thompson's book is that he has gotten inside the Angels, like Harrison Salisbury reporting from Hanoi. His document will make even liberals finally comprehend the powerful attraction to the masculine ego of American fascism. It is only by understanding its excitement from within that responsible minds will be able to cope with the beauty of speed, violence and brotherhood on an actual and not a pious level.

1967

LEROI JONES ("Home"):

Liberal critics who have dismissed Jones because of his

venomous and (most) often inflammatory attacks on white America miss the fine blade of his mind. It can cut, slice and stab through heaps of sentimental blubber like a black dandy's rapier. "By the time this book appears, I will be even blacker," says Jones with understandable humanity, and if that's what he really wants one hopes he now burns with a funky coalblack rage; but other people, while acknowledging the corrupt, comfort-loving whitey target which Jones smears with pleasure, can also see a *writer* scoring points on that ancient antagonist reality because Jones has found a subject that uses all of him. Like Baldwin, especially an earlier Baldwin, Jones throws all of his manifold ambivalent hangups about being alive into the black-white pot and triumphs over them with Walt Whiteman as convenient fallguy. No one, not even Mr. Whiteman, could be quite as black as Jones paints him. But who cares? Because in the process Jones has moved more energy, singed the air with his whirring presence, knifed up every platitude and scorned all benevolence—in short written with cold, adult passion. These essays are hacked out of an iceberg of proud human hatred for the dirty trick played on Jones (by America?) and are not about to melt too easily.

1967

JOHN CLELLON HOLMES ("Nothing More To Declare"):

The most intelligent discussion of the Beat Generation on record; the portraits of Legman, Landesman, Ginsberg and Kerouac are dandies; the book as a whole is an inside personal chart of the last 20 years in U.S. literary and emotional-intellectual life, naming names, describing scenes, combining gossip, news and judgment. The most articulate hipster of them all has finally stripped down to his union suit. Perhaps Holmes's greatest contribution in this book— one which is invaluable and which now makes him one of the acutely withit commentators of our time and place—is

the ability to define states of being that have baffled all who
have been tied to the old definitions. We need Holmes to
lead the majority of us who are occasionally blind into the
future of the New Consciousness, American-style; in this
book he has authoritatively set down his claim to being one
of the really fast guns in the national jungle. Readers who
ignore this volume callously ignore their own lives.

1967

FIELDING DAWSON ("An Emotional Memoir of Franz
Kline"):

Dawson is the man who said that for our period "third-
person is 86'd," meaning shut out of relevance to our needs,
and his firstperson description of an intense personal relationship with one of the Big Three Abstract Expressionist painters (DeKooning and Pollock being the others) proves his
theory. As long as Kline's paintings remain valid, so will this
book. It is raw, embarrassing, tender, organically formed, true
to itself, a work of art as well as history. It was written in
obvious love and sorrow which spreads itself slightly indulgently across the page, but underneath the naked and palpi-
tating heart Dawson reveals is steady courage doing its work.
Among the firstperson American testaments of this time—
survival prose, as it's been called—Dawson's valedictory to
Kline and his own younger self can no more perish than the
living memories that all of us who lived through that period
will carry until our deaths.

1967

MORRIS RENEK ("Siam Miami"):

Renek and his book stink with all of the true novelistic
genes that I can imagine: they are rich, broad, insightful,
juicy, funny, wise, full of rooms and places and the tinkle of
silverware and voices—life, we used to call it. I find scenes
and moments heightened (his love for Dickens?) beyond my
own suspicious willingness to believe, but if there are still

"born" novelists in an age of confession and the exploitation of self Morris Renek is sacred property. There is a mammoth world in his head which demands that he roll it out with bigness. And what a skull it must be! Inside its corridors I hear the roar of the crowd, showbusiness stars broken and made, moneymen on the prowl, every steamy hallucination of this society given its rich due. Balzac and Dickens, Conrad and Dreiser, have a faroff Brooklyn Jewish grandson in Morris Renek and they would understand him from the first sentence to the end—*landsman*, they would say! When Renek's tale is too manufactured or "artificial" for my private sense of reality I look to his source of energy and implication in existence, which is always real, and feel heartened that we have even a few writers who know that their task is to patrol the human waterfront from one end to the other.

1969

MICHAEL DISEND ("Stomping the Goyim"):

I would say that at this moment *Stomping* is the must book of the significant and historically unique Lower East Side; even more than Irving Rosenthal's *Sheeper* and Ronald Sukenick's *Up* the precise state of mind of a prototypical posthipster, post-Jew, multipersonalitied psychedelic man is articulated with keener means and stranger impressiveness than I have experienced it before. I found, to be a drag, empty spaces of just talmudic spacetrip here—appreciation, deep appreciation, on my part rather than engagement—but taken as a whole the graph of the mind that it describes and creates astonishes and dates me (until I had the privilege of catching up through these pages) in a way that I humbly yield to. What in the lack of God's name will human beings become with works like this and Burroughs' as our radar? I fear the future that faces us, but kiss ass on Disend for his black flair and courage in making us know it down to the last unbuttonable button.

1969

part 7

intro

As the culmination of the route that led from the publication of the Cannoneer eight years ago to the necessity (economic, psychological, imaginative, moral) to "take my thing" out of the house and into the cultural streets, first at Swank where I edited an experimental literary section within the body of the magazine, then at Nugget, then a brief whirl as so-called senior editor at Show until it collapsed, I became at 43 a common cityside reporter on the New York Herald Tribune. It was the pragmatic test of ideas about literature-in-action already articulated for their book-section during the two preceding years; but with only a few exceptions the men with whom I worked in the "indoor Yankee stadium" city-room on West 41st St. knew nothing about what I had done for their Sunday book pages (hardnews reporters are reverse snobs), knew nothing about my literary past, could accept me only when I cut the time-space reportorial mustard in terms they understood. To me it was the focal point of every notion I had struggled toward about an imaginative nonfiction that uses every resource of literature aimed at real events and by its point of view and intensity toward the actual makes meaning out of history as it happens—which could in turn influence future events. I felt I was closer to the *source of my being, my literary imagination, the significance of my fate, etc., during the five months from Dec. 5, 1965 to April 24, 1966 when the paper died than at any point in my adult life. The entire experience was controlled euphoria: crashing in at me from every angle were the hungry lives of real people in the some 40 stories that I covered and the meaning (assuming as I do that there was one) of every aspect of their visible actions and personalities was in my hands when I hurried back to the office after an assignment and sat hunched over the machine squeezed between Tim Hutchins and Ralph Chapman wondering how I could whittle this into sense before the deadline. (When I had gotten my lead and the story was moving into the fourth and fifth paragraphs and that redemptive light was beginning to shine at the end of the narrative tunnel—when I knew I was in, and felt saved from that small death which had to be faced down every afternoon gunfighter-style—I used to play with the clock on the south wall as it ground toward the 6:30 deadline by deliberately lighting a cigarette and strolling the 50 yards to the pigpen john for a leisurely pee, knowing I could flirt with time because today at least those black hands were hacking somebody else and leaving me killer-cool.) I never fumbled a story—although I missed a half dozen deadlines for the first edition but usually made the second and had my share of work spiked after five hours' futile labor— except for one where I was later embarrassingly accused by* The Village Voice, *without being named, of informing the police about nude dancers performing at the Bridge Theater in the East Village in order to "get a scoop." The entire episode seems bizarre and cockeyed enough to win the Funny Fuckup Medal of the Week seen at this distance as I sit in a strange hotel room staving off yet another deadline. But it was harrowing enough at the time when through a Hearst-headed assistant city editor I was advised to call the local downtown precinct to find out whether any complaints had been filed about the naked dancers. The station-*

house police, immersed in Nugget pix or their equivalent, had heard nothing about these new pubic expressionists until I questioned them and then they eagerly squeezed the address of the tiny theater out of me while on an open telephone line one of the nervous nude dancers—apprehensive from the start because our photographer had predictably shot cheescake at the theater that afternoon when the group was obviously selling soul—listened to me saying, licked: "If you go to the theater keep my name and the paper's out of this." I should, of course, have hung up on the switchboard sergeant when I realized he knew from nothing but I had already identified myself and the Trib when I called and I froze—then leaked when they told me it was my and the paper's duty to give them the facts. The dancer on the other phone, lying open on the desk, thought I had called the precinct just to inform on them and when I picked it up he told me off in something close to tears and rage and then circulated word among the other dancers that they were being set up for an arrest. I told my city editor that I could not do the story, called co-manager Arthur Sainer at the theater and told him that against my wishes I had given the address of the Bridge to the local bluecoats and to be on the alert that evening, and then I took the back elevator downstairs and started walking in the rain without a hat or coat. I was a fink, actually felt like vomiting at the corner of 40th St. and 7th Ave. but couldn't, and headed downtown in the semistorm (no cab for 13 blocks) to stand by with my cashed paycheck for bail in case the rollers made a bust. To wind this up, I was turned out of the Bridge lobby like a smalltime Judas and feeling green stuck close to my radio all the rest of that miserable night waiting for news of the arrest; it never came and I fell into a haggard smear of sleep at dawn hating the paper, myself, vowing to resign. It was the only assignment I never fulfilled, from Bobby Kennedy to Sing Sing, and it shamed me as it still does in memory because I was thought to have betrayed my own leftish-

avantgarde-East Village identity. There was no arrest, by the way, because the one nude male dancer in the group who had overheard me on the phone ("Wear a jockstrap tonight," I pleaded) and whose whirling testicles and piece were the nub of the issue merely dropped his number that night. Simple. I was considered a sharp if strange reporter by the usual citydesk standards but I was not as good as I wanted to be because each event I covered aroused in me a thicket of thought-emotion-association that I could only deal with technically by scaling the experience down. I could be appropriately sassy, funny on occasion, biting, but the full grand weight of what the business meant to me (the opportunity to act out in print a theoretical obsession about the newspaper as the most effective vehicle of literature in the mass-communications area) was only hinted at in my work; if the paper had not perished I would have spent the next X-number of years working toward the principles I outline in "The Newspaper as Literature" and I would have found the only significant home I've ever known in that scuffed cityroom. After the Tribune *crumbled, and I was too low on the seniority list to follow the troops to the* World Journal Tribune, *I worked for two weeks on the liberal Jewish* New York Post *("The paper's made for you," Breslin told me seriously) covering such stories as changes in the weather and the Sanitation Department's plans for winter. On the thirteenth day I came back to the office hot and tired with a nothing story on striking ballet dancers and was fired in one minute flat by a city editor named John Bott who looked over my shoulder at the colorless paintjob and told me I was trying to get copy into the* Post *that no newspaper in the country would print. I felt like an old man for the first time in my life.*

lindsay's debut:
the mayor and the
gentle practitioners

They crouched, they crawled, they shouted, they stampeded early Saturday morning in the Hotel Americana. And it wasn't a New Year's celebration. Hardly.

It was the hysterical might of New York's radio, television, magazine and newspaper representatives—mass-communications with a High C—that stole the show they had come to cover, roughed up the new Mayor as if he were a plebe and proved that the real story today is hardly the news event but rather the freebooting army of newsmongers themselves.

At 12:09 A.M. on this weird New Year's day, Michael Quill sat down at a long desk at the north end of press headquarters in the Americana's Albert Hall—a fancy name for the basement—and had eight microphones shoved in his face, four TV cameras trained on his balding head and a babble of questions flung into his pauses between sentences. But Mr. Quill knew that he had the upper hand—he was effortlessly

*This was my first lively *Tribune* story; but the city desk was not yet used to my style and it ended up in *The Village Voice*.

making news by saying the strike was on and that he was going to bed—so that the eager-beavers snapping and baying in front of him, and on the sides, had to adjust themselves to his pace.

Besides, he had 10 TWU stonefaces flanking him like a Warner Brothers gangster movie and the sight of all that muscle lent a courteous, or respectful, tone to the questions that was absent from that point on. When Mr. Quill slyly and delightedly tore up the injunction issued against his union before the thirsty TV cameras, his part in the show was over and, like an accomplished actor, he knew when to get off.

"Nobody passes here!" growled a six-foot TWU hardnose to three frenetic radio reporters, thrusting out little microphones to catch a wheeze from Quill as he selfcontentedly made his exit. The radio boys (and one girl) faded like an early snow and the green-buttoned troop encircling Quill brought back charming memories of Hitler's early days in Munich.

It was now the new Mayor's turn to face the eyes and ears of the world. But, poor chap, he was about eight minutes late in getting from the conference room, where he had only suffered the first major defeat in his entire political career.

"Where the hell is he?" shouted a dapper man with earphones clamped over his skull, small black eyes surveying the horizon like Magellan.

"Tell 'em to leave Gabe's mike open," a Channel 4 man in a sharp purple jacket yelled. "This way we can get Gabe out in a hurry when Lindsay shows!"

At least 150 standing, sitting, squatting and jabbering followers of St. Pulitzer showed their impatience until the whipped procession of city officials started out of the conference room toward the press table, led by the crutch-supported Dr. Nathan Feinsinger, Mayor Lindsay's chief mediator.

"Get Gabe out!" cried the Channel 4 purple jacket, and sure enough, like the flying Hertz Rent-a-Car man, Mr. Gabe Pressman suddenly popped into a chair in proper 10-foot range of the NBC-TV camera.

"Thank God we did it," gasped the Channel 4 worrier as the Mayor, Dr. Feinsinger and Theodore Kheel sat down at the press table less than five feet away. "Now Gabe, as soon as they pan Lindsay, they'll break in live!"

"Are they gonna announce where we are, or are they gonna pick it up cold?" asked Gabe as the Mayor, looking as lean and idealistic as young Lindbergh, started to speak about the enormous problem just dumped in his lap.

"As far as they know they'll pick it up cold," said purple jacket, now literally down on his hands and knees before the redeyed TV camera like a member of a religious sect. "Gabe, Gabe, you're on in a minute!"

"It can still be settled," Mayor Lindsay announced strongly, as if aware of his competition, but at that very moment a grey-haired photographer standing some 30 feet to the right of the Mayor jumped back as a flashbulb hit a table and broke, and penetratingly said, "Oy givalt."

"Gabe, you're on," cried Channel 4, while ABC said at precisely the same moment to its John Parsons, "This is it, sweetheart," and CBS called to a headphoned technician wriggling across the carpeted floor like a minelayer, "You got to get closer!"

"The TA has come forward with what could have been a reasonable settlement," Mayor Lindsay was saying, but the goodlooking WINS brunette operating the tape-machine crouched down beside her male colleague and argued, "We've got to move it to the right, can't you see that?"

The special phones of NBC, UPI and CBS on an improvised console to the right of the press table punctuated the Mayor's sentences—"My offer was to submit it to fact-finding and arbitration and retroactivity"—with beautifully clear rings, almost as if to remind the promising newcomer that these world-famous organizations were considering using his words if they came out good enough.

Mayor Lindsay, holding himself in leash, refused only once to be raped of privileged information that could conceivably settle the strike at the bargaining table and which, if he had yielded, would have momentarily jazzed up a 15-minute TV show at 12:55 in the morning. Dr. Feinsinger, who followed the Mayor as Fodder No. 2, also permitted himself only one sharp retort, to Gabe, who on the basis of his wrist-watch needed a spineshattering scoop in the minute and 30 seconds remaining. And Theodore Kheel, playing the unusual role of backstop to Dr. Feinsinger in this particular crisis, contented himself with pursing his bulldog mouth at both the press and his own team. At least, so it appeared.

When the principals finally escaped—Quill blithely off to bed in his suite at the Americana, the Mayor to City Hall and the mediators to some unkinking Scotches-on-the-rocks and a troubled sleep before picking up the cudgels at 10 A.M.—WOR and WMCA microphones dug up TA boss Joseph O'Grady in the back of Albert Hall.

Perhaps the slightest bit pleased at finally getting a little attention, O'Grady was saying over the air in answer to a question, "Well, that's a typical Mike Quill statement—" when all of a sudden it became hard for him to hear his own voice.

This was because a reporter on the UPI special phone only a few feet away was saying loudly and clearly in answer to a question just put to him by his office, "Hell, it's only O'Grady trying to explain what the package was that they offered Quill, who cares now?"

Grown men have gone bruised to psychiatrists for less, but it's hard to beat the good old communications business when it comes to the real callous thing.   Jan. 1, 1966

st. john's school-in-exile opens

The banner of the Catholic academic rebels was planted in the middle of the posh Jamaica Estates section of Queens yesterday and amidst a worldly fanfare of TV lights, Broadway-type publicity, $100,000 homes, precocious kids and avant-garde sculpture, it almost curled up and died.

The Rev. Peter O'Reilly, the plump local chairman of the United Federation of College Teachers, the union representing the dismissed and striking college teachers at St. John's University, formally opened the "university-in-exile" yesterday.

But visions of hairshirts, martyrdom and anguished cries of academic freedom coming from passionate lips should be quickly stricken from every overactive imagination.

The "university-in-exile" is in a fancy private school, called the Parkway School, which is a leisurely 10-minute walk from the main St. John's campus in Queens. This repository of learning was offered to Father O'Reilly and the 90-odd dismissed and striking teachers by director Sid Dorfman, to continue their courses for as long as the dispute with St. John's lasts.

But the 12 students who came for the opening course in

329

"introductory philosophical psychology" had to push their way through a mob of cynical massmedia representatives who outnumbered them 5 to 1. The press, radio and TV had been alerted by the publicity-conscious United Federation of College Teachers that this was to be one of the greatest gestures for intellectual freedom since Martin Luther nailed his historic manifesto to the Wittenberg church door in 1517.

Father O'Reilly held on tightly to his textbook for the day, "The Image of His Maker," by Robert Elward Brennan, but it became merely a solemn prop. He was plunked down in front of the TV cameras and made to repeat like a parrot what he had already said over radio; he was spun this way and then that way by impatient newspaper photographers; and his 12 students learned about as much philosophical psychology from the behavior of the milling communications men, and a carefully contrived "nonevent," as they could ever have gotten from author Brennan.

In the meantime, squadrons of camera-clicking, ooohing-and-aaahing, prattling Parkway School kids—undergoing their own rigorous training in academic freedom at $1,200 per semester—took notes like fiendish child-journalists while an art teacher in a smock cried, "What an exciting day, they are seeing news being made for the first time!"

For Mr. Dorfman, founder of the Parkway School and its nearby twin, the Highland School, it was a family event of great moment. His son and wife beamed at the crush in the hiply art-decorated school basement, while Mr. Dorfman genially welcomed all newcomers as if it were the opening of a new summer vacation resort, saying with direct, athletic heartiness, "I offered Father O'Reilly the school because I have a lot of respect for the principles and people at stake."

Father O'Reilly and a staff of dissident St. John's teachers will attempt to teach courses to former students in history, classics, fine arts, psychology, chemistry, physics, mathematics, Russian and French at the Parkway School every day after 3 P.M., when regular school hours end for the newsloving youngsters. Onward, Christian soldiers!   Jan. 20, 1966

they sang his praises
and his songs

To the whitecollar world he was an arrogant little labor
Hitler, especially when he pulled his final caper and paralyzed
New York for 13 days during the transit strike last month.
But to the men who graduated from overalls to selfrespect
because of his efforts he was the last of the unwhippable Irish
rebels.

The Transport Workers Union of America held an oldfashioned memorial to their fallen leader, Michael J. Quill,
yesterday afternoon at Manhattan Center. Almost 4000 men
and women who had looked up to Mr. Quill as their bold
voice and crafty right hand at the bargaining table for more
than a quarter of a century, saw a parade of celebrated men
give homage to a feisty, difficult, unswerving labor visionary
who founded the TWU in 1934 and guarded it like a child
until he paid the ultimate price and died for it on Jan. 28,
1966.

Ambassador Arthur J. Goldberg, Theodore Kheel, Paul
O'Dwyer, Harry van Arsdale and others testified to his
"uniqueness," his "integrity coupled with sincerity" and cried
the words that roused the hall: "He never sold out the men!"

The feeling that dominated the entire afternoon was
expressed in the banner that hung across the length of the

331

broad stage and said in big, black letters, "He Was Not For
An Age, But For All Time," words that Ben Jonson wrote
after the death of his enigmatic contemporary, William
Shakespeare. However strong, they did not seem out of place
as, one by one, the speakers made their way to the cluster of
microphones in the center of the gladiolus-heaped stage and
spoke words they could never have spoken to the sardonic Mr.
Quill when he was alive.

Ambassador Goldberg: "He came from the Old World to
give light and inspiration to the New World. He was a great
labor leader, like Philip Murray from Scotland, and Sidney
Hillman from Russia, and his best living memorial is the
union he founded."

Michael Mann, AFL-CIO New York regional director:
"He carried over the spirit of rebellion, in its finest sense,
from the green hills of County Kerry to the concrete streets
of New York, which he loved. He was made by the spirit of
the Irish Republican Army."

Albert Shanker, president, Local 2, United Federation of
Teachers: "Michael Quill was a teacher of teachers. The
legacy of collective bargaining for public employees was his
doing."

Paul O'Dwyer, special counsel, TWU: "Michael Quill
didn't have to wait for the civil rights movement. Thirty
years ago the bylaws of his union were nondiscriminatory
and they have stayed that way."

Theodore Kheel, impartial chairman, New York Transit
Industry: "You never read it in the editorials that denounced
him, but he loved this city and this country."

Harry van Arsdale, president, N.Y.C. Central Labor Coun-
cil: "Mike more than anyone else helped us get the taxi
drivers organized. I want you to give $1 a month to start a
Mike Quill Fund for Justice and Education so his light will
never go out."

On the stage, 100 of the men who had come up with him
through the ranks—their hair white, their demeanor almost

churchlike, their hornrimmed spectacles slipping on and off as they stiffly examined scribbled notes before speaking—sat like an honor guard over the memory of their chief. As the memorial program reached its climax with the singing of Irish songs (Matthew Guinan, the man who has succeeded Michael Quill as president of the TWU, told how Mike loved to get a "bunch of the boys together to sing the old songs"), the crowd, 4000 strong, hummed "The Rising of the Moon" and "Kevin Barry" along with the wraithlike Pete Seeger, who strummed the tunes out on his banjo and crooned them in a high voice.

But then came the quiet moment, a thousand miles removed from politics, concerned only with the private man and his private life. From the hidden ranks of honor guests and colleagues on stage stepped Michael Quill's darkhaired, darkeyed, striking Jewish widow, Shirley Quill; his prematurely bald, 26-year-old son, John; and his tiny sister, Mrs. Mary O'Sullivan, who had been flown over from the old country. She is 69 and looked timidly out of place. Both she and portly young John Quill, a plain electrician, silently accepted memorial Bibles from the TWU leadership.

Then Shirley Quill stepped forward, looking like La Passionaria, a double strand of pearls wound around her neck, her black veil flung back, and almost hurled her words into the microphone: "My husband was an impossible-ist, in his vision, in his ideals—an impossible-ist who succeeded!"

The house roared back its understanding.   Feb. 21, 1966

men in bondage on an easter sunday

Ossining, N.Y.—God may be dead or hiding down in that neon-lit circus of the soul called Manhattan, but his traditional image was very much alive up here on Easter Sunday—both inside the walls of Sing Sing and out, both in the secure and in the disturbing sense.

In this quiet town, the conservative Christian element went to church in the overcast late morning, then some saw "The Greatest Story Ever Told" at the Victoria Theater and topped it off with the $4.50 turkey dinner at Pastor's Steak House. Bright new bonnets were heaped on the checkroom counter; and the mothers watched carefully to see that giblet-and-gravy stains were efficiently sponged off eyecatching new dresses on their daughters and tight little three-button suits on their sons.

Inside the flat grey prison compound, where the electric chair has been quiet these past two years, the mood of the day was almost exactly the same—except for the absence of the children. Downstairs in the visitors' room, after morning chapel and the noontime dinner of roast chicken and mashed potatoes, 40 cons in clean white shirts and sharply pressed

335

trousers visited with wives and girlfriends across the tables
that are divided by no screen.

It was a time for reunion—mostly whispered, with hands
doing the most expressive talking.

Out on the ballfield, where the season starts in two weeks,
four lone men with no dependents were loosening up on the
bleak diamond. And in front of the messhall hundreds of prisoners sucked on cigarettes or played cards while waiting for
their Easter movie to begin.

They had seen a double-bill yesterday, "Operation Cross-
bow" and "Follow That Dream," but time hangs heavy for
these 1800 long-termers and Paramount Pictures had sent up
its 10-year-old popularization of "The Ten Commandments"
as an appropriate film for this particular day. At 1 P.M., more
than 1000 of the men began to file into the chapel, now converted into an auditorium, and took hard wooden seats in
front of a white screen with an American flag pinned over it.

Paramount has made a neat $80 million out of its lush reli-
gious fairytale, which was the final life-work of the flamboyant
Cecil B. DeMille, and the skilled business minds who earned
that company a $6 million profit last year thought that this
prison-locked Easter showing would be a wise move in the
national reissue of the film. They were right. But they could
never have anticipated why "The Ten Commandments"
made such a sharp and disturbing impression on the men
packed into the Sing Sing chapel yesterday afternoon.

Although Mr. DeMille was apparently as much boy as he
was man, and fashioned a shallow, brightly colored entertainment out of the enormous metaphysical riddles that surround
the legend of Moses' confrontation with the God of the Old
Testament, the men were gripped to silence by the pictures of
the Israelites under the Egyptian whip.

The reason for their intense silence was not hard to search
for. Eighty percent of the men in that hall, a little over 800,
were either Negro or Puerto Rican—they dominated the audience just as they dominate Sing Sing. And when the Jews in

the film begged for a messiah, someone to deliver them from the impotence of their plight as slaves to the Egyptians, a Negro convict in the audience muttered, "Malcolm was our goddam messiah but he got shot down."

There were wild cheers for the goodlooking women—some of them deep African or Ethiopian—who danced across the screen, and there were homosexually aware laughs when Moses (Charlton Heston) embraced Joshua (John Derek), but it was near to impossible to get a laugh out of the prisoners as they watched scene after scene of the degradation of Moses' people by the Egyptians.

Suddenly, to an observer, all of the lyrics of Negro blues songs and spirituals that identify with "the children of Israel" became concrete as one watched the hunched men in the audience with their eyes riveted on the film. It was not far-fetched to imagine that they were watching a metaphor of their own situation in white America—one that has filled prisons across the country with a frustrated, often hopeless majority of darkskinned people that far outnumber their white counterparts and make U.S. prisons into black Harlems and Spanish Harlems that the average middleclass person never hears about.

That, perhaps, is the most important news one can send out of Ossining at the end of a "traditional" Easter Sunday with all the so-called trimmings.   April 11, 1966

the newspaper as literature/ literature as leadership

To My Fellow Wordmen:

On Oct. 30, 1966 (but it could have been tomorrow), the late *New York World Journal Tribune* carried a page-one story by Jimmy Breslin from Fairfield, California, that told of the arrival at the Travis Air Force Base of four dead Marines from Vietnam. Breslin gave a closeup of exactly what happened as the four aluminum boxes were lifted off the transport plane that brought them in and were taken by covered truck to a mortuary on the air force base. He told how the cold northern California nightwind spun the tags on the metal coffins, how they were trucked in darkness behind the terminal where 165 new soldiers were about to fly off to the same place from where the bodies had come, and how the human remains of these dead Marines—called "H.R." in military shorthand—were gingerly handled by the embarrassed personnel in the mortuary:

"Lift easy," one of them said. "Yeah, lift very
easy," another one said. . . . The airmen
brought the other three cases in and now the
four dead Marines were side by side on the
wooden rack. "There is nothing inside these
boxes, just human remains," one of the airmen
said. "Inside they got a rest for the head and
then just an empty box," another one said.

Breslin tells us that on each aluminum box was stenciled,
"RETURN TO USAF MORTUARY TSN RVN," and in
the last paragraph of his 1800-word story he explains that this
"meant when the bodies of the four Marines were taken out
of the cases, the cases should be put on a plane and returned
to Tan Son Nhut in the Republic of Vietnam, so that the cases
could be used again."

In that flat, open, deceptive (Gertrude Stein and Ernest
Hemingway are stretched out in those "cases," repetitively
tolled three times along with the dead Marines) and yet completely practical tone of voice, Breslin gave a picture of contemporary reality that went beyond the particular Sunday
story he had written. By sticking entirely to the facts and
selecting them with a prose artist's touch—the art in Breslin's
shrewd hands being to underplay details packed with emotional consequence and by flattening them allow their intrinsic value to float clear—he forced his readers to experience
larger meanings than the return of four men, or parts of them,
from Vietnam. The simple details themselves, without any
evidence of strain on Breslin's part (naturalness is his big
trump card as a persuader), became symbolic of the technological impersonality demanded by war in the 60s; of how
men who were alive 24 hours before on distant soil became
converted into neatly packaged meat sent home in the wink
of a mechanical eye; of how the quick and utilitarian techniques for transporting and disposing of this meat becomes

the foreground of a story about death today and makes the luxury of sentiment ridiculous; of how the living try to adjust to the rapid businesslike logistics of human annihilation and the only act of baffled mourning allowed them is to handle a sealed aluminum box gently.

For all they knew there could be dirty underwear in it, so weird, abstract, numbing to the emotions and mind is the way boisterous young bucks fly out from this West Coast terminal and quickly fly back as souls of aluminum.

All this and more can be legitimately read into Breslin's story, and yet he did not have time to calculate all the echoes set up by what he had written; working under a deadline for a daily paper, with his piece due in New York by roughly 5 P.M. on Saturday evening (Oct. 29th) at the latest, he had to write as well as he possibly could about an event dissolving in front of his eyes—like a sharpshooter on the run. (Actually, I heard later from Dick Schaap that Breslin had tried this particular story before and been dissatisfied with it; this was his second run on it, according to Schaap; but since every story a good newspaperman writes is different, like a jazzman cutting several versions of the same tune out of an excess of spirit, it is not unfair to the existential reality of this story's composition to see it as a totally fresh shot out of Breslin's typewriter.)

The details enumerated earlier, with the actual names of the personnel on the air force base to be spelled correctly, the right numbers on the transport plane and the insignia on the mortuary to be set down so accurately that they could stand up in a court of law, constituted his materials. With this data plus the intake of his senses he had to build a story with a purpose and build it quickly; unlike a "pure" fiction writer he could not convert the four dead Marines into 24 to dramatize the scene—although an air force major in the story is actually quoted as saying that there were three separate shipments of aluminum boxes that day—nor could he alter the shape of the terminal or the number of planes parked out in front ready to fly newcomers to the combat area. (For

the record there were two commercial airliners supplied by
TWA and Pan American ready to do this unpublicized
chore, with a third air force transport plane assigned to carry
the equipment.)

But within the circumscribed reality of this particular story,
without violating facts that could be checked by others and
would be hotly scrutinized by those who had actually been on
the air force base that night, Breslin had to write, rewrite,
twist, carve his piece. If he wrote it in a West Coast motel
room after covering the story, as is likely, he probably had no
more than three hours to do approximately 10 wide-margin
double-spaced pages. (Most metropolitan newspapermen tri-
ple-space on four stapled sheets of copy paper with carbons in
between known as "books"; the triple-spacing is to allow for
editing and the extra sheets go to various desks; Breslin's dou-
ble-spacing on one single piece of copy paper at a time indicates the weight he can throw around any New York newspaper office except the *Times*.) Typing in clean bursts with an
aggressiveness and intensity that doesn't appear in the copy,
surrounded by hot, visibly smoking coffee, smoldering cigarettes, his 7½″ x 5″ wire-ringed National notebook and a
nearby telephone which he might have used half a dozen
times to fill in tiny chinks of information—Breslin has the
personal style of a boom-boom MGM supernewspaperman
but each of these props is active in itself or tends to create a
rhythm of action—he had to see into this story with his own
experience-cum-feelers and find the precise way for rendering
a new event that had never crossed his consciousness before in
all its fine relationships. Each story is totally new to the newspaperman or truthteller-on-the-run, even if he has taken a
quick bite out of it before; each time he "covers" or "goes out
on the street" he is faced with unique combinations of history, large or small, and the only way he can confront an
event that he can't wholly anticipate or control is by his technique and finally his depth of perception.

Breslin's depth as a writer (and he can also be shallow and

obvious) reveals itself in the quiet line-by-line way in which he places the significant small detail and the entirely believable, telling quote—"We don't pick them up like freight," one of the defensive airmen tells him in the mortuary that "had white walls and no windows and a heavy air conditioning unit hanging from the ceiling." (Notice how he relies on the "and" to both keep his sentence moving and deal out the necessary facts without pausing; the device can get mechanical—and when a Breslin story fails it can be flatter than stale beer—but what Gertrude Stein and Hemingway never realized was how handy their simplified English would become for journalists who cram sentences to the teeth with fact and are always looking for the most painless way to do the job.)

As a columnist, Breslin is permitted to use the "I" whenever he wants since the very idea of having a column is based upon owning a big "I"; but his best or at least most serious stories direct attention to the scene itself—four dead Marines, a Greenwich Village firehouse that lost half a dozen men in a building cavein, the night at the New York Hilton when Rockefeller heard that he'd won the Governorship for the third time; the more important the event, the less Breslin will inject himself, although he has written totally knockout *New York Magazine* feature stories in the first person that gain their freshness from his willingness to bat out the literal truth about his drinking, rages, tyranny over neighbors-wife-and-family, bad debts, etc. These stories almost never fail to entertain because they shout with honesty of emotion and are never selfconscious. Breslin inherits the oldfashioned newspaper code of suspicion for intellectuals and intellectuality—which has been melting in the last several years with his support of liberal and vaguely avantgarde causes—but the virtue of his show-me-I'm-from-Queens stance, at least in the firstperson pieces, is that it keeps him earthy, tangible, solid and finally modest in a way that a writer who took his mortal being more heavily could not be. Breslin's comparative spiritual modesty as well as his narrowmindedness and occasional noisy rant seems the direct result of his Irish Catholic upbringing, which puts an unquestioned God cleanly above man and permits Breslin to be easy in print about himself because he is not trying to save the world.

From his point of view it would probably be blasphemous and even more important—to that knowing street-urchin eye—inexpressibly stupid.

But if this 37-year-old Babe Ruth, Jr., of the cityroom is ultimately easier to take and "puts a cheaper price on his ass" (to Pete Hamill the key to snapping newspaper prose) than other firstperson blabbers whose confessions appear in Important Books, there is nothing shy about the writing ego that went into "4 Bodies At Midnight," the headline for his dead Marine story. Here, disdaining to use the first person because it would have shown a lack of "class" (to which Breslin is as sensitive as Frank Sinatra—both gangster buffs), he had to project his feelings through the dead kids and the situation itself and did not let himself offer an opinion. In other words, he had to write a *short story* as formal as the kind taught in any fiction class, except his was about people with actual dogtag numbers and a real place still doing its ugly work today. By an unexpected evolution—or is it a revolution?—the American realistic short story from Stephen Crane to post-John O'Hara has now been inherited by the imaginative newspaperman, like Breslin, and all the independent probing of reality that the best native literary artists of the past have achieved can now be tried by a creative reporter without undue sweat.

Not only is there no longer any pretense involved (pretense in the sense that so-called "fine" writing was once a world apart, in a BOOK, while newspaper prose was supposed "to line somebody's birdcage" in Hamill's words), there is a definite advantage to the newspaperman in recreating reality if he uses every conceivable literary avenue open to him; for his job, depending on the intensity of his sense of mission, is to penetrate ever more deeply into the truth of every story—and this can only be done if he has the instruments of language, narrative knowhow, character-development, etc., that until now have always been associated with fiction. ("Every technique of fiction is now available to us," Tom Wolfe said recently. And if Breslin is currently the Kid Ruth of the New Journalism, Wolfe is certainly its ultra flashy-smooth Ted Williams. Wolfe goes on to say: "Stream-of-consciousness and subjective truth is the next breakthrough. Gay Talese's article in *Esquire* in 1958, 'Joe Louis At 50,' is a classic in this direction; Truman Capote, who in my opinion is not a firstrate writer, was only doing in *In Cold Blood* what Talese had done six or seven years before.")

Perhaps there was a time, really, truly, down in the belly, when fiction in America shed more light on the outlook of a generation than nonfiction; but today the application of fictional and avantgarde prose techniques to the actual scene before us seems much more crucially necessary. When Breslin wrote his story about the silent flight of four statistics from Asia to California he was telling us things about the America that each of us must confront on our own—this real-unreal country and each of our lives in it being bound up with a strange war, monsterlike technology, guilt over the death of these four young guys, secret happiness that we escaped their fate, bewilderment toward the future. He was reporting to us from the outer perimeter of our own coolly murderous time, expanding through the clarity of his writing skill our knowledge of what is *actually going on* in places we can't possibly get to but which all add up to our sense of fateful identity as a people.

If for some reason he had written this same story as a fictional sketch—changing names, location, inflating or "working up" the tone while he disguised the specifics as so many unimaginative novelists do for no significant purpose except selfprotection—would he have achieved anything more? The question, admittedly loaded, answers itself. Not only with this kind of story would he have added nothing to the central mood that justly shakes up the reader after finishing it, fictionalizing what was as rich as fiction in his mind to begin with would have disgraced the reality of what he saw. The punch of his story lies in its actuality; although Breslin has a reputation in New York newspaper circles of occasionally "piping" or making up quotes that fit a situation or clinch a scene, this can only be done in small part and in itself is sometimes an act of courage. To put quotes in the mouths of living people is a more audacious act of the imagination than to invent words for people who have never existed, especially when the writer knows these quotes will be read by the participants and he will be judged for it.

Breslin's story *gains* its impact precisely because it is not made up; it can be checked; and it was written out of that dual responsibility which rides the writer-reporter as it doesn't the totally free "creative writer," namely factual justice to his material and yet equal pride in the literary possibilities offered by his imagination. He is playing the most potentially dangerous game of all, writing about real, observable, aftermath-ridden life situations; and yet—to the extent that he is a writer equal in skill and ambition to the best novelists—he has to invest this living material with every bit of his artistic sense, his concern for language, mood, nuance, insight, suspense, moral value. And if he is a genuine firstrate writer, on a par with any who have put their signature on this ruptured time, he has to illuminate the material with his own needle-sharp angle of vision—"material" which is people who are very much alive, nameable, often prominent, people whom he will meet again as a vulnerable man himself caught up in the crosscurrents of contemporary U.S. life.

The reporter-writer does not have the freedom that the oldfashioned novelist or shortstory writer had and still has. He is hemmed in by his awareness of the living characters who make up the cast of each new story. If he wants to satirize them, make them pathetic, select a fact or describe a gesture that will perhaps show them up as frauds he has to be aware (and is soon made aware!) that there will be a kick-back right in the psychic breadbasket. There is a resiliency between what he writes and the public, and if he takes risks either imaginative or moral he does not do it in a vacuum or in the eye of posterity; he is bound to be reacted to with a bang in the present. This means that in the case of a Breslin, Tom Wolfe, Pete Hamill—as well as Murray Kempton and Ralph J. Gleason, the two older pillars of the New Journalism—the literary imagination that each possesses is not allowed the freewheeling of a writer who is not called daily to the bar of justice for his work.

Breslin's artistic imagination in the dead Marine story had to function within the framework of the air base, the number of caskets, the name of the community that houses the base, all the tough facts that constitute the skeleton of every report-er's story; in addition, he had to cope with the intangible human element that hangs over every scrap of type that appears in a newspaper with a byline attached to it. Will he get punched in the mouth after the story appears? Has he wounded someone unintentionally or seriously fucked them up? Is there a possibility of inaccuracy that will backfire and embarrass not only himself and his newspaper but the precar-ious balance of the event involved? Within this network run-ning from potential anxiety to real outward danger to hard-headed responsibility for the factual truth, Breslin or any feel-ing newspaperman tries his creative chutzpah to its limit in order to extract the most he possibly can from a fleeting set of circumstances that will never come again.

Until quite recently it was customarily thought that the place for high imagination in contemporary prosewriting was in fiction—but is this the kind of writing that is most signifi-cant today for the helplessly involved reader who is in a state of flux trying to relate his life to the world? When Establish-ment book critics say that there are no major novelists of the American 60s comparable to the Hemingway-Fitzgerald-Wolfe-Faulkner combine, they mean that none stand as

solid and sharply cut against the waving backdrop of the
shapeless age we inhabit. But these men, in spite of the
bookish glamor attached to their names, were in the most
radical sense *reporters* whose subjectmatter and vision was
too hot or subtle or complicated or violent or lyrical or intractable or challenging for the massmedia of their period.
They had to make up their own stories, based on what
they observed and felt, and publish them as loners who leanly
stood for personal integrity and subjective truth in opposition
to the superficial "objective" journalism of their day. The
exclusion of the deeper half of reality by oldtime journalism
was very much at the bottom of the mystique of the American Novel as it has been sentimentalized in our time—that
only in this medium could the real down-and-dirty story of
the country and the nature of its people be told. If you were a
prosewriter, there was almost a necessity to work in the form
of fiction 20 or 30 years ago because only through it could you
"tell" more than you could in journalism; by inventing characters with madeup names, put in imagined situations, you
could reveal more about being a modern American than in
any other way.

But why should the necessities of the 20s, 30s and 40s
(although the fictional necessity was already fading by the
end of the war) be right for today? The talk in New York
about newspapermen like Breslin, Wolfe, Hamill, the peren-
nial Kempton, Ralph J. Gleason of the San Francisco *Chronicle*, and after that journalists who write for weekly or monthly
publications like Nat Hentoff, Jack Newfield ("The immediacy of TV has created the opening for this kind of writing"),
John Wilcock, Allan Katzman, Richard Goldstein, Gay
Talese, Barbara Long, Michael C. D. Macdonald, Gail
Sheehy, Brian O'Doherty, Paul Krassner, Sid Bernard, Gene
Lees, Lawrence Lipton, Saul Maloff, Jack Kroll, Warren
Hincle, Roger Kahn, Albert Goldman, etc., is where the
immediate interest and excitement lies. The freshness of these
writers, first the daily newspapermen, then the weekly journal-

ists, then the monthly essayists and social observers—include here half-time novelists like Paul Goodman, Harvey Swados, Mailer, Susan Sontag, John Clellon Holmes—is that they are using the eyes and ears that American novelists used 30 years ago upon a uniformly fantastic public reality that millions of people must cope with daily. A current of appreciation flows between their audience and what they have to say; they are "needed" in an acute, shit-cutting way that novelists no longer seem to be, if only because of the time-gap between real action out on the streets and fiction; it is only when the novelist gives us a deeper vision of this evidence before our eyes—like Heller with *Catch-22* or Selby with *Last Exit to Brooklyn*—that the naked individual imagination seems as pertinent as it once was, because it extends our understanding.

With present law what it is, Selby and Heller would have been jailed or murdered by their unforgiving subjects if they wrote their true names and deeds in the same way that they fictionalized them. And John Barth might be expelled from the human race (or at least his university professorship) for his view of it. But in 1967 that is the only practical justification for "fictionalizing"—if it says something that can't possibly be said otherwise. And with the accelerating frankness and freedom of expression that journalists demand today—they are perhaps the most disciplined literary rebels of our time because of their mature sense of fact, the moral radar because they are situated out in front and become the alerted senses for the rest of us—how much *has* to be fictionalized? Reality itself has become so extravagant in its contradictions, absurdities, violence, speed of change, science-fictional technology, weirdness and constant unfamiliarity, that just to match what is with accuracy takes the conscientious reporter into the realms of the Unknown—into what used to be called "the world of the imagination."

And yet THAT is the wild world we all live in today when we just try to play it straight.

If living itself often seems more and more like a nonstop LSD trip—"illogical, surrealistic, and mad" as the 50-year-old Ralph Gleason keeps saying in his nuttily misnamed "On The Town" column in the San Francisco *Chronicle*—what fertile new truths can most fiction writers tell us about a reality that has far outraced them at their own game? How can they compete with the absurd and startling authorship of each new hour? It becomes a diminished echo, the average serious good novel today; but the average sharp piece of New Journalism can at present never become an echo because it keeps moving into this new universe of unreality and exposing it with the zest that Sinclair Lewis once used to tear the hide off Main Street. A new generation of authority-suspicious newspaper-men can only take so much repression and traditional burying of what they know to be true before ripping up clichés in the face of a new scene; no one is in the professional position to see and communicate as much as the daily reporter, and yet up to now he has been handcuffed by the much-used and abused journalistic slogan, "good taste," which until the 60s left the most alive writing in a U.S. newspaper story on the copydesk floor. If I am covering a story about a Washington politician found dead in a screw-a-minute 43d St. hotel with a spade hooker, and I want to write about it truthfully, I have to mention details that would have offended my mother and father (dead these 35 years) because emotionally they couldn't handle this information. Newspapers, geared to the broadest readership of all publications, used to cater to people like my mother and father and yours, and such stories—prostitution, miscegenation, homosexuality, suicide, psychosis among well-known people, etc.—were edited or whitewashed so that the middleclass public could continue its hypocritical idealism in spite of facts which were quite different.

Then, during the first 40 years of this century in America, it was only a minority of the fiction writers, playwrights (practically none before O'Neill) and poets among the users of words who broke this conspiracy of public lying and attempted to show things for what they were. There was a pragmatic reason for our Stephen Cranes, Dreisers, O'Neills, Djuna Barneses, Faulkners, Hemingways. They were necessary if one wanted to know how creatures like oneself actually lived, suffered and died. Hollywood, slick magazines, radio—as well as newspapers—demanded by their cynical manufacture of safe good cheer, Protestant wish-fulfillment and the cleaning-up of evidence that a few brave maniacs of hairy expression take up the burden for all.

But this neat division between purity and compromise doesn't exist any longer—obviously. The current generation brought up under the huge umbrella of the massmedia doesn't despise the sellout aspects of the bigtime action as we 40-and-over puritans did because of our conditioning. As McLuhan suggests, the massmedia are an extension of the rock generation's nervous system—newspapers, movies, TV, radio, records, tapes, every device of communication which reaches millions of people—and it is inconceivable that they are going to romanticize (as we did) the power of a "fine" novel that sells 1500 copies in the wake of the communications hurricane on which they were suckled. No, they want to make it in the public media that this country since World War II has revved up to such a colossal pitch; but they want to do it on the terms that the former generation once thought of only for poetry, novels and serious plays—with total integrity; and right now a struggle for power is going on between the technicians who invented and the advertisers who capitalized on these octopal massmediums and the young visionaries (who might have been novelists 30 years ago) presently using them as hotlines of communication. But it is still the Word, written, spoken, sung, the very Word that has been the most significant instrument for men throughout history, it is that Word as conveyor of reality which is at the heart of this tug of war and through which a new and broader conception of literature is being shaped.

Does the book-reverencing literary critic or any other stubborn protector of the unsacred past realize that Lord Buckley,
Lennie Bruce and Mort Sahl, Joan Baez, Buffie St. Marie and
Bob Dylan, users of pop forms like nightclub comedy and
folkrock preaching, have cut into the serious American literary man's ground by using the massmedia to make knifing
comment of needed immediacy?

And does the Harvard doctor of letters recognize that a
Jimmy Breslin or Pete Hamill, two cocky Irish parochial-
school boys off the greater New York streets, are using that
traditional literary doormat, the newspaper, to get to reality-
through-language much more quickly than is done through
books?

Sure they do; but they don't know quite how to handle it.

As you doubtless know, Matthew Arnold called
19th-century journalism "literature [written] in a hurry," a
famous phrase that until now has reflected the sense of utilitarianism and literary inferiority felt by most journalists when
they compared themselves to "writers." In Manhattan newspaper (and weekly magazine) shops you'll find veterans who
spit on their work and automatically say that the importance
of today's newspaper is to provide the wrapper for a smelly
flounder tomorrow. The movie-portraits are for real, folks:
no one is more snottily and superficially cynical about both
reality and writing than the oldtime, ex-alcoholic, security-
obsessed newspaper grandad whom you'll run into on the
overnight rewrite desk of a New York paper. He drools about
Mencken or Hemingway or James Gould Cozzens, but it
never crosses his mind that he could have done comparable
work within the limits of his own job; from his point of view
newspapering is merely Grinding It Out under the humbling
restrictions of time, space, subjectmatter and childishly basic
English; he thinks newspaper work "ruins your prose" and
any idea that every story—even an obituary—can be inter-
preted, shaded, significantly woven, carrying a human center
and an implicit judgment on experience, has long since been

shut out in the empty night of unthought while grandad figures out new ways to pad the overtime sheet.

But this hard-guy-with-soul-of-mush attitude, this fatalistic acceptance and sneering embrace of the Grub Street rhythm of newspapering, is the dying style of a generation who looked at literature through the intimidated eyes of being "hacks," as they saw themselves, or "clerks of fact" as Pete Hamill has beautifully put it; selfmocking errand boys without a grain of conviction, carrying into print the latest fart of some celebrity of politics, entertainment or high (low) finance and being embittered because the Name was up there in lights that they helped plug in while they were condemned to doing whitecollar porter work in the cityroom. Traditionally, the average cityside newspaperman was a machine, a phone-bully, a sidewalk-buttonholer, a privacy-invader, a freebie-collector and not a writer at all—he had a formula for processing his information (much of it dumped on him by publicity men) and was not encouraged to depart from it. It is no wonder at all that the combination of what he saw—and the reporter has entré into every doorway of life without exception if he chooses to use it—coupled with the injunction not to express it produced that style of the Big Sneer which gave him his uniqueness as an American type. But underneath the cocked fedora and the rest of the so-called glamor crust you could find a man who thought of himself as a failure by the worldly standards pounded into his being by his work—money, achievement and status.

Newspaper offices were known in the trade as being comfortable, in-the-know flophouses where losers came to trickle out their lives; alcoholics floated on the assurance of seniority granted them by the once-righteous power of the American Newspaper Guild and those who weren't alcoholics floated just the same, notching up Army-style credits and cautious little nesteggs against the last winter of enfeeblement and the final smirk. The idea that they might be frontrunners snaring and interpreting reality as it broke before their eyes would have been a joke to the majority of these putdown experts who envied the stars on the world stage that they covered, but never conceived that they themselves were in the position to make history and not merely record it.

But this lock on the imagination of the old cigar-chewing bigots—and their young imitators who snipe and curse at easy targets to prove that they are really in The Business—in no way deterred the balling sense of opportunity felt by a nuclear-goosed generation of newcomers now in their 30s (Breslin, Wolfe, Hamill, Gay Talese, Alfred G. Aronowitz, Dick Schaap, Eliot Fremont-Smith, Larry Merchant, Kenneth Gross, Vincent Canby, Mike Royko, Nicholas von Hoffman, etc.) and the two intransigent standouts 49 and 50 respectively (Murray Kempton and Ralph J. Gleason) who realized in differing ways what could be done within the dulling graveyard of a newspaper. Certainly there had been great inspirations in the profession only recently dead or played out: Heywood Broun (admired by Gleason), Westbrook Pegler (ditto for Kempton, Hamill and Wolfe in spite of W.P.'s politics), H.L. Mencken ("a favorite," Wolfe), Damon Runyon, Jimmy Cannon and even Walter Winchell (the last two hugely appreciated by Hamill for their language and Cannon in particular for his jazzy literary flair). But most of these older writers, however superpro in the daily journalism of their day, hit their high moments with the "crusading" approach that has been the essence of the American newspaper religion since Lincoln Steffens. If the large majority of professional reporters and editors of news have developed a protective sneer to cope with the stuffed urinal of human avarice, weakness and folly into which they've been dunked, the minority of newsmen whose names stand out from the past have always had their moral indignation heightened and made sharply eloquent by what they've been exposed to.

It commands one's respect, this unique kind of moral courage, and it is central to the oldfashioned idea of the press as watchdog to the community—more often a capped-tooth watchdog, unfortunately—but it is not at the heart of the style that lies waiting for the total reporters of the immediate future. This new style or revolution in reportorial values— which can be seen in varying part in Breslin (the novelistic fullness of his recreation of reality); Wolfe (the rhythmic montage of disjointed contemporary phenomena); Hamill (sophisticated realism which brings an urban snarl to bear on the absurdity of what he covers); Kempton (an elegance of mind and irony trained on the soiled collar of events); Gleason (his unkidding notion that the world today is insane and his enthusiastic tubthumping for popular avantgardists who can cut a path to the future)—goes far beyond the public role of pointing a finger at specific fraud or deceit, which has usually been the American journalist's finest hour from Steffens to Pegler. It rather points the finger at Self (both the writer's and the reader's) in relation to the World Out There; it concerns the *whole man*—the acting out in print, as Hamill intuitively senses on certain stories, of the subjective being as it collides with objective happenings. A good example would be the vulgarity and possibly the evil of Johnson's 1966 Asian tour as seen through Hamill's personal eyes ("... a non-event") and then communicated to a public of half a million or more people through the *New York Post*. If the New Journalist is the outrider for news of reality itself—since we live in an age where the interaction between public events and private response is becoming the whole mortal show for everyone, the anonymous as well as the notorious, all of whom live under the threat of each new day's surprises—then it should be clear why the specific villain-baiting of a Pegler or, occasionally, Kempton is a cowboy-and-Indians game compared to the infinity of inner and outer space that the newspaperman has now inherited. When the New Journalist goes out to cover a story today he is handling nothing less than the time in which he lives; no matter how trivial his story, if his frame of reference is broad as well as acute, he can bring to bear upon it his own fate as a riddled modern man and relate

it to the similarly riddled lives of his readers. It is no longer
the mere formal outlines of an experience that we expect
from a Breslin, Wolfe or Hamill, but its entire quality, overtones and undertones, in a word the "saturation reporting"
(Wolfe's phrase) that we used to get from novelists but now
need daily to understand the untrustworthy world in which
our own small destinies are being negotiated.

This need to know our fate may be more intense than ever
before—the "officialese" of which Orwell contemptuously
spoke has grown thicker and demands immediate translation
if men's minds are not to be permanently blown by impene-
trable doubletalk—but the literary elite in this country has
long shied away from American journalism in its crass or bull-
dog-edition actuality. Truman Capote, upon the publication
of *In Cold Blood,* took great strenuous pains to distinguish
what he was doing (and did very fastidiously well) from what
the unelegant New Journalists were attempting to do every
day on cheaper paper; their stuff was "just journalism," while
his was "Art," dig?

*But was it art in the most profound sense, which entails
great risk, a new point of view, and above all the conviction to
change the world to your way of seeing?*

With the division of literary labor between the truckdrivers
and the high princes of words—so common in our country for
the last 25 or 30 years—the university, the abstract novel
(Barth, Hawkes, Sontag, etc.) and literary theory have claimed
the more refined or at least better-trained minds while it has
been left to the guy next door to wade into the enormous literary problem of trying to tell the whole truth in the newspapers. Wolfe, 36, is a Yale Ph.D. in American Studies—true;
but Breslin, Hamill and Gleason never graduated from college
(Hamill, the 32-year-old whizkid, never even finished highschool) and Kempton apprenticed for what is currently the
most mandarin style in daily journalism by being a grubby
assistant labor reporter. These men learned by writing under
the pinched code, the brutal deadlines and the unflinching

pragmatism that characterizes all newspaper work; now—
suddenly—the literary doors of their profession have been
kicked wider open than at any time in the past and they have
been catapulted into becoming spokesmen whose role and responsibility to truth has grown enormously. It is not unfair to
say that as writers they are more pertinent to this time of permanent crisis than eight- or nine-tenths of the straight literary
figures who read them regularly every afternoon and then
patronize them in the evening over cocktails.

And yet—if one could undo years of aloofness, fear, luxu-
rious introspection, sheltered alienation, university tenure, all
the proud and wanly smiling snobbery that went with being
a Serious American Writer of this period just ending—what
better place for truly significant prose than the daily newspaper? Why shouldn't it seem the most logical place in the
world for writers who teethed on fictional naturalism-realism
to test their concepts of reality upon alive characters and
report their findings to a huge captive audience that has to
listen merely to get the news? More than that, the journalistic stakes are a thousand times greater than in the past
because of the immediate reverberation of an original statement today: if Harrison Salisbury shook up the Washington
power machine with his *Times* reports of the U.S. bombing
of Hanoi, and William Manchester threw a gritty bomb into
national Democratic politics with his imaginative and yet
factual portrait of *The Death of a President,* consider the
power that our most eminent prosewriters could finally
wield in their own country by being the most sensitive con-
ductors for news, the transmitters of verbal reality for the
nation.

Power is not to be despised in a culture that uses it like
America; and writers, too long the weak and easily seduced
stepsisters of the national family, are not to be condemned for
craving it; when H. L. Mencken said of this country and Poe,
"They let him die like a cat up an alley," he was merely con-
cretizing the hatred that literary artists have always felt in this

society toward a citizenry that has found them ornamental
rather than basic. But what could possibly be more basic
than this generation's Poes and Melvilles (or Ray Bradburys
and Saul Bellows) applying their vision of existence to news
as it breaks, reading individual values into what is now a
mechanical UPI report, interviewing Johnson as candidly as
Brady photographed Lincoln, finally breaking out of the profound isolation of their heads and gambling their point of
view on its involvement with events? News has *become* reality
for millions in this Age of Journalism; but what if this reality—a mine disaster, a nuclear test under the Atlantic, the
death of Anne Sheridan, a Harlem riot—were to be both
accurately and originally reported at the very moment that it
happened (not three months later in *Esquire*) by an Ellison
or Kerouac or Jean Stafford?

Suppose, in other words, that our very understanding of
what is news was to be overturned by coverage that made
uncommon human sense as well as giving the facts, and that
our information was no longer flat and closed but fully dimensional and open—as open and revealing and meaningful as
the writer could make it by pouring his spirit into a union
with the event? Have you ever stopped to think what could
happen to the programmed newspaper reader if the finest lit-
rary talent was used to illuminate even the most perfunctory
one-paragraph auto accident out on the street, how the closed
or small mind would be jolted by a recognition of the mutual
dependence of all our beings if a writer who cared interposed
the warm hands of his typewriter between the cold statistic
and fact-numbed heads?

The "symbolic action" that literary artists have frustratedly
contented themselves with in a book would take a radical
turn into monumental real action if they could dominate the
sources of news, not only in the press, but in the fields of
spoken literature as well—radio and TV. To be novelistically
engaged with one's time in the manner of the early Malraux,
Koestler and Camus is an undeniably great modern primitive

example; but now there is a real chance that the masses' version of truth, of what is, of reality itself, can be revolutionized
if men and women of proven artistic vision step down from
their rickety subjective towers of private being into the com-
munal ego-socialism of daily journalism. The artificial split
between literature and journalism has never seemed more
beside the point as the human race staggers into the last
third of the 20th century not really knowing if it will survive
or what kind of freaky mutation it will become. If such
encompassing selfdoubt has eaten into the race, isn't it inevitable that it has affected literature as well, that the so-called
transiency of journalism is no greater than the seeming irrelevance of most literature today? The step from a Jimmy Breslin "up" to Robert Lowell is no longer the giant step that it
might once have been when newspapermen stood in awe of
honest-to-gawd writers; the best of the New Journalists are
already writers equal in their way to any of their generation;
but the step from Robert Lowell "down" to a Jimmy Breslin
has implications that go beyond writing to the possibility of
the artist affecting the reaction to events themselves by shaping the significance of daily reality with his own hand. Since
the New Journalists have gone like pilgrims to literature to
learn the techniques for being faithful to all that they alone
are in a position to see, and sweat daily to give added dimension, nuance, perspective and insight to their stories, let
once-mighty literature swallow its whitefaced pride and give
its mythic propensity to journalism—the *de facto* literature
of our time.

If this seems like a special curving of the truth, consider the
fact that at least 30 underground weekly and biweekly newspapers—from such respectable rebels as *The Village Voice*
and the Los Angeles *Free Press* to the latest *Rat* and
Oracle—have sprung up like bayonets in the last 10 (especially the last five) years out of the same soil that once produced little magazines. Why have they replaced their toy tiger
literary counterparts, or if not entirely replaced them at least

been the strongest force for "new," "different," "anti-Establishment" writing in the last decade? Because (in essence) it is only by usurping the public sources of news or actuality itself—and newspapers more than any other publications have always been the official version of reality, the standard of sanity, the middleclass scale of justice—that fedup young writer-journalists can advance a totally liberated view of the contemporary scene which challenges the entire range of assumed belief. A strictly imaginative work, with no literal frame of reference outside the author's mind, can be evaded today by a defensive reader who claims it has no relevance for him; but how can any reader evade a typical L.A. *Free Press* story about two cops who were found stashing marijuana for themselves which they had confiscated from some young hippies during a bust?

If the 20s were the supreme time of technical experimentation and overthrow in literature, the 60s are the comparably radical decade for the revolution in human values and the breakout in personal lifestyle; it is no longer the pure "literary" expression of the private mind that grabs most of us, but rather the outspoken public declaration of the most hidden energies of individual being that have been crouching in the shadowed doorways of our society. Artists, and especially literary artists, have in the American past been the belligerent walking illustrations of a totally free individualism because they would have suffocated without it; now an entire generation of longhaired Flower Children (to use one of their fast-changing names) has taken over what were essentially the antiauthority attitudes of bohemia and the artist; and the significant word-artist himself—with exceptions like Allen Ginsberg, Mailer, Bobby Dylan, bruised but embracing Jewish sprinters who can identify more easily with change than their more stolid gentile brethren—has stood uncomfortably tight in the face of the very journalistic-pop forms where he is most vitally needed.

For the last two centuries the "artist" has been the mar-

tyred holy man of secular life (Van Gogh's ear, Nietzsche's
insanity, Rimbaud's cancer, Kafka's tortured mental maze,
Melville's polar isolation, the list of hell's angels is endless)
whose vision of perfection ate into existence long after he was
wiped out of the race as a blot on his generation. This was the
reverse fairytale formula, that the genuine artist be despised
or misunderstood during his lifetime and then haunt men forever from the untouchable penthouse of his grave. Anyone
who presumed to be an artist took ironic comfort from the
grotesque set of groundrules laid down over the last 150 or so
years and prepared himself for misery with his work as his
only blessing. The contemporary artist knew too much about
the lives of his bitched breed in the past to expect anything
different for himself; "silence, exile and cunning," as defiant
Jimmy Joyce put it, were his strategems, his work was the
goal, and death was his friend because they lived on such close
bedroom terms until the work was done. This, in a bitter nut-
shell, was the diagram of most outstanding literary artists'
earthly existences.

But the world has changed and the diagram must change
also.

The lonely dedication of the artist pursuing his chimera no
longer impresses us the same way it once did; it is a still-shot
from the past, as out of style as a silent movie; mankind's
survival itself, mentally as well as bodily, morally as well as
materially, hopefully as well as horribly, seems much more
crucial as we survey the climate of emergency that clobbers
each heart and soul alive right now. The "heroic" suffering
and victimization that once distinguished the artist's life has
now become the property of everyman-everywoman in this
bleak Beckett playlet called Existence, 67. The neurotic tor-
ments that once clung to the artist as to a lover are now
democratically spread among the race at large. In other
words, the artist's lot has now become the human predica-
ment, they are one, and any artist worth the name must
now attempt to solve the riddle of the world because there

is no longer any other theme worthy of him. But if his tor-
ment is now shared by mankind at large, his imagination
and the ability to make it tangible are still his alone until
every human alive learns the trick of converting pain into
fame; and they have not yet been used upon the mass-communication techniques (journalism in all its forms) that
dominate this period as he has formerly used them on traditional stuff like clay, canvas and book.

Art, the most independently truthful form of human
expression, was not made to hang on a wall or hide in a page
but rather to show duller eyes a more radical and truer version
of the life slipping through each generation's hands. For it to
speak today—rather than be spoken about and not experienced at full volume—it has ready and waiting for it the outlets of press and electronic journalism; and on the reading-
listening-looking end it has for the first time in history a mass
audience of millions of individuals milling about in noisy desperation, confused, nihilistic, disgusted with political leadership, laughing at formal religion, looking for jet-age proph-
ets from Tim Leary to Bobby Kennedy who will lead them
to the promised land.

But modern literature and art has always been both more
truthful and more accurate in its views of the contemporary
crisis than any charismatic personality who flits across the
headlines.

It has been the most penetrating and significant use of the
imagination known to us.

Isn't the time ready for its potential to explode into the
center of society via the journalism that has become literature
for the majority, so that the human animal may finally know
what the "landmine" (the word is Isaac Babel's) of great
writing can do when it is hooked up to presidents, govern-
ments, prices, power, murder and every variety of antiparadise
that clubs us daily? What is art for, from Shakespeare to
Terry Southern, if not to transform the world by example?
And if Camus is coming to be recognized as much as a spirit-

ual leader as a rare, exalted writer, why can't we begin to see that the word-artist in action in this time *is* the new spiritual leader by virtue of the technological wings that carry what he says?

Jimmy Breslin, cute anti-intellectual that he can be, nevertheless once wrote a disgusted *WJT* column about the misuse and abuse of languge by a machine politician who had the indifferent arrogance to run for office when he could barely speak intelligibly. Norman Mailer wrote an equivalent piece about the prose of LBJ. What they were saying is that language is the clearest indication of being in this time and that they as writers were by their own words superior to the individuals they were writing about. But the implications extend beyond Breslin, Mailer or any single individual; what it seems to mean practically speaking is that articulate leadership has been thrust upon the writer in the authority-empty vacuum of this period; and the most effective way for it to reveal itself is in the mirror of the daily press where the intelligence and sensibility of the writer-artist can carve the very news of the world each day into a revelation that will in turn *act* upon history intsead of merely reflect it. What else but actuality itself—and what is "news" in our time but actuality compressed to a boil?—is worthy of the revolutionary insight that the literary artist has always lined his work with but until now has never had the chance to impose upon the literalness of events? It is no longer just a technical literary question of "fiction" vs. "nonfiction"; the essential issue that creative writers are now faced with is whether the literary-artistic imagination is to be effective in creating a new view of reality that does not shrink the potentialities of being alive in the 20th century or whether it is to be wasted on a pen-pusher's slavish copying of a life which is no longer tolerable according to the deepest needs of men.

If writers of the highest rank were to invade journalism as did E. E. Cummings, James Agee and Albert Camus—and if multimedia journalists are in fact the current "arbiters of reality" (the phrase was first used by a reporter on *The New York Times* about his own paper)—then it is inevitable that the original point of view of the creative writer trained upon people and events in the news has to open new possibilities in every newspaper reader's concept of the real and hence in himself. We writers, in other words, now have the long-sought-for opportunity to basically influence men's conception of the present and therefore the immediate future on a *mass scale* if we are not too proud or frail to enter into the race for moral and ideological power through our daily work in the massmedia. If we show our gossamer stuff in the day-to-day terms that the majority of people understand—pitting our skill and insight and freshness of seeing against the raw acts of this time that make up the news and undermining today's brute reality by our verbal projection of a greater one —there is nothing that can stop our long-postponed hunger for ultimate justice and beauty here and now from becoming a radical force in the life-game. If you agree with me that art is the only untainted vision of truth that can be made demonstrable to all, and if we demonstrate it upon the daily happenings of this time in the journalistic forms that capsulize authenticity for the terse minds of modern men, how can we dodge the fact that we have an alchemic dream within our grasp—the transmutation of base everyday matter into the poem of life?

We may well be on the doorstep of that necesssary leap into the future when the world itself is literally governed by art, or truth made manifest, because there is nowhere else to turn and everywhere to go.

Sincerely,

Seymour Krim

1967

postscript

It was inevitable that I would one day use the new dimension that daily newspaper work gave me and try to relate it to my own total existence. I am literally embarking for Europe and new alternatives as this is written and might very well end up on the Paris *International Herald Tribune* to put my "journalit" mania into deadline-action one more time; but if I ever again work on a daily paper I will have to crack the American Noosepaper Guild taboo of using the character of myself in relation to the people I write about. I must get down in the grass and interact with my subjects or my stories will be false to one half of their reality.

This combination of subjectivity and objectivity, of being myself but not dominating others in my work, of the actual current that flows in daily life between self and other selves, came to me when I took my voice out of the cityroom and back into my own private identity. The discipline of writing for the dailies led to economy of expression and alertness to every quiver on the external scene, but it suppressed my internal life or thinned it out to the point where I became a professional observer rather than a personally involved participant. The intimate pieces of reporting that end this journey-in-progress were written in the postnewspaper days just past when I was a person free of every outwardly imposed responsibility and you can see the soul's slanting signature coming back to what had been tight journalistic performance.

When you are unequipped to be free this world is full of sweating dread, believe me, and this entire book has an under-lying story of a spiritually naked man coping with his life by finding the way into the ultimate public reality whose confir-mation he needed in order to survive. With that tour of duty behind him—behind me—I can now be as authentically free as my imagination can reach and also as sensitive to what is outside me as my need for others and my technical training in expressing that need has finally equipped me. I sail to my own future and that of the history of my frantic time as aware of my place as I ever have been; whether I fill it depends on the unknown in whose dangerous element I swim with love but also with a flat smiling knowledge of the chances.

brother dave at 38

McReynolds has lived in the same apartment for 10 years; a four-room railroad flat hollowed out of the tenement jungle of E. 4th St., and while he plays Lotte Lenya and other sharply defined communicators on his record player and tapes—there's always sound going in McR.'s presence—the street down below is belching and stewing in its own disorganized life. Gypsies, hippies, bent synagogue Jews, PRs, spades, thousands of kids and bawling mamas keep up a drumbeat of noise and action around Mollie's Trucking and the abandoned ABC Stage City and the Palm Casino while the street heaves up crushed beer cans and ruined overturned chairs; you catfoot through this mess into the long, hopeless, loser hallways of McReynolds' building and up four flights and then—voilà!—you're in Dave's pad, which is a different world.

The cookbooks hit me first. McReynolds enjoys cooking and he has five hefty tomes on the subject bulging out from a top shelf, setting the style for a shelter inside a hurricane. In opposition to the drab hallways, the crap on the stairs, snotted kleenex, junk, McReynolds' livingroom is alive with bright yellows and reds; lots of green plants, two cool aristocratic Siamese cats (Loki and Bast, how d'ya do?), Lenya

hoarsing out the tough Brecht lyrics on the machine, Dave
cleaning up the room with those quick, abrupt movements
that defeat the eye. Talking as he makes the bed: "I was supposed to go up to Boston for the Spock trial—it's stupid, their
trying him on conspiracy charges for the Dec. 5th action on
Whitehall St. which I organized—but I'm not going to make
it today, anyway. Couldn't raise anyone on the phone up
there."

Dave is standing there—just for a slight second, because
he's always in motion, putting the cigarette in the holder,
pouring a white Alameda wine for himself, running a dust-
cloth along a book-and-record shelf ("The place hasn't been
cleaned for weeks, excuse me")—and I observe him with a
hard eye. Hard because I want to see where he's at, what he's
become, how it is with him. I've known McReynolds for
almost 10 years when we both came out of our separate camps
to support the Beat Generation—he from the socialist movement, I as an escapee from the *Commentary-Partisan Review*
Yiddish intellectual bag—and I trust him as a brother. A distant one, we have different things to do and he has gone far-
ther into his political identity than probably I have into my
literary one even though I'm eight years older, but still a
brother: two aliens, two missionaries, two explorers dissatisfied with the dull land we had already staked out, we met on
the goofy Beat barricades and stuck up for Gregory ("Little
Mafia") Corso. Brothers from about as opposite ends of the
American spectrum as you can get; see each other once a
year, maybe, and now I see that Brother Dave has developed
a slight pot under that dirty T-shirt, a little more hair has
vanished from the front of that stern, imperious head, but
it's been replaced by sidewhiskers, beard and mustache which
he picked up in Sweden last summer ("I like it because it
fills out my face; your face is too broad for the sidehair, on
you I'd just put the beard-mustache combination").

Dave is unfreezing the chicken, checking the French gour-
met cookbook as if it were his beloved New Testament—he

was a Baptist churchworker before he became a professional radical politician—and while he talks, the elegant cigarette-holder bobbing up and down in the middle of the young forest on his face, I notice the clear blue veins running across the slender muscles of his arms. They are definite, incisive, unmistakable; everything about Brother Dave is clearcut, from the tall willow tree of his build to the long bare feet, including the way he talks:

"I've been field secretary of the War Resister's League now for about seven years. They pay me $100 a weeek plus about $25 in expenses. The apartment costs $27 a month. That's it. When I get hardup for money I sometimes wish I could write an article for $1,000 but I freeze. I can only write for the *Voice* or the L.A. *Free Press* where I know my audience; otherwise I get rejected and I can't take that. I'm not a professional writer. I'm a politician, an organizer and a leader. I have to be a leader and I've learned enormously from A. J. Muste, Bayard [Rustin], and Norman [Thomas]. Identify leaders and you're safe. You know where they stand. If you interfere with people, you're not a leader. When I was a youngster I couldn't climb the tree that was sort of a totem of our tribe, but I sat in the crotch halfway up and the other kids crowned me with a wreath as king of the tribe because I wanted to be the king even though other boys could climb all the way to the top. That didn't matter. There is no society without leaders, it's the role of shaman, and people want it as much as the leader does. A. J. was a fox as well as a saint, the most impressive leader I've yet come across. Bayard said in effect, don't trust me, I'm a conman, a thief, a non-saint—now let's talk! I loved that down-to-earth approach, it was tactically sound, and I miss Bayard very much now that he's out of the Movement and apparently ashamed to speak to us. It's tragic—he belongs in the streets organizing things. He'll support Humphrey, he gets money for his Institute from the trade unions, it's a shame because in my opinion he's a genius. Norman is basically conservative but a true leader

because of the trust he inspired; he'll be an organizer till the
day of his death, bless him."

Dave is now chopping onions, salad ingredients, offering
herbs to be smelled, getting the stove going, asking his "children" (the two cats) if they stole his red address-phone book,
dialing a number that doesn't answer and talking politics as
naturally as a bookie talks numbers:

"It's tragic that there's a split between PFP [Peace & Freedom Party] and FPP [Freedom & Peace Party]. But I
was at Albany and there was no alternative but to leave. FPP
is not Communist, but the Communists have close ties with
them through Lydia Williams and others and now have a
potentially huge role in the Black community. I would like
to heal the split with FPP and settle for a formulation with
the Black caucus which is less than one man, one vote. I
might accept a Black veto power just like the Jewish bloc had
in the Socialist Party. You can't be totally legalistic if you're
trying to build a mass party and have to make concessions so
the blacks and Puerto Ricans can be protected. The major
parties do this already; but I think the blacks should grow up
and stop demanding 50% of the vote. Ossie Davis and Spock
are not CP and spoke before the FPP convention because of
their connection with the National Committee for New Politics—the Chicago debacle, remember? There is a New Left-
Ramparts element in the FPP as well as the CP, but compared to us they're a straw house. We have the live bodies,
independents like yourself, the new faces and we actually
came within five votes of winning the day at Albany even
though they had the chairman and tried to drum through
their proposals without discussion. You must remember that
the CP is against minor party action, they would have preferred a King-Spock ticket and now that that's out of the
question they'll probably back Humphrey against Nixon. The
CP is oldfashioned, dogmatic, reactionary, but they have at
least 10,000 members left and their influence is strong in New
York state. Do democrats with a small d have the willpower

to work with them in the PFP? That's the challenge. I dis-
agree with the ISC [Independent Socialist Club] about their
hard-line anti-Communism even though I'm close to them on
other issues. The ISC has no more than 200 people in the
entire country, if that, and yet they were the biggest force in
establishing the PFP in California. But they're hard-core, I
know they're not pacifists. But you need a broad coalition that
includes ISC, CP and PL [Progressive Labor] and hopefully all
those McCarthy people when and if Gene loses. Peace and
Freedom set something loose; I never thought they'd get on
the ballot on the Coast and I was beautifully wrong; I thought
we'd be dead when Johnson asked for negotiations and we're
not. There is no genuine radical movement now without the
hope of a PFP coalition. The CP is corrupt. The trade union
movement sold out. The Socialist Party is down to no members. The black militants might go into a private enterprise
bag unless we lay the basis for a broad party. We have to run
people for Congress and local assembly, have a guy who represents community interests like Vito Marcantonio who
couldn't be bought and was a true tribune of the people even
though he had no party. Running Cleaver for President is a
joke, politically speaking. Gregory would be better, but he
refuses to be represented by a party."

We sit down at the kitchen table and dig into the rice and
chicken; no bread, which is why my pot is bigger than Dave's.
I like it. The dressing on the salad puts an edge on my teeth.
The chicken is saucy enough to make it at a pretty good
French restaurant, which should give Brother Dave an occu-
pation if he ever gets weary of politics. In between bites:

"Right now the PFP is essentially middleclass and naive. A
radical formation means you don't vote for major party candi-
dates under any circumstances. But the truth is that we who
have been in politics (I've been in 20 years now) don't know
for certain where things are going. The atmosphere is revolutionary and nihilist; revolution without a program. We used
to be a small tidy movement. Today radicalism is larger.

We're confused and anyone who says he isn't earns my contempt. At Columbia—was amnesty good or bad? I don't know. I admire the kids but I'm baffled by them too. Also, I don't want to get beaten up by the cops. I'm not prepared to say they are right. But I'm an organizer, not an intellectual. I'm not good at developing new ideas; I need to have people talk so I can make up my mind. I miss talking to Bayard. I want to talk to Abbie Hoffman and Jerry Rubin and find out the Yippie position. I don't like their kids who beg for money on St. Marks Place. I'm getting older, I sometimes actually feel like 70."

It's hard for me to accept that (am I being sentimental?) but I understand his fatigue; Brother Dave is making more coffee, scouring the cooking pans, trying that not-answering number again, and all the while telling me things I never knew for certain before in the decade that I've known him:

"My heritage is Scotch-Irish-English-Dutch. My father is a Goldwaterite, although he wouldn't admit it, and worked as an advertising salesman before he retired. I have one brother, Marty, 35, who works for UPI in Buenos Aires. A sister, Elizabeth, who's a housewife—she's 31. They're sympathetic to what I've done with my life. But my family is symbolic, almost a perfect illustration, of the great changes that have come to America. My grandparents came to California at the turn of the century in a covered wagon from Kansas and now they see jet planes overhead! We never had much money, or say we were never rich, but four of my ancestors came over on the Mayflower. My own politics flow from my early involvement with the Christian church. I always believed in the four great Gospels of the New Testament, but when I was 17 and on the verge of agnosticism I read them freshly and found they were radical in the greatest sense. They are still my cornerstone but I am no longer a Christian because it excludes other beliefs; I am now interested in Buddhism and Hinduism. Ten years ago I took peyote and had a crucial experience in which I faced death. I now know that I will die, my ego will die, but my unconscious will flow back to life and in that sense I know there's a life after death. The night of my peyote experience I had a frightening debate between my unconscious and my conscious; my unconscious wanted the collective embrace of death and I told it I was not prepared to die yet. It was a crisis night and it made me realize from that time forward until now that the neurotic who seeks to preserve his ego and avoid risk will die without having given anything to life. I now live with the awareness that every day can be your last day. I am terrified of dying and my life is trying not to die. But the only way you can not die, in the ultimate sense, is to realize what Jesus was talking about when he said, 'If you lose your life for my sake you will find yourself.' It means to me that you lose your ego for the perfect order that rests behind the accidents of time and place. That goes on forever; 'you' won't be there to appreciate it but it will include the best of you. I now try to do everything as if it were worth doing in the last 24 hours of my life."

Around midnight I say so long to Brother Dave and he gives me a gentle, reserved smile and apologizes for talking so much. It's an unnecessary apology. I have come precisely to get him to open up the valves of his soul, and I feel rewarded—not only by the frankness of the rapping but by knowing that spiritual men and women are today the greatest wealth that the left possesses. From A. J. the fox to Brother Dave the straight-talking missionary the best of religion nowadays (I think as I pick my way through the crud of E. 4th St.) is in action, in the world, and will remain there from now on. The crud vanishes or at least I don't see it because I feel good knowing that when Dave "dies" another Dave will take his place and another and another. We are not entirely alone.

1968

when we went to john steinbeck's funeral service, this is what happened:

There was no announcement on the little black church bulletin board (with white letters) out in front. I said to Chayevsky: "Maybe it's private." We had not been invited.

But the church doors opened for us as if we had been spotted through a peephole and several well-dressed men bowed us in. The church was only a third full. Chayevsky recognized Frank Loesser, the Broadway-Hollywood songwriter, and shook his hand as an usher took us to an empty pew far back from the altar.

The altar was banked with more than 100 red and white flowers. The smell was too sweet.

The service was swift and formal. The preacher said we were all dust. We had to stand up and then kneel on a little cushion inside the pew, two willing Jewish boys going through unfamiliar ceremonies. But feeling right about it, somehow.

375

Henry Fonda, who played Tom Joad in the movie of *The Grapes of Wrath*, came out to the pulpit right of the altar and without any introduction read three poems that Steinbeck had liked; none contemporary, one of them bad writing by Tennyson. There was no audio. We could only hear Fonda every fifth word or so. We whispered that he'd lost a lot of hair, natural in a man over 60 but still a shock to the eye in a movie star we remembered from our highschool days.

The six pallbearers carried John Steinbeck's coffin, closed, down the aisle from the altar as soon as the preacher said the final words. The service had taken 14 minutes. I missed Fonda or someone reading some of Steinbeck's prose; but the *Times* coverage told me the next morning that Steinbeck himself had wanted the cold simplicity of a formal Episcopal service. I was terribly sorry that Steinbeck had wanted this. I wanted Steinbeck himself at this last hour, his own humane prose. The carrying of the coffin was remarkable. Loesser, Edward Albee, the other four pallbearers did not touch the coffin with their hands. It rested only on their shoulders, three on each side. It was the high moment of the service as they walked with measured sure step down the length of the church with John resting secure on their shoulders and all of us watching from our pews.

Chayevsky introduced me to Budd Schulberg, prematurely grey, before we reached the door on the way out; Schulberg's wife was the only person in the church with real tears squirting out of her eyes and down her cheeks, wrecking her mascara.

The photographers, TV and still, were waiting like assassins outside the door on the cold slate street. John O'Hara, the millionaire hermit novelist, sort of staggered down the churchsteps in front of me; his legs buckled as he reached the final step. He looked smaller than I would have thought from gossip about him as a barroom brawler 30 years ago. His Rolls Royce was waiting for him in front of the church. He was wearing a natty doublebreasted grey-check suit, ears sticking out like Gable and Mailer (before the long hairdo), eyes on the steps, speaking to no one. Like Breslin, there is still a wideeyed altar boy look on his round aged kid's face. Alert, but a stone misanthrope—that was the message.

I waited down below, against a car, deciding not to accompany Chayevsky "backstage" to speak to Mrs. Steinbeck. He knew Steinbeck as a semidrunk on the fashionable supperclub circuit. I'd never met him; but I knew him as a writer from the West who once meant something in this country and meant something to me—30stime that will never come again. Like Sinclair Lewis, he had lost it by the time he won the Nobel but no young man who had wanted to be an American Novelist in the late 30s could forget Big John. I recalled a picture of him in a long-yellowed *World Telegram* when he had come to town in a workshirt for the stage opening of *Of Mice and Men*. I waited against the car.

Walter Cronkite, unexpectedly, came down the steps and walked very unselfconsciously past the 15-20 slobs waiting to ooh and ahh over the more recognizable celebrities. Didn't bat an eye and looked sincere about having come to pay his respects, which is what Chayevsky and I had done, only that. Cronkite looked small too.

Leonard Lyons, who really liked Steinbeck, stood on the churchsteps with his great nose sniffing the air. He seemed unmoved. He was tailored to the teeth, as usual. I wonder how many funerals he has to go to these days and what he thinks as they carry his friends out one by one. But Leonard is tough; you'll never know from looking at him, Mr. Deception.

I didn't see Albee again. Chayevsky had said Albee was losing his looks but he looked good to me carrying John on his shoulder. Two nights before, I had heard Albee was making a wild scene; now at the service he looked like he was as dignified a vestryman as T.S. Eliot ever was for the Church of England; being an American, I dig severe contrasts and liked these cool contradictions in Albee. He showed great poise while carrying John in his box. An odd father-son friendship,

theirs, almost bizarre given their separate writings—but it
worked, from what I've heard.

Chayevsky came bundling down the steps, I was freezing by
now. The photographers had drifted away. O'Hara and his
Rolls and a few other chauffered cars had vanished. Chayevsky said: "I only met Mrs. Steinbeck once before this but she
remembered me." I like Paddy, among other reasons, because
he is very straight, boyish. "She told me not to forget him." I
said: "That's sort of pathetic." He didn't come up out of his
own thoughts: "She said, 'Please, please don't forget him.' "

We both had to piss; went to a nearby luncheonette two
blocks south on Madison and both tried to reach the urinal but
it could only hold one at a time. Chayevsky pissed first because
of his rank uptown. I was glad he and I had lifted ourselves up
out of the lousy small routine of our lives and gone to pay our
respects to the dead writer from the Salinas Valley in California, two New York bullshitters feeling good we had done so
over our coffee. I stood with him for almost 20 minutes while
he tried to get a cab back to his office on 7th Ave. and wres-
tle with the plot of a militant student murder-comedy he's
writing. He had tried it out on me before the service, over
nova scotia at a deli, as he often does; I gave him a thought
which he turned into a useful idea, that brain of his always
working like a sewing machine.

I walked and walked, zigzagging from Madison south over
to 2nd, glad I was walking and taking an eighth of an inch off
my gut, maybe; but I also thought that Steinbeck's passing
meant that so much of my early feeling about this country
was dead, too, also part of my early identity, and I was living
in a bright strange foreign new world all on my own without a
past. Poor bastards, all of us.

1969